Social Development in Youth: Structure and Content

Contributions to Human Development

Vol. 5

Series Editor
J.A. Meacham, Washington, D.C.

S. Karger · Basel · München · Paris · London · New York · Sydney

Social Development in Youth: Structure and Content

Volume Editors·
J.A. Meacham and *N.R. Santilli,* Washington, D.C.

2 figures and 18 tables, 1981

S. Karger · Basel · München · Paris · London · New York · Sydney

Contributions to Human Development

Vol. 3: Patterns of Aging. Findings from the Bonn Longitudinal Study of Aging. Thomae, H., Bonn (ed.)
VIII + 178 p., 12 fig., 51 tab., 1976. ISBN 3-8055-2292-4
Vol. 4: The Mechanism of Evolution: A New Look at Old Ideas. Wolsky, M. de I. and Wolsky, A., New York (eds.)
VIII + 160 p., 3 fig., 3 tab., 1976. ISBN 3-8055-2347-5

National Library of Medicine, Cataloging in Publication
Social development in youth: structure and content / volume editors,
J.A. Meacham and N.R. Santilli. - Basel; New York: Karger, 1981.
(Contributions to human development; v. 5)
1. Child Development 2. Personality Development - in adolescence
I. Meacham, J.A. II. Santilli, N.R. III. Series
W1 C0778S v. 5 WS 462 S678
ISBN 3-8055-2868-X

Printed in Switzerland by Basler Zeitung, Basel
ISBN 3-8055-2868-X

Contents

Preface

A variety of issues regarding social and personality development in youth is currently being examined from the perspective of *Jean Piaget's* structuralist theory of development. Among these are identity achievement, perspective taking, social relations, self-concept, friendship, interpretation of poetry, moral judgment, and moral action. The authors in this volume consider ways in which the structuralist approach may be applied to achieve a better understanding of these and related topics. This volume will be of interest to researchers and students in the disciplines of psychology, sociology, and education, and indirectly to teachers, counselors, and parents of adolescents. As a textbook, the volume provides a unique collection of original chapters to accompany the book by *Inhelder and Piaget* [1958].

All the chapters were submitted originally to the journal *Human Development,* have survived the usual review process, and have been strengthened in the light of suggestions from anonymous reviewers. Although these chapters might well have been published separately over the course of several issues of the journal, the fact that all the chapters address similar themes in social and personality development in youth was the impetus for bringing them together in a single volume (the chapter by *Hardy-Brown* is an exception, having appeared previously in *Human Development*). It is hoped that publication of the chapters in this monograph series accompanying *Human Development* will make them more readily accessible for serious comparison and criticism, as well as stimulate the construction of more advanced models and interpretations. Together, the chapters provide a more comprehensive treatment of social and personality development in youth than could any one of the chapters by itself.

The course of development in childhood and adolescence, according to *Piaget*, can be described as a sequence of stages. The last of these, the stage of formal operations, is characterized by abilities to consider the real as a special case among the infinite possibilities in a given situation, and to reflect upon the logical operations acquired in the preceding stage. Conceptually, formal operations represents a significant advance beyond the stage of concrete operations, and it is difficult to imagine an adult fully participating in life without having attained formal operations. The first chapter by *Tomlinson-Keasey and Eisert* provides a useful description of four distinct models of the relationship between formal operations and development in various domains: the total integration model, the cognitive core model, the content-free organizational core model, and the independent functioning model. Data on affective and cognitive development in college students are employed to evaluate these four models.

In the following chapter, *Demetriou and Efklides* propose a detailed framework for conceptualizing the extent to which formal operational thought underlies performance in various domains. They distinguish two levels of thought, the strategic level and the level of tactics. The level of tactics is further differentiated, with different structures corresponding to different domains of application: relational, correlational-probabilistic, and experimental. The experimental, in particular, is directed towards hypothesis formation, experimentation, and the drawing of inferences in social situations. The relationship between the strategic and tactical levels, as presented by *Demetriou and Efklides*, appears similar to the role of gamma compensations in coordinating partial systems of knowledge with totalities [*Furth*, 1981; *Moesinger*, 1978].

Demetriou and Efklides propose assessment of formal operational performance along two dimensions, yielding a vertical score that indicates completeness of structural development, and a horizontal score that indicates extension of structure to various content domains that may be more or less familiar to the individual. Thus, the horizontal score provides a means of exploring *Piaget's* [1972] earlier suggestion that individuals will be more capable of formal operational thinking when the content is familiar and of interest. For example, lawyers will likely reason at a formal operational level regarding civil rights, physicists regarding relativity, etc. The problem of assessment is also addressed in the chapter by *Chapman. Chapman* raises the question, within the framework of *Juan Pascual-Leone's* theory of constructive operators [*Chapman*, 1981], why children with apparent sufficient structural capacity still do not succeed at various tasks. Answering this question requires an evaluation of the cognitive demands of various tasks independently of the content of those tasks. *Chapman* provides such a rigorous assessment for various measures of perspective taking. Clearly, his procedures could be readily extended to issues of identity, social relations, and epistemology in adolescence.

The following two chapters are detailed explorations of the relationship between formal operations and two specific content domains. The necessity of formal operations for identity achievement, as described by *Erik Erikson*, is considered by *Berzonsky and Barclay*. Their conclusion is consistent with that of *Blasi and Hoeffel* [1974], who suggested that social and personality development may not necessarily be tied to the structure of formal operations. However, *Berzonsky and Barclay* explore a possible role for formal operations in the assessment of hypotheses and the resolution of conflicts that arise in the course of identity achievement. In the following chapter, *Hardy-Brown* explores the relationship between formal operations and interpretation of poetry by college students – an imaginative extension of *Piaget's* work.

The chapter by *Conn* provides an interesting discussion of the relationship between moral judgment and moral action in *Lawrence Kohlberg's* theory of moral reasoning. Beginning with the nature of stage six postconventional thought and the development of universal ethical principles, *Conn* delineates four issues that may be problematic for *Kohlberg's* description of postconventional thought as bridging the gap between moral judgment and moral action. In particular, the relationship between structure and content is crucial in considering what constitutes appropriate moral judgment and action. The discussion of moral development is continued in the seventh chapter by *Thorlindsson and Wieting*, who focus upon the reciprocal influences of cognitive development and the social environment of the child in influencing moral reasoning. Specifically, they provide an integration of *Piaget's* distinction between morality of constraint and morality of reciprocity, with *Basil Bernstein's* characterization of family interaction as position oriented or person oriented. Data on mother-child interactions, gathered from high-school and college students in Iceland, support the view that thought derives from the structure of interpersonal relations.

The preceding conclusion is consistent with the thesis advanced by

Youniss [1980], who provides evidence that friendship relations, such as those among peers, are equally critical in development with authority relations, such as children have with adults. This thesis, a synthesis of the perspective of *Piaget* with that of *Harry Stack Sullivan*, provides a framework for the chapter by *Volpe.* Instead of focusing upon other persons or the self as the unit of analysis, *Volpe* explores the development of the self-concept by considering the type of relationship – constraint or reciprocity – in which the individual is engaged. *Volpe* provides data to support the conclusion that the development of the self-concept is equally influenced by relations of constraint with parents and relations of reciprocity with peers in adolescence.

In previous research, *Furth* [1980] has investigated the development of the child's understanding of money, school, and various other social institutions. This work is extended in the chapter by *McConville and Furth*, in which adolescents' understanding of different social rule systems is considered in the light of their judgments of rule violations and explanations regarding the nature of the violations. Five different rule systems are considered: legal, ascriptive, moral, conventional, and interpersonal. This volume concludes with a forward-looking chapter by *Kitchener and Kitchener*, who raise questions not about the necessity of formal operations for social and personality development, but instead about the sufficiency of formal operations for describing the thought of adolescents and adults in daily life, in scientific and philosophical discussions, etc. They provide evidence for the importance of inductive reasoning and metaphysical and epistemological assumptions in adult thought.

Together, the chapters in this volume provide an elaboration of questions raised earlier by *Piaget* [1972] regarding the universality of formal operations and the generalizability of formal operations across various content domains. If, as *Piaget* suggested, formal operations are not readily applied in some domains, such as those in which the individual lacks experience and interest, then perhaps development proceeds in various domains at rather different rates. Is social and personality development in youth necessarily tied to the structure of formal operations? How can the individual's familiarity with an interest in various content domains be assessed, so that predictions as to capability for formal operational thought may be verified? What are the dimensions of content that might influence the timing of the generalization of formal operations? Is the theory of formal operations sufficient to account for adolescent and adult thought, including practical, social, and philosophical problems [*Neimark*, 1979]? If not, what additional individual capabilities are required? These and related questions regarding structure and content are all addressed within the present volume.

As editors of this volume, we wish to acknowledge with gratitude the thoughtful criticisms and suggestions of the many anonymous reviewers of these chapters, as well as the support provided in the preparation of this volume by The Boys Town Center for the Study of Youth Development, The Catholic University of America.

References

Blasi, A.; Hoeffel, E.C.: Adolescence and formal operations. Hum. Dev. *17:* 344–363 (1974).

Chapman, M.: Pascual-Leone's theory of constructive operators: An introduction. Hum. Dev. *24:* 145–155 (1981).

Furth, H.G.: The world of grown-ups: Children's conceptions of society (Elsevier, New York 1980).

Furth, H.G.: Piaget's new equilibration model; in Furth, Piaget and knowledge; 2nd ed. (University of Chicago Press, Chicago 1981).

Inhelder, B.; Piaget, J.: The growth of logical thinking from childhood to adolescence (Basic Books, New York 1958).

Moessinger, P.: Piaget on equilibration. Hum. Dev. *21:* 255–267 (1978).

Neimark, E.D.: Current status of formal operations research. Hum. Dev. *22:* 60–67 (1979).

Piaget, J.: Intellectual evolution from adolescence to adulthood. Hum. Dev. *15:* 1–12 (1972).

Youniss, J.: Parents and peers in social development. A Sullivan-Piaget perspective (University of Chicago Press, Chicago 1980).

J.A. Meacham
N.R. Santilli

Contr. hum. Dev., vol. 5, pp. 1–19 (Karger, Basel 1981)

From a 'Structure d'Ensemble' to Separate Organizations for Cognitive and Affective Development

C. Tomlinson-Keasey, Debra C. Eisert

University of California at Riverside, Calif., USA; Duke University Medical Center, Durham, N.C., USA

The *structure d'ensemble* that Piaget presents as the touchstone of his theory has been acclaimed by psychologists with a molar view of development at the same time that it has been questioned by psychologists with a more molecular point of view. Recent reviews by *Brainerd* [1978] and *Tomlinson-Keasey* [1981] present the differing points of contention. One aspect of a *structure d'ensemble* that has received scant attention theoretically is the relationship between cognitive development and affective development. Although Piaget was asked to speak on the relationships between these two kinds of knowledge, he did so only rarely [*Piaget*, 1951, 1962, 1972a] and his comments have been of a general nature.

The essence of these comments is to view affective variables as an energizing force that can facilitate or inhibit exploration and hence influence cognitive development [*Inhelder and Piaget*, 1958]. *Piaget* [1951] also contends that affect and cognition are parallel and interdependent; and are subject to the same functionally invariant processes of development.

'Actions related to others are like other actions. They tend to be reproduced (reproductive assimilation), and to discover new ones (generalizing assimilation), whether it be the case of an affection, an aggressive tendency, or any other. It is the same assimilation because personal schemas, like all others, are both intellectual and affective. We do not love without seeking to understand, and we do not even hate without a subtle use of judgment. Thus when we speak of "affective schemas" it must be understood that what is meant is merely the affective aspect of schemas which are also intellectual.'

Piaget makes the additional point that affective and motivational forces do not create structures as such but that the development of cognitive structures is accompanied by parallel forms of affective organization, as when adolescents develop highly structured value systems to complement their sophisticated logical understanding. In some sense, it was unreasonable to expect him to explain the acquisition of knowledge in the social and interpersonal worlds since it was tangential to his primary interest, genetic epistimology. It is not surprising then that both *Flavell* [1963] and *Langer* [1969] view the affective component as one which will continue to require theoretical explication. The present chapter is an examination of the possible theoretical relationships that exist between cognitive and affective development. It accepts, as its point of departure, the view that cognition develops through a series of structurally coherent and distinct phases. The question that is examined, given this premise, is how other kinds of development might be related to the cognitive structures that develop. After presenting four different models of the relationship between cognition and affect, evidence relevant to the models is presented and evaluated.

Perhaps it is best to begin by delineating what is meant by affective development. On occasion when Piaget talked about affect, he seemed to mean physiological arousal that had no specific pattern [*Mandler,* 1975]. At other times, however, he seemed to infer a pattern to the affect. For example in 1951 *Piaget* argued that: 'Since affective life is adaptation, it also implies continual assimilation of present situations to earlier ones – assimilation which gives rise to affective schemas or relatively stable modes of feeling and reacting – and continual accommodation of these schemas to the present situation.'

This latter sense of affect in which interpersonal perceptions, attitudes, and feelings do have an organization is the one that is intended throughout this chapter. The major part of the paper compares and contrasts the acquisition of these patterns with the cognitive development that takes place.

It is necessary also to distinguish affective development from the rapidly growing literature on social development. As indicated by *Shantz* [1975] social cognitions are focused on the child's conception of other people. The affective patterns that are charted here are people's views of themselves and their interaction with others. Still, the theoretical arguments made here might very well be applied to social development [see *Kuhn,* 1978].

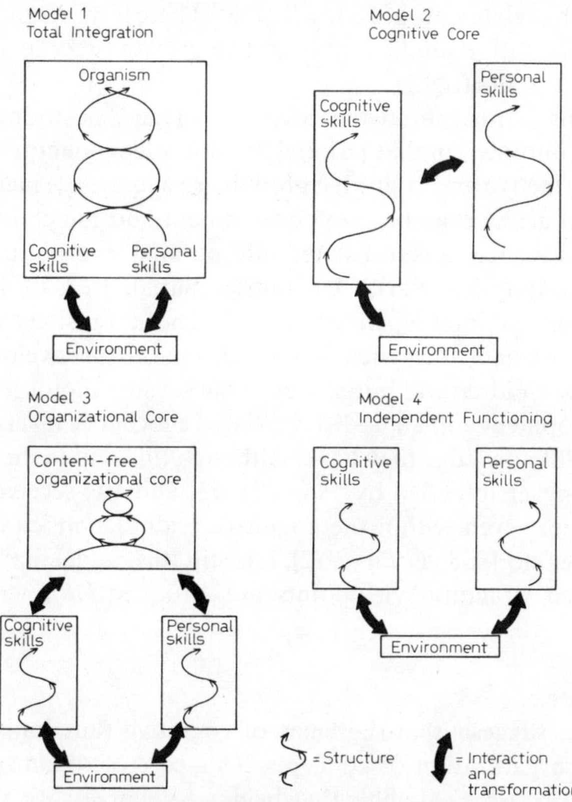

Fig. 1. Four models of the relationship between cognitive and personal knowledge.

Four Models of Structural Development

(1) Total Integration.

There are at least four models that could be used to conceptualize the relationship between cognitive and affective patterns of development. The first model looks at cognition and affect being totally integrated within a *structure d'ensemble*. As such, when progress is made in the cognitive realm, other aspects of development would, by definition, adhere to the pace established by the cognitive system. Likewise, any progress made in the affective realm would be accompanied by similar advances in cognitive functioning. Development in all areas – cognitive, affective, and social – is inextricably meshed and progress in one area is matched by related progress in all areas. There is no requirement in the Total Integration model that cognitive growth precede advances in the affective realm (fig. 1).

This model seems to incorporate the essence of Piaget's position as it has been globally outlined, in that parallel and interdependent relationships between affective and cognitive growth are acquired [Piaget, 1951]. Emotions and affect can energize development and the child's progress in the cognitive realm is translated into parallel levels of understanding in the nonphysical world. The notion that all areas of development are parallel and interdependent has often been translated in this model to a requirement for synchrony in all phases of development. In other words, children will initially be at the sensory motor level in cognitive development and an undifferentiated egocentric level in the kinds of personal knowledge they have. Although this requirement for synchrony was never intended by *Piaget* [1955] and has received little empirical support even within the cognitive realm [*Almy* et al., 1966, 1970, *Hooper* et al., 1978; *Little,* 1972], it is still this model that is usually evoked when structural viewpoints are critiqued [*Brainerd,* 1978].

(2) Cognitive Core.

A second model suggests that the heart of cognitive functioning consists of a stable organization of concepts. This core of organized knowledge is the *structure d'ensemble* that begins to evolve with the child's first physical encounters with the environment during the sensori-motor period. Progress at this core conceptual level must precede any progress in ancillary areas like affective development. Hence developmental change in affective areas necessarily lags behind cognitive development. An often quoted example notes that until the child has mastered a cognitive understanding of objects, attachments to people are theoretically not possible. There are two additional aspects of this model that need to be made clear. The first is that this model requires that development proceed in a single direction. Disequilibrium from exploration and interaction with the environment leads to cognitive growth and this progress is translated subsequently into new affective views of the world. There is little the environment can do to alter affective development directly. Any change in that system must be mediated by the cognitive core. The fact that there is minimal feedback from affective to cognitive development leads to a second, often implicit, corollary to this model – namely that affective development is somehow not as well organized as cognition.

The thrust of this theoretical perspective can be seen in several different kinds of research. The interface between cognitive development and moral development has been depicted in this way [*Kuhn* et al. 1977; *Tomlinson-Keasey and Keasey,* 1974], with investigators arguing that a formal level of thought is a necessary prelude to principled moral judgments, but that, in and of itself, formal thought is not sufficient to insure such judgments. In general then, cognitive progress, or, more exactly, the lack of it, is a severely limiting factor in affective growth. A similar distinction has been made between competence in certain cognitive areas and performance [*Moshman,* 1977; *Neimark,* 1979]. In making this distinction investigators argue that the competence to perform a given operation exists at some core level but that this competence has not been translated or adapted to the same level of skill in another content area or another realm of functioning. In general, theorists of a cognitive-developmental bent are likely to be attracted to this model because of their interest in cognition. However, there are some empirical data from the literature on infant development that argue against the cognitive core model. The finding that infants develop person permanence, for instance, before they consistently show object permanence [*Bell,* 1970] has been interpreted as evidence against the cognitive core model. To those who hold this model, however, this evidence merely demonstrates the fact that the mother is seen initially as an object and that the development of person permanence is therefore a cognitive attainment which is translated later into a more affective form of attachment.

The Cognitive Core model also seems to be consistent with Piaget's general framework since the two kinds of development are parallel and interdependent. The major difference between the Cognitive Core model and the Total Integration model is that this model not only accepts a lack of snychrony between cognitive and affective development, but incorporates it into the model.

(3) Organizational Core.

A third model suggests that the *structure d'ensemble* is an organizational core that is, as far as possible, content free. Cognitive and affective development both represent organizations that are ancillary to this core functioning but which possess an additional fund of organized knowledge that is more specific. So, for example, a child may, at the organizational core, develop a content-free notion about classification. This, no doubt, occurs in tandem with exploration of the environment. But once this system of organization (classification) is available, the child can apply it to a variety of experiences. Hence objects might be classed as long, short, wide, or narrow and humans might be classed as male, female, adult, or child, etc. In this model, progress in both the cognitive and affective realms is determined by interaction with the environment and these ancillary systems of knowledge can function somewhat exclusively if the ongoing exploration is strictly cognitive or strictly affective. But there is also the possibility of a constant two-way flow of information between the organizational core and the ancillary areas. This enables the organizational core to constantly influence and be influenced by any form of interaction with the environment. The cognitive and personal systems can also interact with the environment simultaneously.

Unlike the Total Integration model there is no expectation in this model that progress in one realm will be accompanied by progress in another. Also, unlike the Total Integration or Cognitive Core models, this model allows for disproportionate growth of either the cognitive or affective system. Using this model one can imagine a personally inept professor who functions at very sophisticated cognitive levels. This caricature could also be explained using the Cognitive Core model. However, the reverse, a sensitive, affectively sophisticated individual who cannot conserve volume is not possible in the Cognitive Core model. These kinds of major imbalances between functional areas would, however, be the exception rather than the rule since both interact with the organizational core.

Whether or not this model is consistent with Piaget's general views is a difficult question. Certainly, the two systems can exhibit parallel and interdependent development. In addition, this model incorporates the kind of *structure d'ensemble* that Genevan psychologists have always depicted – an organization that is an abstracted and integrated coding of the individual's various interactions with the environment [*Overton*, 1975; *Piaget*, 1970]. On the other hand, this model allows for development in one area that proceeds with little generalization to other areas. Some of Piaget's writings offer this as a possibility [*Piaget*, 1972b], but his position is typically interpreted as more closely resembling the Cognitive Core model [*Piaget*, 1971, p. 150]: 'It is indeed worth noting that in every domain cognitive functions constitute invariants which are vital to their functioning, even in situations where immediate experience does not seem to make them necessary.'

(4) Independent Functioning.

A fourth model advocates separate structured wholes for the two areas of functioning. Each of the areas of development would proceed in a manner unrelated to and unbiased by the other. There is still an organization within each of the systems but there is no linkage except that both would operate on many of the same environmental settings. It should be emphasized that this model still allows for correspondences between the two areas of functioning simply because both organizations act in tandem so much of the time. But the correspondence exists because of overlapping information that the two systems are processing, not because of communication links or organizations between the two systems. Of course, using this model one would predict many more major discrepancies between cognitive and affective development. It also follows that the environmental interaction assumes a more critical role in this model since there is no way for information gathered in one system to be transformed into information that is applicable to another system. This model is the only one of the four that is clearly excluded by Piaget's parallel but interdependent criteria. In this model cognitive and affective progress occur independently. Still this model is often invoked by developmental psychologists by default. It is common to present Piaget's view of cognitive development and Erikson's view of affective development with little note of any correspondence or communication between the two. Two major exceptions to this are the work of *Loevinger* [1976] and the recent surge of interest in attachment, where cognitive aspects of attachment are recognized as part and parcel of the attachment process [*Bower*, 1977; *Bell*, 1970].

Transforming Information

The four models that have been presented differ along several dimensions: (a) the relationship between cognitive and affective development; (b) the form of the organized structure; (c) the form of the interaction of that structure with the environment, and (d) the way that information is transformed and communicated throughout the developing organization. This final component, the transformation of information, is critical to a complete understanding of development. As *Riegel and Rosenwald* [1975, p. xiii] argued: 'Neither a pure structuralist's approach (which would be comparable to an inspection of the separate frames of a film strip) nor a pure transformationalist's approach (which would analyze the flow of movements in the film without any separate inspection of the frames) can lead to a satisfactory interpretation of the individual, of society, and their changes. What we should aim to study are structural transformations or transforming structures.'

A structural position that makes no provision for transforming information becomes a static, cumbersome model that lacks the adaptability inherent to development. Hence, a consideration of how the four models incorporate transformations of information is necessary. In the Total Integration model transformations of information occur as the integrated structure deals with the environment. As the organism explores, the structure influences the nature of the exploration and the transformations that result. Presumably, all transformations that occur following exploration are completed in the cognitive and affective domains simultaneously. So, in this model there is only one avenue for transforming information. Hence, this one link assumes a great deal of importance.

In the Cognitive Core model, the concepts that have been derived direct the child's interactions with the environment. Transformations of information occur readily between this cognitive structure and the child's explorations. In this model, moreover, there is an additional avenue for the transformation of information when the cognitive structure communicates with other areas of functioning. Presumably, then, once children have mastered the classification of objects, they will transform the classification scheme into one that can sort out dimensions of people.

In the Organizational Core model, the possibilities for transforming information are even greater. Transformations can occur at the level of specific systems interacting with the environment. Further opportunities for transformations exist in the two-way communication system between the organizational core and the ancillary systems. This model, then, has built into it several possibilities for flexibly manipulating information garnered from the environment. The fourth model, independent organizations, has a single avenue for each of the separate organizational systems to interact with the environment, and no mechanism exists for transforming information from one realm to another.

Evaluating the Models

Four models have been presented demonstrating differing ways in which both the structures and the transformations necessary to explain cognitive and affective development can be viewed. The task that remains is to begin to evaluate these models by assessing cognitive and affective growth at different times. Such an evaluation is extremely complex because there is no way to measure cognitive organization or affective organization directly. To measure the cognitive skill of classification, for example, children are asked to classify something - blocks, animals, shapes, etc. This assessment moves away from the theoretical realm of content-free cognitive schemes and into an assessment of classification skills in a particular area of knowledge. Thus, the distinction between a cognitive organization like classification and the ability of a subject to classify material in a particular area becomes blurred. The effect of this confounding can be seen in several controversies in the cognitive-developmental literature. Critics of the research in formal operational thought have argued that the conclusions about logical skills that have been drawn from these experiments are invalid because the tasks used rely too heavily on knowledge of the physical world [see *Neimark,* 1975 for a discussion]. Formal operational thought can obviously occur in contexts that do not require knowledge of the physical world.

The importance of this controversy for the current study is that measuring cognitive skills requires a context, and it is easy to confuse cognitive competence with performance in a particular area. It is also clear from this research that the particular task chosen to measure cognitive skill can dramatically affect the conclusions that are drawn about cognitive organization [*Bracewell and Hidi,* 1974; *Capon and Kuhn,* 1979; *Kuhn and Brannock,* 1977; *Sinnott,* 1975].

The problem is even more difficult when the measurement of affect is involved. As with cognition, we must choose a task that will measure affect, and that task becomes, rightly or wrongly, an important part of the assessment of the subject's affective development. Unlike cognitive tasks, though, we rarely ask subjects to demonstrate affect the way we

Table I. Design of study

	1975–1976 (n = 55)			1976–1977 (n = 34)	
	fall	spring		fall	spring
Omnibus Personality Inventory	×		Omnibus Personality Inventory	×	
Conceptual complexity	×	×	Ego development	×	×
Formal operations	×	×	Watson-Glazer critical thinking appraisal	×	×
American College Test	×		American College Test	×	

ask them to demonstrate classification. Instead of asking subjects to display their anger or their feelings directly, we ask them to respond to items like 'At times I feel like smashing things'. These indirect measures tell us how subjects *think* they feel, not how they really feel.

These controversies in the literature highlight the distinction that needs to be made between theoretical views of cognitive and affective development and the measurement of cognition and affect. Cognition certainly includes knowledge of the physical world, and that is how it is most often measured; but cognition can also include kowledge of social and interpersonal events. Affect, on the other hand, suggests an emotional involvement that is most characteristic of, but not limited to, events in the personal realm. Affect, however, is most often measured through indirect assessments that have strong cognitive overtones.

In the present study, we were interested in whether affective development demonstrates an organization similar to the organization that has been found in cognitive development. The data gathered include several measures of the cognitive and affective performance of college freshmen, and were collected with an eye toward evaluating the four theoretical models that have been presented. The measures selected were deemed to be the most appropriate measures available for answering the questions that were being asked. It should be understood, however, that the affective measures used were indirect measures of affective organization, and that the cognitive measures assessed cognition in a limited number of contexts.

The different assessments of cognition and affect that were used are indicated in table I. During the first year of the study, two measures of affective development - the Omnibus Personality Inventory (OPI) and a measure of Conceptual Complexity [*Harvey* et al., 1961; *Shroder*, 1971] - and two measures of cognitive skills - a test of formal operational thought and the ACT - were administered. During the second year, the OPI was given again, with a measure of Ego Development [*Loevinger*, 1976] to assess affective dimensions. The cognitive measures during the second year were the *Watson and Glazer* [1964] Critical Thinking Appraisal and the ACT.

The OPI, used during both years of the study, consists of 14 subscales covering various aspects of personality. Several of these scales deal with personal issues that are analogs of the abstract thinking skills that we see in the cognitive stage of formal operations. The *Thinking Introversion* subscale, for example, measures a preference for reflection and abstract thought. Persons scoring high on *Theoretical Orientation* indicate a preference for using the scientific method. High scores on *Estheticism* indicate an interest in diverse phenomena and enjoyment of novel ideas and situations. The high end of the *Complexity* scale reflects an experimental and flexible orientation toward reality rather than a fixed way of viewing and organizing phenomena. Finally, high scorers on *Autonomy* are characteristically nonauthoritarian in their thinking and tolerant of other viewpoints. A sixth scale, *Practical Outlook*, measures interest in practical, concrete accomplishments and hence should be negatively correlated with formal thought.

Theoretically, the measure of a subject's Conceptual Complexity [*Harvey* et al., 1961] should tap, in the interpersonal area, the multifaceted thinking skills that are characteristic of formal operations. The Conceptual Complexity test concerns the adult's ability to conceptualize issues of interpersonal concern on succeedingly abstract planes. Responses to sentence stems are categorized into one of four stages. The lowest stage suggests that a student conceptualizes issues regarding self-other in black and white terms and is very concrete about the material and facts that are part of the clear-cut and often simplistic handling of an issue. At the other end of the scale, responses are characterized by a careful weighing of a variety of variables. Interpersonal concern is now conceptualized in much more abstract and differentiated terms and an attempt is made to analyze and integrate all of the variables that are relevant to the problem. The stage-like theoretical basis of the Conceptual Complexity measure, the clear necessity to see issues as multifaceted, and the movement toward a more flexible interpersonal orientation suggest that there is an underlying structural similarity between conceptual complexity and formal operational thinking skills.

Loevinger's [1976] assessment of ego development follows a developmental framework complete with structural characteristics and incorporating underlying changes in personality structure. These facets of her theory seem to mimic in the affective realm the kinds of changes that Piaget has suggested in the cognitive realm. All three of the measures of affective development that were used in the present study require the same kinds of abstractions and considerations of multiple variables that are necessary in formal operational thinking. Hence, the performance of college students on these measures should highlight structural similarities or differences.

The cognitive assessments were also selected for their ability to depict the organization of underlying logical skills. Formal operational thought was assessed by a paper and pencil measure developed by *Tomlinson-Keasey* [see *Eisert and Tomlinson-Keasey,* 1978]. This measure was derived from Inhelder and Piaget's classic experiments in formal operations and has received independent validation with college students [*Arnold* et al., 1980]. The Watson-Glazer Critical Thinking Appraisal was chosen because it is standardized and could provide normative data on logical skills that the test of formal operations lacked. Finally, college level entry skills in the cognitive area were measured by the ACT. These tests were selected with the expectation that they could be used to examine relationships that existed between the affective and cognitive systems that are in constant flux in most 18-year-old college students.

By examining the strengths of the correlations between the cognitive and affective functioning of college students, we can begin to test the four models presented. Figure 2 depicts four correlation vectors that can represent the degree of relationship between cognitive and affective measures. Vectors 1 and 4 would be the correlations between affective and cognitive measures at the same point in time while vectors 2 and 3 represent the correlations when measures are obtained at different times. Model 1, the Total Integration model, argues for synchronous development in the cognitive and affective areas. Hence, the correlations between cognitive and affective development should be highest when they are assessed at the same point – either vector 1 or 4. Vectors 2 and 3 depict assessments at different times and these correlations should be lower if cognitive and affective progress are well inte-

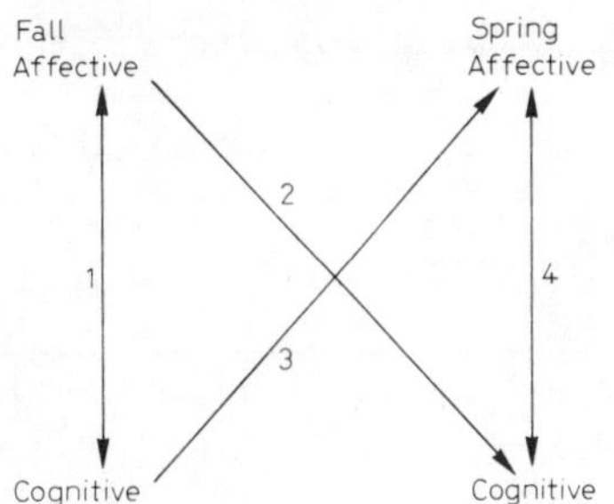

Fig. 2. Correlation vectors showing the patters of correlations that are predicted by the four models.

grated. The Cognitive Core model would predict a smaller correlation between tests given at the same time. But, since cognitive functioning is seen as preceding and paving the way for affective development, there should be a higher correlation between cognitive tests given at time 1 and affective measures administered at time 2 (vector 3). No similar relationship beetwen affective measures given at time 1 and cognitive tests given at time 2 (vector 2) should exist since affective development must await progress in the cognitive realm. Predictions from the Organizational Core model are a bit more difficult since the relationship between the two developing systems can vary so much. Certainly this model would not predict correlations between affective and cognitive measures given at the same time to be as high as in model 1. Moderate correlations in both vectors 2 and 3 would reflect the functional relationship predicted by this model. In model 4, Independent Organization, random, scattered relationships would be expected in all four vectors. There would be no reason to predict either cognitive or affective predominance or more or less relationship between measures given at the same time.

A look at the data gathered during the first year indicated that the correlations between the subscales of the OPI and formal thought were not very strong when both tests were given in the fall. The only significant relationship was a negative one between *Practical Outlook* and *Formal Operations* (see table II). The relationships between the OPI given in the fall and the formal operational test given during the spring were stronger. *Practical Outlook* was again negatively correlated with formal operational thought. *Autonomy, Estheticism,* and *Thinking In-*

Table II. Correlations between measures of cognition and personal knowledge

OPI subscale	Formal operations		Watson-Glazer	
	pretest (n=36)	posttest (n=33)	pretest (n=34)	posttest (n=34)
Thinking intraversion	0.06	0.30*	0.17	0.14
Theoretical orientation	0.20	0.23	0.16	0.34*
Estheticism	0.11	0.38*	0.02	-0.07
Autonomy	0.24	0.41*	0.29*	0.45*
Complexity	-0.07	-0.09	-0.14	0.20
Practical outlook	-0.37*	-0.42*	-0.14	0.28*

* $p < 0.05$.

troversion were positively related. This pattern of correlations indicates a stronger relationship between the affective and cognitive areas from fall to spring than when both tests were taken in the fall. The lack of significant relationships between formal operations and the OPI given at the same time (vector 1) suggests that, at least in this case, the Total Integration model was not supported. Since the Cognitive Core model expressly prohibits high level affective skills from preceding formal operational cognitions, the Cognitive Core model was also refuted. The second year evaluation, which used different measures but had the same goals, indicated a pattern of findings quite similar to the above. The OPI subscales predicted how students would perform during the spring administration of the Watson-Glazer better than it predicted the fall performance.

Since the OPI was only given during the fall, there was no possibility of using it to examine how cognitive change during the year influenced affective growth. However, the Conceptual Complexity and Ego Development assessments that were given both fall and spring can speak to the issue. The correlations between Ego Development and the Watson-Glazer measure of cognitive development are presented in table III. The only significant correlation was beetwen the cognitive pretest and the ego development posttest (0.26). The correlation between an affective pretest and a cognitive posttest was negligible (0.07). This pattern of results fits the predictions that would be made using a Cognitive Core model. The relationships between conceptual complex-

Table III. Correlations between measures of cognitive and personal knowledge, administered at the same and different times

	Watson-Glazer$_1$ (n=98)	Watson-Glazer$_2$ (n=98)
Ego development$_1$	0.14	0.07
Ego development$_2$	0.26*	0.17
	Formal operations$_1$ (n=56)	Formal operations$_2$ (n=56)
Conceptual complexity$_1$	0.17	0.28*
Conceptual complexity$_2$	0.27*	0.30*

* $p < 0.05$.

Table IV. Correlations between ACT and measures of personal knowledge

	ACT English	ACT Math	ACT Composite
Ego development$_1$	0.43*	0.27*	0.35*
Ego development$_2$	0.36*	0.25*	0.31*
Conceptual complexity$_1$	0.05	0.18	0.08
Conceptual complexity$_2$	0.07	0.04	0.03

* $p < 0.05$.

ity and formal operations (see table III) were not as clear. Three of the four vectors yielded significant, but modest correlations. This pattern of results seems most consonant with the Organizational Core model.

The ACT scores from the spring before the student entered college were significantly related to performance on affective development measures the following year. Regression analyses showed that the ACT composite, the ACT math, and the ACT English scores correlated significantly with the Loevinger fall and spring scores (see table IV). This is clearly the kind of result one would predict from the Cognitive Core model. Such a result is also compatible with the Organizational Core model. If the same pattern held on another assessment of affective growth the next year, one might feel some confidence in the relationships expressed. However, students' scores on the ACT did not predict scores on cognitive complexity the following year.

Trying to assess all of these results in terms of the models presented is extremely difficult since there are cautions about the models, the tests, the predictions, and the results which need to be mentioned. In the first place, the models as presented are purposefully stylized. As such, aspects of interest are emphasized and other aspects are minimized. Differences have been deliberately overdrawn between the models so that predictions could be made. A second caution concerns the tests. All of the assessments were assumed to be reasonable indices of either an affective or a cognitive system. Still, it must be remembered that the measures are not pure assessments of cognitive or affective organization. To move from the data obtained by such inexact measures to an evaluation of theoretical models of cognitive and affective organization involves some risk, because one is required to step back from the data and look for patterns and similarities. Such an approach is only a beginning in the effort to pin down the organization that many investigators see as being central to cognitive and affective functioning.

A third caution is related to predictions derived from the models. One of the predictions in the Cognitive Core model is that cognitive skills precede affective demonstrations of the same knowledge. But what does precede mean? Does cognitive progress precede affective progress by an hour, a day, a year or 5 years? Obviously the time period required to translate cognitive accomplishments into affective skills varies. But as it varies, so must the predictions from the model.

Despite these cautions, there are some important findings. The first model, Total Integration, received little empirical support. In some sense this is theoretically the purest model; perhaps that is why it is so easy to refute. Before dispensing with this model entirely, we will mention again the caution about the tests that were used. They are clearly imperfect measures and one could argue that these imperfections mask the total integration that exists. This argument is not very compelling since correlations were higher when tests were given at different times than when they were given at the same time. The Cognitive Core model seems to impose some unrealistic restrictions on development in a variety of areas. Some of the data from the present study indicate that high levels of functioning in the affective area existed prior to similar attainments in the cognitive realm. Model 4, Independent Functioning, poses some problems since there are really few predictions that can be drawn from it. However, the lack of any testable predictions would, in and of itself, discourage one from advocating it. The random relationships that would be expected can be refuted if systematic and predictable correspondences are found between a variety of cognitive and affective measures. This study is a beginning in that direction.

We are left then with model 3 which suggests an Organizational Core that interacts with more specific systems that are developing. This model is also difficult to disprove because it trades on moderate correlations and several feedback systems. The results of the present study can certainly be happily accommodated under the umbrella of this model. We also think that this model can be defended as a structural one. However, differences in skill and attainment, which in the past have posed problems for structural models, can still be explained. Another advantage of this model is a format which can accommodate other developing systems, such as language or moral development. Ultimately descriptions of cognitive development, affective development, social development, etc. must be merged to account for human development. An organizational core model could be the candidate that could accomplish this merger.

Summary

The relationship between cognitive development and affective development is examined via four theoretically distinct models suggested by cognitive-developmental research. In each model, the role of an organizing structure is considered as are the kinds of transformations of information that would be necessary. Two sets of data gathered on college students are examined to see whether these data support one of the models proposed. It is concluded that the most satisfactory model is an Organizational Core model. Such a model allows for a content-free organization of knowledge that then influences an individual's functioning in many content areas. This model also allows for major imbalances between individual areas of functioning, and for continuous transformations of information from the organizational core to specific areas of functioning.

References

Almy, M.; Chittenden, E.; Miller, P.: Young children's thinking. Studies of some aspects of Piaget's theory (Teachers College Press, New York 1966).

Almy, M.; Dimitrovsky, L.; Hardeman, M.; Gordis, F.; Chittenden, E.; Elliott, D.: Logical thinking in second grade (Teachers College Press, New York 1970).

Arnold, D.; Lonky, E.; Kaus, C.; Eckstein, M.: The relationship of two measures of formal operations and psychometric intelligence. Meet. Eastern Psychological Ass., Hartford 1980.

Bell, S.: The development of the concept of the object as related to infant-mother attachment. Child Dev. *41:*291-311 (1970).

Bower, T.G.R.: A primer of infant development (Freeman, San Francisco 1977).

Bracewell, R.; Hidi, S.: The solution of an interential problem as a function of stimulus materials. J. exp. Psychol. *26:*480-488 (1974).

Brainerd, C.: The stage question in cognitive developmental theory. Behav. Brain Sci. *2:* 173-213 (1978).

Capon, N.; Kuhn, D.: Logical reasoning in the supermarket: Adult females' use of a proportional reasoning strategy in an everyday context. Devl Psychol. *15:* 450-452 (1979).

Eisert, D.; Tomlinson-Keasey, C.: Cognitive and interpersonal growth during the college freshman year: A structural analysis. Percept. Mot. Skills *46:*995-1005 (1978).

Flavell, J.: The developmental psychology of Jean Piaget (Van Nostrand, Princeton 1963).

Harvey, O.; Hunt, D.; Schroder, H.: Conceptual systems and personality organization (Wiley, New York 1961).

Hauser, S.: Loevinger's model and measure of ego development. A critical review. Psychol. Bull. *83:*928-955 (1976).

Hoffman, M.: Moral development; in Mussen, Carmichael's Manual of Child Psychology (Wiley, New York 1970).

Hooper, F.; Toniolo, T.; Sipple, T.: A longitudinal analysis of logical reasoning relationships: conservation and transitive inference. Devl Psychol. *14:*678-682 (1978).

Inhelder, B.; Piaget, J.: The growth of logical thinking from childhood to adolescence (Basic Books, New York 1958).

Kuhn, D.: Mechanisms of cognitive and social development: One psychology or two? Hum. Dev. *21:*92-118 (1978).

Kuhn, D.; Brannock, J.: Development of the isolation of variables scheme in experimental and 'natural experiment' contexts. Devl Psychol. *13:*9-14 (1977).

Kuhn, D.; Langer, J.; Kohlberg, L.; Haan, N.: The development of formal operations in logical and moral judgement. Genet. Psychol. Monogr. *95:*97-188 (1977).

Langer, J.: Theories of development (Holt, Rinehart & Winston, New York 1969).

Little, A.: A longitudinal study of cognitive development in young children. Child Dev. *43:*1124-1134 (1972).

Loevinger, J.: Ego development (Jossey-Bass, San Francisco 1976).

Mandler, G.: Mind and emotion (Wiley, New York 1975).

Moshman, D.: Consolidation and stage formation in the emergence of formal operations. Devl Psychol. *13:*95-100 (1977).

Neimark, E.: Intellectual development during adolescence; In Horowitz, Review of child development research, vol. 4 (University of Chicago Press, Chicago 1975).

Neimark, E.: Current status of formal operations research. Hum. Dev. *22:*60-67 (1979).

Neimark, E.: Intellectual development in the exceptional adolescent as viewed within a Piagetian framework. Exceptional Ed. (in press).

Overton, W.: General systems, structure, and development; in Riegel, Rosenwald, Structure and transformation. Developmental and historical aspects (Wiley, New York 1975).

Piaget, J.: Plays, dreams, and imitation in childhood (Norton, New York 1951).

Piaget, J.: Les stades du développement intellectuel de l'enfant et de l'adolescent; dans Osterrieth, Le problème des stades en psychologie de l'enfant (Presses universitaire de France, Paris 1955).

Piaget, J.: Les relations entre l'affectivité et l'intelligence dans le développement de l'enfant (CDV, Paris 1962).

Piaget, J.: Structuralism (Basic Books, New York 1970).

Piaget, J.: Biology and knowledge (University of Chicago Press, Chicago 1971).

Piaget, J.: Intellectual evolution from adolescence to adulthood. Hum. Dev. *15:* 1–12 (1972a).

Piaget, J.: The relation of affectivity to intelligence in the mental development of the child; in Harrison, McDermott, Childhood psychopathology (International Universities Press, New York 1972b).

Riegel, K.; Rosenwald, G.: Structure and transformation. Developmental and historical aspects (Wiley, New York 1975).

Schroder, H.: Conceptual complexity and personality organization; in Schroder, Suedfeld, Personality theory and information processing (Ronald Press, New York 1971).

Shantz, C.: The development of social cognition; in Hetherington, Review of child development research, vol. 5 (University of Chicago Press, Chicago 1975).

Sinnott, J.: Everyday thinking and Piagetian operativity in adults. Hum. Dev. *18:* 430–443 (1975).

Tomlinson-Keasey, C.: Structures, functions, and stages. A trio of unsolved issues in formal operations; in Modgil, Modgil, Piaget 1896–1980: Consensus and Controversy (Humanities Press, Atlantic Highlands 1981).

Tomlinson-Keasey, C.; Eisert, D.; Kahle, L.; Hardy-Brown, K.; Keasey, B.: The structure of concrete operational thought. Child Dev. *50:* 1153–1163 (1979).

Tomlinson-Keasey, C.; Keasey, C.: The mediating role of cognitive development in moral development. Child Dev. *45:* 291–299 (1974).

Watson, G.; Glazer, E.: Critical thinking appraisal manual (Harcourt, Brace, & World, New York 1964).

Contr. hum. Dev., vol. 5, pp. 20–46 (Karger, Basel 1981)

The Structure of Formal Operations: The Ideal of the Whole and the Reality of the Parts

Andreas Demetriou, Anastasia Efklides
Aristotelian University of Thessaloniki, Greece

Inhelder and Piaget's [1958] *The Growth of Logical Thinking* is one of the major contributions to our understanding of the mechanisms and the forms of the construction of knowledge. By assuming that the *structure d'ensemble* of the formal stage results from the integration of the partial structures of concrete thinking, *Inhelder and Piaget* showed how functioning with concrete reality might be transformed into functioning with both actualities and abstract entities. Thus, the most important characteristic of formal thought is that it is free from content restrictions, since its main objects are pure possibilities or realities considered as possibilities.

The *structure d'ensemble* to which these major cognitive transformations are reduced is analyzed by *Piaget* in terms of two basic logical structures: the lattice structure and the INRC group structure. In terms of competence [cf. *Flavell and Wohlwill,* 1969] or structural possibility [*Inhelder and Piaget,* 1958, p. 260], these structures model the following formal thought capacities: The lattice structure underlies the subject's capacity, given a set of variables, to produce by hypothetico-deductive reasoning every possible relation that might be found between these variables and their products. It also underlies the capacity to subject these inter-propositional formulations to systematic and exhaustive experimental testing. The actualization of both abilities proceeds in a binary combinatorial way. The INRC group structure serves a double function. On one hand, the propositional transformations that lead to hypothesis formation are INRC operations. Similarly, the experimental testing of hypotheses either by exclusion (negation) or by neutralization (reciprocity) of variables is guaranteed by the attainment of

INRC operations. On the other hand, this structure determines the subject's understanding of the various exactly compensated relations that connect the factors constituting various physical systems (balances, systems of double reference, etc.)

Three major derivations can be deduced from the above Piagetian assumptions [*Inhelder and Piaget,* 1958]: first, all aspects of formal thought should appear synchronously and they should evolve at the same pace [p. 317]. Second, the formal subject should solve all kinds of problems demanding any aspect of formal thought. This is so because 'it is as if the system of possible operations were an internal network along which a given thought content, once it had engaged the network, spread out immediately in all directions' [p. 265]. Third, formal thinking is the thinking of adulthood because its equilibrium potentialities can compensate for any external disturbance [p. 332].

However, none of these assumptions has been demonstrated sufficiently. *Inhelder and Piaget* [1958] nowhere clarify whether the same individual has been tested in all tasks representing the various aspects of the assumed lattice-INRC structure; furthermore, no adult subjects have been examined either. Therefore, it seems that the first two assumptions are theoretically derived from the 'formality property' of this structure rather than empirically highlighted. Similarly, the third assumption seems to be a derivation of the almost omnipotent equilibration potentialities of this structure rather than empirically evidenced.

As a consequence some major criticisms have been leveled against *Piaget's* theory of formal thought. Firstly, some authors [*Bruner,* 1959; *Flavell,* 1963, 1977; *Strauss and Kroy,* 1977] have argued that *Piaget's* theory fails to differentiate between the general orientation of thought to problems demanding logical thinking and the specific processes and operations functioning as tools for the solution of particular problems. Secondly, a number of authors [*Braine,* 1978; *Flavell,* 1963; *Lunzer,* 1965; *Parsons,* 1960], arguing on logical and psychological grounds, have questioned the possibility of finding such a strict and clear connection between the two components of formal thought, i.e., the lattice and the INRC group structures. Thirdly, some other authors [*Blasi and Hoeffel,* 1974; *Bruner,* 1959; *Riegel,* 1973] have argued that formal thought does not capture the whole range of everyday adaptive functioning, since a considerable number of well-functioning adults do not attain the formal stage [cf. *Hooper and Sheehan,* 1977].

Because of the accumulated evidence validating the above criticism [cf. *Blasi and Hoeffel*, 1974; *Hooper and Sheehan*, 1977; *Neimark*, 1975a], *Piaget* [1972] admitted that under adverse conditions formal thought may never appear. More importantly, he argued that while formal thought constitutes a proper developmental stage it may, nevertheless, be realized only in relation to the special educational and life experiences of a given subject or population. However, *Piaget* did not change his theory in regard to the psychological reality of a *unique and unifying* lattice-INRC *structure d'ensemble*. *Piaget* seems to adhere to it even though he reduced the generality of its domain of application.

Given this state of affairs, the aim of this chapter is to discuss empirical research related to formal operations in order to identify the empirically justified organization of the various formal thought capacities; to trace their developmental sequence; and to suggest possible causal factors accounting for this organization and sequencing. Thus, the structure of the chapter will be the following: firstly, we shall distinguish two levels in formal thought development, a strategic level and a level of tactics. The various tactics will be demarcated in respect to their logical constitution and their domain of application. Once demarcated, tactics will be called 'spheres of formal thought'. This term conveys the assumption that, on the one hand, various particular thought capacities are connected to form more general thought capacities; yet, on the other hand, these more general capacities can coexist in partial segregation. Secondly, we shall try to relate the various levels and spheres with the Piagetian *structure d'ensemble* and a certain inter- and intrasphere sequence will be proposed. Finally, a tentative model, aiming to direct future research on formal thought, will be put forward.

Differentiating the Structure d'Ensemble *of Formal Thought*

As it is to be shown, *Piaget's structure d'ensemble* is an epistemological ideal of limited psychological value. It is possible, however, to identify partial structures within the total structure, which could account for the cases where limited application of formal operations is empirically revealed. The criteria for such a delimitation are twofold: firstly, they are criteria pertaining to the phenomena and the objects which are cognizable by a given set of cognitive abilities, i.e., to its domain of application. Secondly, they are criteria referring to the processes, rules or operations that define the functioning of this set of cognitive abilities in relation to its domain of application. That is, each set of cognitive abilities consists of operations and objects - actual or mental - upon which these operations apply.

The adoption of these criteria implies that, given two environmental domains, *x* and *y*, differing in organization, complexity, etc., two different cognitive structures, X and Y, might be generated which also differ in their organization, complexity, etc. and also in their order of attainment, the more complex following the simpler ones.

It should be noted that though such a conception of formal thought organization is in contradiction to *Piaget's* specific formal thought theory, it does not, however, contradict *Piaget's* overall theory of development [*Piaget,* 1970, 1971]. *Piaget* clearly conceives development as a product of the developing organism's interaction with the various aspects of its environment. Yet environment is not uniform; it consists of various realms (e.g., physical vs. social environments), each one supposedly having different structures and posing different demands on the individual. It is plausible then to assume that the organism's interaction with these realms will produce different cognitive structures to match the special demands [*Labouvie-Vief,* 1980; *Riegel,* 1973; *Turiel,* 1978]. But as the individual lives in the world as a whole and not in isolated compartments of it, one should assume that before these special structures can be formed, the individual's growing general experience will provide an overall problem-solving orientation. This in its turn will gradually be differentiated and crystallized, if needed, in specific abilities relevant to the specific world demands.

Thus, we shall now turn to the substantiation of the distinction of two levels in formal thought, starting from a basal level of functioning and coming to a second, more refined and, thus, differentiable level.

Levels in Formal Thought

We have already referred to the distinction between the strategic level and the level of tactics. The possibility of such a distinction was first noted by *Bruner* [1959], but the distinction has also been drawn by *Flavell* [1963], pp. 438–440; 1977, pp. 117–118]. *Strauss and Kroy* [1977] have also conceived formal thought as developing in 'layers' by appealing to the principles of modal logic. Nevertheless, we shall take

Flavell's account as a reference point because it appears conceptually clearer and empirically more sound.

According to *Flavell's* account, the attainment of the strategic level of formal thought marks the achievement of three interdependent abilities. First, when approaching a given problem, thought proceeds from the possible to the real; second, as a consequence, the subject understands the need to operate not just on actual entities but mainly on thought products; third, the subject's approach is already hypothetico-deductive in character. While this attainment is an advance over concrete thought, it does not, however, guarantee once and for all the subject's full formal attainment of the various Piagetian formal operational schemata. These schemata belong to the level of tactics and they are subsequently acquired in a sense independent of each other.

It is our contention that empirical evidence validates this distinction, but it also suggests important modifications concerning the structural constitution of the two levels. Moreover, there is now evidence indicating the operation of causal factors in the acquisition and structure of these levels.

The Strategic Level

Three complementary sources of evidence seem to provide support to the distinction between the strategic and the tactical level of formal thought and to their order of attainment. The first source of evidence, deriving from the performance of children up to the age of 10 years, shows that performance which for *Piaget and Inhelder* is characteristic of the formal level, in fact appears earlier, i.e., at the concrete operations level; we refer here to performance under the guidance of theories formed in relation to the problems posed. However, these theories are too close to the phenomenal aspect of data and they are, therefore, too rigid and uncompromising, more often hindering than guiding correct performance [*Karmiloff-Smith and Inhelder,* 1974]. In a similar vein, *Lunzer* [1976] reports findings indicating that at about this age children begin to *accept the lack of closure* in respect to available information. That is, they are prone to think that they have to turn to alternative sources of information when the first-hand information cannot lead to the solution of a given problem.

According to the second source of evidence [*Demetriou and Efklides,* 1979], illiterate adults were able, when prompted, to deal with formal problems although such problems were formulated in terms of ideal possibilities. In addition, the same adults were able, just as the children referred to above, to manipulate mentally alternative aspects of the task in hand and to suggest 'theories' concerning the interplay of such aspects. Yet, they were unable to plan and put into effect a test of their theory, although they were aware that such testing was necessary before they arrived at their final judgment. According to the third source of evidence, even sophisticated adults are unable to handle efficiently a number of classical formal or other complex logical tasks [*Wason*, 1977].

Therefore, it is reasonable to suggest that there may exist a developmental level which extends beyond the level of simple classification, ordering and drawing correspondences. Such a level seems to pave the way for the various Piagetian formal operational abilities by widening the array of objects and situations that thought should be able to handle and by providing, at the same time, a basic processing approach. As a consequence, the strategic level functions as a necessary but not sufficient condition, simply opening the possibility for the attainment of tactics.

Specifically, the findings referred to above suggest that the positive aspects, on the one hand, and the negative aspects, on the other, of the strategic level are the following. Firstly, the subject at this level is able, in part, to detach himself or herself from the givens of the specific problems with the purpose of organizing them on a 'theoretical' level before proceeding to direct performance on them. However, if the subjects are functioning only at this level, they are unable to detach completely from the reality of those givens in order to generate the apparently nonpragmatic interrelations. As a consequence, to return to *Flavell*, thought at this level proceeds from the possible to the real but is not ready to accept unrealistic possibilities.

Secondly, the subject probably understands, according to *Flavell*, that the problem's data as they are given and as they have been organized by the subject are different entities and that in order to find the solution required he or she has to implement performance primarily stemming from these theoretical organizations. However, the subject at this level is incapable of planning and materializing alternative procedures of testing his or her conceptions [*Demetriou und Efklides*, 1979]. This might be an indication that the subject is still unable to differentiate clearly between possibility and reality as realms obeying different laws, the one logical and the other causal. Thus, it does not come to his or her mind that alternative testing procedures are the means through which the coordination between the logical and the causal could be effected. As a consequence, we do not agree with *Flavell* that the subject's reasoning processes could be properly conceived of as hypothetico-deductive, if by this term we mean reasoning processes giving precise form to the various relations constituting the unbound world of the possible.

When and under what conditions is this strategic orientation formed? The findings of *Karmiloff-Smith and Inhelder* [1974] as well as those reported by *Lunzer* [1976] imply that this development may appear before the various concrete groupings come to their developmental end points. Consequently, the first manifestations of formal thought cannot be ascribed to the integration of the concrete groupings as Piagetian theory asserts. Instead one might assume that a probable cause of this development is the diversification of thought that is being exhibited – and possibly effected – through the mastery of some basic concrete abilities, e.g., the various conservation concepts. That is, one could assume that the processes leading to these concepts, and also the concepts themselves, once acquired, show the child that even though reality can appear in alternative facets, its essence can only be grasped through the reduction of these facets to a rule explicating their production mechanism. As a consequence, the child who has to deal with other problems that appear at first as complex and 'non-revealing' transfers to these problems an attitude of taking some distance from the problems in order to envisage possible alternative facets which may lead to the solution sought. We are not convinced that there is any need to bind this attitude to the formation of, say, the ability to carry out co-univocal multiplication of classes and relations and the like which seem to pose heavy demands even on adults [cf. *Flavell,* 1963]. Thus, basic concrete abilities seem sufficient for the formation of a formal featuring orientation. The more complex concrete abilities may be necessary for the formation of the advanced formal abilities belonging to the level of tactics. In accord with these speculations *Luria* [1976] showed with naive adult subjects that active involvement in social programming as well as some years of some sort of formal education diversifies thinking; as a result these subjects were able to escape from their personal experience and to transcend the givens of the problems posed to them, accepting them and treating them as objects of thought activity.

When is this strategic attainment transformed into the various abilities constituting the level of tactics? In this respect an extended period of education, sometimes well beyond the years of Western secondary education, and life in a complex environment (e.g., urban vs. rural) appear to be more important precipitants than age itself [cf. *Hooper and Sheehan,* 1977; *Neimark,* 1975a].

The Level of Tactics

By 'tactics' we mean the various formal operational abilities which constitute the spheres of formal thought, to be analyzed below, and which are at the disposal of the individual in order to cope effectively with various complex physical and social situations. However, it should be noted that the analysis in this chapter is limited to the interaction of the individual with the physical environment.

Differentiation of the Lattice-INRC Structure d'Ensemble *into Thought Spheres*

We shall now concentrate on *Piaget's* basic assumption concerning operational and performance homogeneity of the constituent aspects of the *structure d'ensemble.*

Let us start by considering what abilities are essentially expressed by the INRC group structure. This structure models formal thought's flexibility to grasp, through the interwined application of negation and reciprocity, the identity of effects of various operations, actions or factors, in respect to specifiable results, and to bring them together in a single mental scheme. This scheme functions as an economical framework able to be used as an interpretative tool when it is required to understand an isolated state of these operations, actions or factors, or to initiate overt performance in relation to them.

Lattice structure seems to be an umbrella covering a set of different abilities. These abilities, taken together, constitute the complete scientific capacity underlying Western experimental sciences. That is, the lattice structure consists, firstly, of the ability to set up alternative hypotheses possibly accounting for a given set of variables; secondly, the ability to devise and implement ways of testing these hypotheses; thirdly, the ability to interpret exhaustively the results obtained in order to confirm or disprove the initial hypotheses.

This analysis suggests an important difference between the thought abilities modeled by the two structures. The INRC group-like abilities appear to be mainly synthetic or convergent. Given two operations or two factors, application of the INRC group will result in their *reduction* to a relation which resolves them in a single mental product. Conversely, the lattice-like abilities appear to be mainly analytic or divergent. That is, given a certain relation, their application will result in the *production* of the set of all possible relations in which the factors constituting the initial relation might appear.

Following these distinctions, we can delimit the domain of application of the abilities underlying the two structures. The first one applies to the functioning of various physical systems where the factors operating compensate each other in various but equivalent ways (e.g., balances, seesaws, etc.). That is, it applies to the various relations existing in the physical world. Because of the equivalence of the transformations constituting this structure, we can assume that they ultimately lead to the formation of mathematical relations such as the concept of ratio (direct covariation of relations) and proportion (inverse covariation of relations). Thus, the abilities underlying the INRC group in relation to their application domain will be called from now on the *relational sphere* of formal thought. It includes the following formal operational schemata: proportions, coordination of two systems of reference, relativity of motion, mechanical equilibrium and multiplicative compensations [*Inhelder and Piaget*, 1958, pp. 307–329].

The domain of application of the lattice-like abilities encompasses every aspect of reality, physical or social, and it is consequently wider. This is so because these abilities function as a complex device generating plans and providing methods for realizing these plans in order to satisfy a 'searching' attitude on the part of the subject. Thus, we shall refer to this set of abilities as the *experimental sphere*. It includes the Piagetian combinatorial operations schema.

The fusion of the abilities pertaining to the above-mentioned spheres results in a third sphere. Its characteristic abilities refer to the conception of the correlations between events or phenomena and also to the conception of the probabilities of an event or phenomenon. This *correlational-probabilistic sphere* presupposes the abilities of the other two spheres because if a subject is to be able to conceive the probability of an event or its correlation to some other event the following requirements should be met. Firstly, the subject should be able to generate the possibilities of these events through hypothetico-deductive reasoning insofar as the probability of an event can only be estimated in relation to the whole set of possibilities the given event belongs to (experimental sphere). Secondly, the products of this analysis should be relationally processed so as to lead to a mathematical formulation expressing the degree and the direction of the probability or the covariation of the relations produced (relational sphere). This sphere should also concern understanding of social and physical phenomena and it includes the Piagetian formal schemata of correlations and probabilities. Such an analysis, implying the existence of thought spheres differing in their logical constitution and/or their domains of application, indicates that the Piagetian assumption of homogeneity in formal operational performance is not justified. Thus, we shall now turn to the examination of the empirical status of the proposed spheres.

Do There Exist Spheres in Formal Thought?

A number of researchers have directly studied the psychological reality of the *structure d'ensemble* of formal operations. The tasks were selected from the repertoire of *Inhelder and Piaget* [1958] so as to represent more than one aspect of the lattice-INRC group structure and, consequently, more than one of the spheres delimited above. However, it should be noted that a problem with most of the studies to be referred to [e.g., *Bart*, 1971; *Jackson*, 1965; *Kuhn* et al., 1977; *Lovell*, 1961; *Lovell and Shields*, 1967; *Neimark*, 1970, 1975b] is that they concentrated on adolescent and college populations and only a few (e.g., *Demetriou and Efklides*, 1979; *Dulit*, 1975; *Smedslund*, 1963] present data concerning adulthood, which is presumably the period of mature formal functioning; moreover, longitudinal evidence is quite scarce [*Kuhn* et al., 1977; *Neimark*, 1975b].

Nevertheless, many of these studies directly support the assumption according to which formal thought can be analyzed in terms of separate abilities similar to the spheres proposed here and the others can be so interpreted. The longitudinal [*Kuhn* et al., 1977; *Neimark*, 1975b] and cross-sectional [*Neimark*, 1970] findings indicate developmental differentiation between the experimental and the correlational-probabilistic sphere. The evidence from *Demetriou and Efklides* [1979], concerning adult subjects coming from various backgrounds, strongly indicates that even at the level of adulthood the relational abilities remain separate from the experimental abilities. In this respect it is highly instructive that *Shayer* [1979], after a refined analysis of the tasks used in component variables, concluded that 'tasks involving the equilibrium of physical systems are to some extent differentiated from the others which more obviously require logical reasoning' [p. 271]. Similarly, *Ross* et al. [1976] found no training transfer between the balance and the pendulum tasks, representing the relational and the experimental spheres, respectively.

However, a number of studies did find a single factor underlying performance on tasks representing the first and the second sphere [e.g., *Bart,* 1971; *Lovell and Shields,* 1967] or all three spheres [*Lovell,* 1961]. Two things should be noted in respect to these studies. First, even in the studies of *Bart* [1971] and *Lovell* [1961], two of the most commonly cited references in support of the homogeneity assumption, the correlation between tasks nested within the limits of the same sphere is higher than the correlation between tasks representing more than one sphere. Second, relatively high correlations between tasks representing different spheres should not be unexpected because all three spheres stem by *differentiation* from a single overall capacity, that of the strategic level. This means that 'once a certain level of maturity has been achieved (say in one sphere) it becomes capable of serving as one of the developmental bridges to (or "mediators" of) the attainment' [*Flavell,* 1972, p. 311] or the functioning of another sphere without one being an integral or inclusive part of the other.

Sequence in the Achievement of Formal Thought Spheres

The sequencing of the three formal thought spheres essentially refers to the order in which the strategic level of formal thought is differentiated into the various formal thought abilities composing the level of tactics; such an assumption stands in contrast to *Piaget's* assumption that the various aspects of formal thought should appear in synchrony. There is empirical evidence now (see the references cited below) indicating that this is not the case. Thus, insofar as the various tasks of *Inhelder and Piaget* [1958] can be considered as equivalently reliable measures of the various abilities constituting these spheres [cf. *Flavell,* 1971, 1977, for a discussion of the tasks sensitivity problem], we can take the existing evidence as indicating some sort of sphere sequencing within the overall stage of formal thought.

The attainment sequence proposed is the following: relational, experimental, correlational-probabilistic. The relational sphere should come before the others on the developmental scene because it appears logically simpler than the other two and it has a more limited domain of application. That is, once the thought of the subject has become flexible enough to transcend reality and form models in which alternative representations of reality can fit (the strategic level), then it should be able to develop a framework in which present appearances of reality can be located and related with other relevant but momentarily unseen appearances. The placement of the relational abilities in their simpler manifestations before the other formal abilities is also implied in *Piaget's* writings [cf. *Inhelder and Piaget*, 1958, p. 36]. *Piaget* considers that volume conservation, which is the first manifestation of the INRC integration, is achieved at the *beginning* of the formal stage, i.e., at about the age of 11 years. The precedence of this mental construction in respect to volume conservation has been amply verified by subsequent research [*Elkind*, 1962; *Lovell and Ogilvie*, 1961; *Lunzer*, 1960].

However, the ability to represent and coordinate present and nonpresent states of reality is not sufficient for effective experimental performance. The subject has to hierarchize conceptions, to formulate alternative hypotheses, to implement complementary experimental procedures and finally to integrate the results of experimentation with the experimental hypotheses, in order to select among his conceptions those that interpret the phenomenon under study. On the other hand, the development of the third sphere at a formal level presupposes that the first two are at a formal level. In accord with these considerations are the findings of *Demetriou and Efklides* [1979] that the attainment of the experimental sphere is more difficult than that of the relational sphere. In this respect, *Kuhn* et al. [1979] and *Moshman* [1979] have shown that the various experimental abilities, far from being universal even among college students, develop slowly, mostly after the age of about 15 years. On the other hand, *Kuhn* et al. [1977] and *Neimark* [1975b] showed longitudinally that the correlational-probabilistic sphere comes after the first two. It is suggestive that, in agreement with these findings, correlational and probabilistic estimates are not always reliable even among specialists within the field of their professional speciality [cf. *Shaklee*, 1979; *Smedslund*, 1963].

However, it must be stressed that the attainment order proposed above refers to the simplest manifestations of the three spheres. The problem of the possible transposition of order of their various component abilities during development will be discussed later, once each sphere has been analyzed in its constituent steps. The same problem has to be considered in relation to the tasks addressed to the testing of the various spheres.

Developmental Steps within the Formal Thought Spheres

Relational sphere

The fusion of inversion and reciprocity in a single system permitting the *qualitative* understanding of the inverse and compensatory relations involved in various systems is just the first step in the development of this sphere. The next step should be the elaboration of this system in a mathematical form permitting the quantitative grasping of proportionality [cf. *Demetriou and Efklides*, 1979]. Along this path, direct proportionality (ratio concepts) comes first, whereas inverse proportionality follows [*Roberge and Flexer*, 1979].

An explanation of this order might be that, however reversible thought may become, the inverse direction is more difficult than the direct: in the case of direct proportionality once a higher order relation has been grasped (i.e., that two sets of data covary, in the same direction), it is applied on another set of data in the form in which it has been abstracted; in the case of inverse proportionality the abstraction of the higher order relation does not suffice. Its direction has to be specified separately for the two sets of data and conceived in two directions, one opposite to the other. Thus, inverse proportionality appears as mentally more loaded than direct proportionality.

A third step seems to be [cf. *Sternberg and Rifkin*, 1979] the extension of these relational abilities to the simultaneous handling of more than four factors or two relations at a time. Inversion and reciprocity of weights *or* distances in the balance task, for example, should be easier than the same operations applied simultaneously to the various intra- and interinversions and reciprocities of weights *and* distances or to double systems of reference. These cases may even exceed the modeling potential of the INRC group structure according to *Parsons's* [1960] logical arguments. No study has dealt with this problem systematically as yet.

Experimental sphere

The concentration of investigators mainly on the abilities allocated within the limits of the experimental sphere permits its more detailed analysis. Thus, the existing evidence strongly suggests that the experimental sphere can be analyzed into the following, more or less, distinct constituent abilities.

The first ability seems to be *hypothesis formation*. It can be defined as the ability to conceive possibilities and to formulate them into precise verbal statements as this can be realized through the setting of alternative solutions to actual problems able to be empirically tested. Consequently, it can be considered as stemming directly from the strategic level. The second constituent ability is the *experimentation* ability. It can be defined as the ability to materialize hypotheses in the form of complementary experiments; this is equivalent to finding ways of giving actual form to the world of the possible and it can be effected through the application on coexistent variables of the scheme 'all other things being equal' as it has been reduced by *Piaget* to the attainment of the combinatorial formal scheme. The third ability constituting this sphere is the 'exploitation' of the results gathered in the form of *drawing correct inferences* from these results. It can be defined as the ability to coordinate the hypotheses formulated with the results gathered, in order to form a precise theory expressing and explaining the laws governing the phenomenon studied.

It will become evident that the existing findings indicate that the development of each of these three abilities progresses along three steps. These are: (a) absence – even though the subject may operate on the strategic level; (b) incomplete or impaired presence, and (c) full presence. The various empirically identified combinations among the evolutionary steps of the above abilities form the overall developmental pattern of the experimental sphere. This pattern seems to coincide in its evolution with the five Piagetian substages regarding formal thought development even though it provides a new meaning to the constitution of these substages. This pattern is as follows.

First, all three abilities are absent. That is, if hypothesis formation is absent, then it is highly improbable that the subject will carry out planned experimentation. Instead, the subject will either refuse to try any form of testing or will immediately start random experimentation (almost every study referred to in this paper reports relevant evidence) being, as a consequence, unable to reach any conclusions concerning causal relations. In such a case the researchers will assign the subject's performance to substage I of *Piaget's* stage system.

A possible reason for this absence - besides the general reasons concerning the transition from the strategic level to the level of tactics - may be the subject's lack of practice in deductive reasoning itself [*Markoulis*, 1979] and/or in experimental work, particularly if the subject's difficulties are on the performance rather than on the competence side [*Kuhn* et al., 1979]. As a consequence, the subject simply does not know why it would be valuable to determine from the start alternative solutions concerning the task given to him.

Second, hypothesis formation may be present but incomplete. Thus, the subject is unable to alternatively define the possible roles of the various variables and their interactions even though he or she is able to identify the variables and to conceive their particular effects separately. In such a case, there are subjects refusing to resort to any kind of experimentation and certainly drawing of inferences [*Demetriou and Efklides*, 1979], causing their assignment to the substage II-A of *Piaget's* stage system. There are subjects, however, who try to check their hypotheses. In this case ensuing experimentation is necessarily also incomplete as hypotheses direct experimental testing to simple classifications, correspondences, etc. of the variables at hand. The subject is led, therefore, by his or her performance to an incomplete conception of the causal interplay of the variables involved, i.e., to incomplete inferences. These subjects are usually assigned to the substage II-B of *Piaget's* stage system.

A possible reason for the incomplete presence of hypothesis formation is verbal poverty, insofar as verbal poverty is a decisive factor in advanced hypothetico-deductive reasoning [*Case and Collinson*, 1962; *Furth and Younnis*, 1971; *Lawson and Shepherd*, 1979]. That is, because of insufficient mastery of the verbal instrument the subject cannot stabilize what he conceives in exact verbal statements as able to direct him or her to the controls needed to obtain the necessary information [see *Demetriou and Efklides*, 1979, regarding performance of semi-illiterates on the combination of chemicals task]. As far as the incomplete presence of the experimentation is concerned, it may be due to the possibility that the subject has not yet attained a falsification strategy that, if present, would lead him or her to the search for falsifying evidence. *Moshman* [1979] showed in this respect that the falsification strategy is a late achievement in the process of formal thought development, following content-based hypothesis-testing (that could probably be allocated at the strategic level) and verification strategy. Finally, decisive reasons concerning the incomplete presence of both hypothesis formation and experimentation seem to be the lack of familiarity with the content of the tasks [*Linn,* 1977; *Lunzer,* et al. 1972; *Kuhn* et al., 1979; *Neimark,* 1970], or such personality traits as field dependence [*Linn,* 1978], or even the person's adopted social role that favors males in respect to formal thought attainment [*Demetriou and Efklides,* 1979; *Elkind,* 1962].

Third, hypothesis formation may be fully present, as it has been defined before. It coexists, however, with incomplete experimentation and drawing of inferences. *Piaget* [1958, p. 78] was the first to indicate in this respect that propositional reasoning at the first substage of formal thought is superior to the ways of experimental proof. In fact, a number of studies [cf. *Demetriou and Efklides,* 1979; *Lunzer,* 1973] have shown that the ability to conceive and define fully the various alternative, possibly causal explanations of a given problem does not automatically imply the complete unfolding of the techniques able to lead to the information necessary for the confirmation of the relevant and the discarding of the irrelevant hypotheses. Moreover, experimentation may be fully present with hypothesis formation leading, as a consequence, to the gathering of the data sufficient for the testing of the truth state of the hypotheses. Nevertheless, there are subjects who do not manage to draw the correct inferences from their experimentation, evidencing incomplete inferencing abilities [*Linn,* 1978; *Lovell,* 1961; *Jackson,* 1965; *Pulos and Linn,* 1978; *Somerville,* 1974]. In the case of both combinations the subject's performance will be assigned by the researchers to substage III-A of *Piaget's* stage system.

Empirical evidence suggests two possible reasons causing the above combinations of steps. First, while familiarity seems to facilitate hypothesis formation and experimentation, it seems, however, to act in the reverse direction in respect to the drawing of inferences. This seems to be due to the possibility that the existence of preconceptions about the behavior of the factors in a given problem and about their interrelations hinders the subject from correctly estimating their behavior as it has been revealed by, and only by, the experiments performed. Thus, instead of taking the opportunity to advance knowledge through the experiments, the subject reverts to his or her preconceptions, and being disinclined to give them up, tries 'logically' to rule out the 'exceptions' found [cf. *Demetriou and Efklides,* 1979; *Karmiloff-Smith and Inhelder,* 1974]. Second, the subject may not have a nonverification insight, i.e., he or she does not realize 'that hypotheses are not conclusively verified by supporting evidence' [*Moshman,* 1979, p. 104]. As a consequence, the subject overestimates the meaning of confirmatory evidence and/or underestimates the meaning of negative evidence.

Finally, a subject may perform on the third step (or state) of all three abilities, justifying assignment to the III-B substage of *Piaget's* stage system. In such a case, there is no need to suppose that the subject should necessarily produce the complete truth-functional tables. *Bynum* et al. [1972] showed that the complete range of the 16 interpropositional combinations does not exist even in the representative protocol of *Inhelder and Piaget* [1958]. Instead, very few (implication, disjunction, incompatability) are usually used by the subjects [*Weitz* et al., 1973], and even these are of differential difficulty [*Dale,* 1970; *Markoulis,* 1979; *Somerville,* 1974]. Therefore, a subject can be considered as fully formal in respect to the abilities under consideration if he or she can define the various factors of the problem relatively independent of the number of the interpropositional operations which can be found in his or her analyses. These findings, together with the disconnection found between the relational and the experimental sphere, provide justification to the assumption put forward before that the attainment of the complete truth-functional table cannot be guaranteed by the attainment of INRC structure-like capacities underlying the conception of physical compensatory relations.

Correlational-Probabilistic Sphere

The shortage of data concerning this sphere does not permit an analysis similar to that attempted in respect to the relational and the experimental spheres. The few – to our knowledge – existing studies [e.g., *Lovell,* 1961; *Neimark,* 1975a, b; *Kuhn* et al., 1977] simply report correlations of tasks representing this sphere with tasks representing the other two spheres. They do not provide data and analyses concerning the possible component abilities in a manner permitting the sequencing of or the differentiation of difficulty of these abilities. There are, however, some indications that probability either precedes correlation [*Neimark*, 1975b] or, in any case, does not appear after correlation [*Vu*, 1978].

Thus, for the time being, the developmental sequences presented by *Inhelder and Piaget* [1958] and *Piaget and Inhelder* [1975] and their relevant theory should be accepted as the only framework able to direct further research in respect to these abilities.

A Model for Studying Formal Thought Development

The analysis of formal thought in levels and spheres resulted in the compartmentalization of what had been conceived of by *Piaget* as a uniform and homogeneous entity. This compartmentalization was based on psycho-logical and functional considerations. However, any model aiming to account for the development and the functioning of thought abilities ought to take into consideration the various possible interrelationships linking the presumably partial abilities and the way they may interact to support each other as they are moving towards their developmental end points. Therefore, the following proposals are directed to this end: to direct research to the study of the segregation and the interaction between abilities *within* and *between* spheres.

Estimation of Formal Thought Development within Spheres

A scale of any formal thought sphere development should be able to yield two kinds of developmental scores. The first one should be a score able to express the degree to which a given subject has attained the range of the steps across which the various constituent abilities of a given sphere evolve. Thus, this score has to be conceived as a value expressing the ratio of the subject's actual steps of attainment to the ideal constitution of the sphere under consideration. Consequently, this score can be conceived as a vertical score representing the dimension of *completeness* in respect to a given sphere. It should be evident from this definition that this vertical score ideally expresses the subject's competence beyond any performance lapses.

Therefore, in order to succeed in estimating this score for a given subject and a given sphere we need to administer the ideally familiar, functionally relevant, interesting, etc., tasks for that particular subject; these tasks ought to be the ideally 'pure' tasks requiring the abilities of this and only this sphere for their solution.[1] Evidently this enterprise will become possible when researchers directly address themselves to the problem of estimating the above variables in order to develop task categories with well-specified relationships with various ages, cultural, social and professional frameworks in respect to these variables.

The estimation of this vertical score does not seem to present any major problems in the case of a sphere, such as the relational, that develops across a single sequence of steps. In such a case the subject's actual steps of attainment divided by the total steps constituting the sphere produce the vertical score. The estimation of this score, however, is more complicated in the case of spheres, like the experimental, that develop across more than one sequence of steps. In these cases we have to combine the various steps and sequences in order to obtain more general sequences that on one hand simplify our task and on the other represent more fully the whole range of the subject's functioning with regard to this sphere. By way of example, this is what we have essentially done with regard to the experimental sphere where the empirically justifiable step combinations coincided with the Piagetian stage system producing a five-step sequence. In any case, however, the values of this score range from zero to one, expressing the subject's competence in respect to the given sphere from complete absence to complete presence.

The second score should be a value expressing the degree to which the above attainment - whichever it is - is transferable over various contents. Consequently, this is a horizontal score expressing the dimension of *extension* of a given sphere. This horizontal score should be conceived as a ratio of the score that the subject attains on task categories that are evidently not familiar, relevant, etc., to him, to his vertical score that has been estimated according to the specifications described above. Thus, this score also ranges from zero to 1 to indicate performance from complete inability to operate with unfamiliar contents to an ideal applicability where the subject's attainment does not suffer from any content restrictions. By way of example, if a subject having a vertical score to 0.5 manages to obtain the same score on a task category justifiably nonfamiliar to him, he has to be ascribed a horizontal score

[1] We raise this point because researchers should be aware that most of the classical formal tasks require the abilities of more than one sphere if they are going to be solved at a formal level. A detailed analysis of the logical and psychological demands of these tasks can be obtained from the authors.

equal to 1; conversely, if this subject obtained a vertical score equal to 1 but a score equal to 0.5 on the nonfamiliar task category he has to be ascribed a horizontal score equal to 0.5.

It should be noted that the estimation of the horizontal score presupposes that the score which the subject attains on a task belonging to a task category not familiar to him should not exceed his vertical score; in this case the horizontal score values would be greater than one. As a consequence, strict measures have to be taken in order to give the subject tasks that, on one hand, tap the same sphere as the tasks used for the estimation of the vertical score but, on the other, are evidently less familiar to the subject.

The differentiation between these two dimensions seems necessary because it provides the possibility of accounting for a number of theoretical assumptions that have not yet been exhaustively investigated and also for the empirical data already collected. First, it would be theoretically possible to have subjects attaining high vertical scores but very low horizontal scores; this possibility is the one usually offered as an explanation for the strong familiarity effects found by many studies (see the references cited above in this respect). That is, the subjects found as nonformal by these studies could function formally if more familiar tasks were addressed to them. This assumption, in its extreme form, would imply that the developmental path of a given sphere should be taken from the beginning whenever the subject has to deal with a new and unfamiliar content [cf. *Sticht,* 1971]. Thus, this assumption asserts that the attainment of a high vertical score does not set up a minimum limit for the relevant horizontal score.

This assumption is obviously contrary to the theory of formal thought of *Inhelder and Piaget* [1958] in which the conception of a horizontal dimension is completely nonexistent. It is, nevertheless, relevant to *Piaget's* [1972] recent speculations. In this article, by advocating specialization and interest restrictions to formal thought, *Piaget* in fact introduces such a horizontal dimension. However, he left its possible relationships to the vertical dimension completely unspecified.

The second assumption is the inverse of the first one. That is, we could assume that there exist subjects operating on a low formal level on every task that could be administered to them; in other words, a low vertical score does not set up a maximum limit for the relevant horizontal score. In fact, this assumption seems also empirically justified. Besides the reported homogeneity of performance across various classical tasks (see the references cited above in this respect), there are now data indicating homogeneity of performance across such diverse examinations as classical formal tasks and 'literary thought' tasks [*Hardy-Brown*, 1979]. Assuming that the tasks used by these studies were not equivalently familiar, etc., to the subjects, we have to take the evidence produced by them as indicating that the assumption of complete dissociation between the horizontal and the vertical dimension is untenable.

To resolve this contradictory state of affairs we are forced to assume a compromizing possibility. That is, according to a third assumption, when a given subject attains a relatively high vertical score - any specification at the moment would be arbitrary - he will also achieve a relatively high horizontal score; however, his horizontal score should be lower than his vertical score but tending - asymptotically - to reach the same value as the vertical score rises. The postulation of this kind of interdependence is particularly validated by findings showing that simple practice on formal tasks by subjects having attained a minimum level of competence can dramatically reduce any familiarity effects that previously hindered formal performance [*Kuhn* et al., 1979]. We may hypothesize in respect to these cases that the subjects found as non-fully formal on the pretests used could be diagnosed as formal, if more appropriate (i.e., directly addressed to the estimation of the vertical dimension) tasks were used. Of similar type are the findings that led *Lunzer* [1976] to assume that as formal thought grows it causes *improvement in learning ability*.

It should be noted at this point that this assumption does not preclude a complementary one: that is, as the horizontal score rises, it pushes up the vertical score; in other words, if we measure the vertical score after a period of practice with tasks pertaining to the estimation of the horizontal score, we shall find the vertical score higher than it was before the period of practice. However, this assumption amounts to the previous one because after practice the part of the horizontal dimension that corresponds to the tasks used for practice is being absorbed by the vertical dimension. This implies that the extension of a sphere cannot be potentially exhausted.

Evidently, the testing of this assumption can only be effected by studies organized according to the suggestions proposed before, i.e., by studies able to clearly reveal the subjects' vertical and horizontal scores. In this case the two scores have to be considered as representing two *different* developmental sequences that can be placed into one-to-one correspondence in order to test the degree to which the dimension of extension attains the level that has been attained by the dimension of completeness. This means that we could estimate the probability of equivalence in the level attained by the two dimensions or their variability, according to the procedures proposed by *Wohlwill* [1973]. According to the relationship between the two dimensions specified above, in the case of probability estimates we have to predict that the probability of equivalence in levels rises, or in the case of variability estimates the variability between levels decreases, as the vertical score rises.

Estimation of Formal Thought Development across Spheres

This enterprise should lead to the estimation of an *overall* vertical score and an *overall* horizontal score for a given subject. These scores have to be obtained by some process of averaging the subject's specific vertical and horizontal scores for each of the three formal thought spheres. Then, the averaging of these two overall scores will yield the subject's general formal score that represents formal ability across spheres and across dimensions. By appropriately manipulating these various particular and overall scores against each other, we may succeed in our task of determining the degree to which the various dimensions of each sphere depend upon the various dimensions of the other spheres, and the degree to which a given dimension of a given sphere contributes to the subject's general formal thought attainment.

Evidently, the estimation of formal thought development across spheres cannot be based only on 'pure' tasks; we also need tasks requiring the abilities of more than one sphere for their solution (e.g., the 'shadows' task requires the abilities of both the relational and the experimental sphere). By addressing these tasks together with pure ones we may reveal the extent to which the characteristic abilities of one sphere are mobilized by or mediate the implementation of the abilities pertaining to the other spheres.

It should be noted at the end that this enterprise cannot have any serious possibility of success as two important problems remain unresolved. That is, we cannot satisfactorily understand, let alone measure, the between spheres interaction before we know first, the developmental starting and end points, and second, the exact step or substage constitution of each sphere. Certainly, our task will prove to be extremely difficult if the developmental trajectories and constitution of the various spheres do not coincide, as seems to be the case according to the assumptions put forward in this chapter.

Conclusion

The account we have tried to develop in this chapter about formal thought leans on two main points. First, formal thought development takes place on two levels, those of strategy and tactics. The strategic level, although it seems to appear before the completion of concrete thinking proper, marks a qualitative shift in respect to it as it raises actualities to the level of thought objects that may alternatively be approached and processed. Thus, the strategic level opens the way for the attainment of tactics. Second, the tactical abilities, far beyond forming an identifiable *structure d'ensemble*, seem to fall within the limits of more restricted structural entities or spheres of thought, evidently differing in their application domain, their logical constitution and complexity, and their age of formation.

This account has three main implications for *Piaget's* theory. First, the transition from the concrete to the formal stage, contrary to *Piaget's* theory, cannot be ascribed to the integration of the various groupings constituting concrete thought because the first manifestations of formal thought take place before these groupings come to their developmental end points.

The second implication concerns the Piagetian ideal of the structured whole and it comes from the empirical reality of the parts. That is, as the evidence reviewed casts serious doubts about the existence of a lattice-INRC structural network along which the various contents spread out in all directions, this network automatically loses its ability to predict and/or explain the development and the functional status of any thought ability by reference to some other thought ability. Therefore, we need to substitute for the Piagetian model one which can account for the interrelationships of various thought abilities within their psycho-logical and domain limits. This model ought to systematically connect competence with performance factors.

The above implications together amount to a third one: if the transition from concrete to formal functioning takes place in a different way from the one postulated by *Piaget* and if the various perturbations of external reality – because of the above reasons – are not equivalently compensated for at the level of formal thought proper, then the meaning of Piagetian equilibrium does not seem valid either as an overall powerful motor of development or as an overall embracing state expressing the competence of the final stage of cognitive development. Therefore, if we need to keep this concept, we probably have to specify more than one equilibrium mechanism which is responsible for advancing thought entities that are directed towards unreduceable developmental end states (consider as an example of this possibility the various formal thought spheres, or even assume that concrete thinking is not finally absorbed by formal functioning). At the level of the interaction between these entities, we may not as much need an equilibrium mechanism as the specification of the mediation mechanisms that determine the mobilization of the abilities constituting one entity by another one for the sake of its effective functioning.

Summary

A survey of the theoretical and research literature concerning *Piaget's* theory of formal operations reveals that two basic levels of formal thought functioning can be distinguished: a strategic level and a level of tactics, the second stemming from the first. The tactics employed on various occasions may differ in their structure according to their domain of application. Thus, within the tactics level, abilities with an INRC group-like structure are employed in problems regarding relations and proportions. Abilities with lattice-like structure are employed in the domains of the physical and the social world where hypothesis formation, experimentation and inference drawing are required. Both abilities are required for the handling of correlation and probability problems. Within these ability spheres a number of developmental steps can also be distinguished. A model is put forward to account for the pattern of these partial formal thought structures across a number of dimensions.

References

Bart, W.M.: The factor structure of formal operations. Br. J. Educ. Psychol. *41:* 70–77 (1971).

Blasi, A.; Hoeffel, E.C.: Adolescence and formal operations. Hum. Dev. *17:* 344–363 (1974).

Braine, M.D.S.: On the relation between the natural logic of reasoning and standard logic. Psychol. Rev. *85:* 1–21 (1978).

Bruner, J.S.: Inhelder and Piaget's 'The growth of logical thinking'. I. A psychologist's viewpoint. Br. J. Psychol. *50:* 363–370 (1959).

Bynum, T.W.; Thomas, J.A.; Weitz, L.J.: Truth-functional logic in formal operational thinking: Inhelder and Piaget's evidence. Devl. Psychol. *7:* 129–132 (1972).

Case, R.D.; Collinson, J.M.: The development of formal thinking in verbal comprehension. Br. J. Educ. Psychol. *32:* 103–111 (1962).

Dale, L.G.: The growth of systematic thinking: replication and analysis of Piaget's first chemical experiment. Aust. J. Psychol. *22:* 277–286 (1979).

Demetriou, A.; Efklides, A.: Formal operational thinking in young adults as a function of education and sex. Int. J. Psychol. *14:* 141–253 (1979).

Dulit, E.: Adolescent thinking à la Piaget: the formal stage; in Grinder, Studies in adolescence. A book of readings in adolescent development (MacMillan, New York 1975).

Elkind, D.: Quantity conceptions in college students. J. soc. Psychol. *57:* 459–465 (1962).

Flavell, J.H.: The developmental psychology of Jean Piaget (Van Nostrand, New York 1963).

Flavell, J.H.: Stage-related properties of cognitive development. Cognitive Psychol. *2:* 421–453 (1971).

Flavell, J.H.: An analysis of cognitive-developmental sequences. Genet. Psychol. Monogr. *86:* 279–350 (1972).

Flavell, J.H.: Cognitive development (Prentice-Hall, Englewood Cliffs 1977).

Flavell, J.H.; Wohlwill, J.F.: Formal and functional aspects of cognitive development; in Elkind, Flavell, Studies in cognitive development: essays in honor of Jean Piaget (Oxford University Press, New York 1969).

Furth, H.G.; Youniss, J.: Formal operations and language. A comparison of deaf and hearing adolescents. Int. J. Psychol. *6:* 49–64 (1971).

Hardy-Brown, K.: Formal operations and the issue of generalizability: the analysis of poetry by college students. Hum. Dev. *22:* 127–136 (1979).

Hooper, F.H.; Sheehan, N.W.: Logical concept attainment during the aging years. Issues in the neo-Piagetian research literature; in Overton, Gallagher, Knowledge and development, vol. 1 (Plenum Press, New York 1977).

Inhelder, B.; Piaget, J.: The growth of logical thinking from childhood to adolescence (Basic Books, New York 1958).

Jackson, S.: The growth of logical thinking in normal and sub-normal children. Br. J. Educ. Psychol. *35:* 255–258 (1965).

Karmiloff-Smith, A.; Inhelder, B.: If you want to go ahead, get a theory. Cognition *3:* 195–212 (1974).

Kuhn, D.; Ho, V.; Adams, C.: Formal reasoning among pre- and late adolescents. Child Dev. *50:* 1128–1135 (1979).

Kuhn, D; Langer, J.; Kohlberg, L.; Haan, N.S.: The development of formal operations in logical and moral judgement. Genet. Psychol. Monogr. *95:* 97–188 (1977).

Labouvie-Vief, G.: Beyond formal operations: Uses and limits of pure logic in life-span development. Hum. Dev. *23:* 141–161 (1980).

Lawson, A.E.; Shepherd, G.D.: Written language maturity and formal reasoning in male and female adolescents. Lang. Speech *22:* 117–127 (1979).

Linn, M.C.: Scientific reasoning: influences on task performance and response categorization. Sci. Educ. *61:* 357–369 (1977).

Linn, M.C.: Influence of cognitive style and training on tasks requiring the separation of variables schema. Child Dev. *49:* 874–877 (1978).

Lovell, K.: A follow-up study of Inhelder and Piaget's 'The growth of logical thinking'. Br. J. Psychol. *52:* 143–153 (1961).

Lovell, K.; Ogilvie, E.: The growth of the concept of volume in junior high school children. J. Child Psychol. Psychiat. *2:* 118–126 (1961).

Lovell, K.; Shields, J.B.: Some aspects of a study of the gifted child. Br. J. educ. Psychol. *37:* 201–208 (1967).

Lunzer, E.A.: Some points of Piagetian theory in the light of experimental evidence. J. Child Psychol. Psychiat. *1:* 191–202 (1960).

Lunzer, E.A.: Problems of formal reasoning in test situations. Monogr. Soc. Res. Child Dev. *30:* 19–46 (1965).

Lunzer, E.A.: The development of formal reasoning: some recent experiments and their implications; in Frey, Lang, Cognitive processes science instruction (Huber, Bern 1973).

Lunzer, E.A.: The development of advanced reasoning abilities. Ital. J. Psychol. *3:* 369–390 (1976).

Lunzer, E.A.; Harrison, C.; Davey, M.: The four-card problem and the generality of formal reasoning. Q. Jl. exp. Psychol. *24:* 326–339 (1972).

Luria, A.R.: Cognitive development: its cultural and social foundations (Harvard University Press, Cambridge 1976).

Markoulis, D.: The effect of language practice and familiarity with deductive modes of thinking on the reasoning ability of children. Views Lang. Lang. Teaching *5:* 115–126 (1979).

Moshman, D.: Development of formal hypothesis-testing ability. Devl. Psychol. *15:* 104–112 (1979).

Neimark, E.D.: A preliminary search for formal operations structures. J. gen. Psychol. *116:* 223–232 (1979).

Neimark, E.D.: Intellectual development during adolescence; in Horowitz, Review of child development research, vol. 4, pp. 541–594 (University of Chicago Press, Chicago 1975a).

Neimark, E.D.: Longitudinal development of formal operations thought. Genet. Psychol. Monogr. *91:* 171–225 (1975b).

Parsons, C.: Inhelder and Piaget's 'The growth of logical thinking'. II. A logician's viewpoint. Br. J. Psychol. *51:* 75–84 (1960).

Piaget, J.: Piaget's theory; in Mussen, Carmichael's manual of child psychology, vol. 1 (Wiley, New York 1970).

Piaget, J.: Biology and knowledge (Routledge & Kegan Paul, London 1971).

Piaget, J.: Intellectual evolution from adolescence to adulthood. Hum. Dev. *15:* 1–12 (1972).

Piaget, J.; Inhelder, B.: The origin of the idea of chance in children (Routledge & Kegan Paul, London 1975).

Pulos, S.M.; Linn, M.C.: Pitfalls and pendulums. Formal Oper. *1:* 9–11 (1978).

Riegel, K.F.: Dialectic operations. The final period of cognitive development. Hum. Dev. *16:* 346–370 (1973).

Roberge, J.J.; Flexer, B.K.: Further examination of formal operational reasoning abilities. Child Dev. *50:* 478–484 (1979).

Ross, R.J.; Hubbell, C.; Ross, C.G.; Thompson, M.: The training and transfer of formal thinking tasks in college students. Genet. Psychol. Monogr. *93:* 171–187 (1976).

Shaklee, H.: Bounded rationality and cognitive development: upper limits of growth? Cognitive Psychol. *11:* 327–345 (1979).

Shayer, M.: Has Piaget's construct of formal operational thinking any utility? Br. J. educ. Psychol. *49:* 265–276 (1979).

Smedslund, J.: The concept of correlation in adults. Scand. J. Psychol. *4:* 165–173 (1963).

Somerville, S.C.: The pendulum problem: patterns of performance defining developmental stages. Br. J. educ. Psychol. *44:* 266–281 (1974).

Sternberg, R.J.; Rifkin, B.: The development of analogical reasoning processes. J. exp. Child Psychol. *27:* 195–232 (1979).

Sticht, T.G.: Comments on Kenneth Lovell's paper: does learning recapitulate ontogeny?; in Green, Ford, Flamer, Measurement and Piaget (McGraw-Hill, New York 1971).

Strauss, S.; Kroy, M.: The child as logician or methodologist? A critique of formal operations. Hum. Dev. *20:* 102–117 (1977).

Turiel, E.: The development of concepts of social structure: social convention; in Glick, Clarke-Stewart, The development of social understanding (Gardner Press, New York 1978).

Vu, N.V.: Piaget's formal operations and the acquisition of the probability and correlation concepts by students in a statistics class. Formal Oper. *1:* 7–9 (1978).

Wason, P.: The theory of formal operations – a critique; in Geber, Piaget and knowing. Studies in genetic epistemology (Routledge & Kegan Paul, London 1977).

Weitz, L.J.; Bynum, T.W.; Thomas, J.A.: Piaget's system of 16 binary operations: an empirical investigations. J. gen. Psychol. *123:* 279–284 (1973).

Wohlwill, J.F.: The study of behavioural development (Academic Press, New York 1973).

Contr. hum. Dev., vol. 5, pp. 47–63 (Karger, Basel 1981)

Egocentrism and Mental Capacity: A NeoPiagetian Analysis

Michael Chapman[1]

National Institute of Mental Health, Bethesda, Md., USA

Following *Piaget* [1950], the prevailing view among cognitive developmentalists has been that the development of both logical and social cognition is a function of decentration [*Chandler*, 1977; *Feffer*, 1970; *Flavell* et al., 1968; *Looft*, 1972]. Young children are unable to solve certain logical problems like conservation because they tend to center on one aspect of the stimulus display (height of a column of liquid) to the exclusion of others (width). Similarly, young children are unable to take the perspectives of others because they center on what they perceive from their own point of view. This reasoning has been supported by evidence that perspective taking develops around the age of 7–8 years, when other concrete operational skills involving decentration are also known to develop [*Feffer*, 1959, 1970; *Feffer and Gourevitch*, 1960; *Flavell* et al., 1968; *Piaget and Inhelder*, 1967; *Selman and Byrne*, 1974].

In contrast, other investigators have reported that if tasks are sufficiently simplified, even very young children seem capable of inferring others' perspectives [*Borke*, 1971, 1973; *Mossler*, et al., 1976]. In a study by *Borke* [1971], 3- to 8-year-olds were told simple stories in which the main characters experience various emotions, and the results showed that even 3½-year-old children could correctly identify happy, sad, and angry situations. *Borke* [1971, p. 269] concluded that these results 'challenge Piaget's position that the child between the ages of 2 and 7

[1] The author would like to thank *Christine Grewell* for her assistance in administering the tasks, and *Lynn Barganier, Ellen von Brandt, Geri Cooperman*, and *Eunice Kennelly* for coding.

years is primarily egocentric and unable to take another person's point of view'.

This conclusion was challenged in turn by *Chandler and Greenspan* [1972], who argued that nonegocentric thought involves taking another person's perspective when that perspective is *different from one's own*. *Borke's* subjects could have responded correctly simply by anticipating their own reactions to the story situations; her procedure did not require children to assume perspectives different from their own. In testing this interpretation, *Chandler and Greenspan* told 6- to 13-year-olds stories in which a main character experiences an incident leading to an emotional reaction. A late arriving bystander witnesses the protagonist's emotional state but not the event that caused it. Children are asked what the bystander thinks about the protagonist's expressed feelings. 85% of the 6-year-olds tested made egocentric intrusions: they confused their own perspective with that of the bystander, attributing to him knowledge of events which preceded his arrival. *Chandler and Greenspan* conclude that while young children may indeed be capable of anticipating the emotional reactions of others, the ability to assume a perspective different from one's own is a relatively late development.

In subsequent papers, *Borke* [1972, 1978] replied that young children fail perspective-taking tasks like that of *Chandler and Greenspan* because such tasks require too much of children's cognitive abilities, not because these children are incapable of understanding the experience of others. Evidence that even very young children are capable of empathic responses implies that 'previous conclusions regarding early egocentrism resulted from children's inability to perform on tasks which were cognitively too difficult for them, rather than from any inherently egocentric orientation on the part of young children' [*Borke*, 1978, p. 38].

Stating the problem in terms of 'egocentrism' versus 'cognitive difficulty', however, glosses over more fundamental ambiguities surrounding these concepts. 'Egocentrism' and 'decentration' may be taken as either descriptive or explanatory terms. It is one thing to describe children's responses as centering on their own perspective. But it is quite another thing to explain those responses as the result of an underlying inability to decenter. Empirically, it is disputable whether performances on different perspective-taking tasks can be explained in terms of any single underlying construct [*Rubin*, 1973, 1978]. The concept of 'cognitive difficulty' suffers from a similar lack of specificity. It may be intuitively obvious that tasks can be made more or less difficult by adding or subtracting stimulus elements and response requirements. But without some objective criterion for cognitive demand, it will not be clear whether young children fail a task because of its 'difficulty' or because of its particular content. In order to answer this question, a better understanding of the cognitive operations used in perspective taking would seem to be necessary.

One attempt to clarify the concept of cognitive demand and its importance for development is represented in *Pascual-Leone's* Theory of Constructive Operators [*Case*, 1974; *Chapman*, 1981; *Pascual-Leone*, 1970]. Briefly, the theory explains children's performances as resulting from the interaction of learning, development, and task content. Specifically, children's performances will be successful only if they have already acquired the specific schemes necessary for a successful performance and if they have also developed sufficient mental capacity (*M* power) to coordinate the *number* of individual schemes necessary for successful performance (*M* demand). In a number of studies, *M* power has been found to be linearly related to age. During the sensorimotor period, children develop sufficient *M* power to sustain certain executive processes, including the representation of an end to be achieved and the selection of the means appropriate to that end. The amount of *M* power used for the executive is constant across tasks and is represented by the letter *e*. The number of additional schemes that a subject is capable of activating is represented by the letter k, so that the subject's total *M* power is e + k. At age 3–4 years, *M* power equals $e + 1$, and k increases by one scheme approximately every 2 years thereafter until age 15–16 years when *M* power reaches its maximum growth at $e + 7$. [For a fuller introduction to the theory, see *Chapman*, 1981.]

The present study was based on the idea that the relative 'difficulty' of different perspective-taking tasks could be interpreted as differences in *M* demand: children could identify the emotions appropriate to story situations [*Borke*, 1971] at an earlier age than they could distinguish their own perspective from that of another [*Chandler and Greenspan*, 1972], because fewer schemes must be coordinated in the former task as compared to the latter. The first step in testing this hypothesis is determining precisely what schemes are necessary in order to achieve successful performances in the *Borke* and *Chandler* tasks.

Task Analysis

In *Borke's* [1971; undated] Interpersonal Perception Task, children are first asked to identify the emotions expressed in four outline drawings of a child's face (happy, sad, afraid, mad). If they can do this successfully, they are told a number of simple stories in which the main character is likely to feel one of these four emotions. For each story, they are asked to point to the drawing which best represents the main character's feelings and to justify their choices. Examples of stories corresponding to each emotion are the following: (a) 'Show me how Nancy would feel if her mother was going to take her some place she liked to go.' (b) 'Show me how Nancy would feel if she wanted to do something and her mother said "No".' (c) 'Show me how Nancy would feel if she dreamed that a tiger was chasing her.' (d) 'Show me how Nancy would feel if she fell and hurt herself.'

The question is what children must minimally know in order to respond correctly and how this knowledge is schematically represented. First, they must understand the question posed by the examiner. In Constructive Operator Theory, this comprehension of the problem *qua* problem is a function of the executive. Second, children must know that certain events are likely to lead to particular emotions. This knowledge may be a product of their own experience or communicated to them by another person. In either case, it is represented as a causal-affective scheme linking objects, situations, or events with their probable affective consequences. The content of the task executive ε_T and the causal-affective scheme φ_{FEEL} relevant to the *Borke* task may be formally represented as follows:

$$\varepsilon_T: \ldots, o_i \xrightarrow{?} FEEL(P_A,x), \ldots \quad (1)$$

$$\varphi_{FEEL}: o_i \rightarrow FEEL(P_j,a_s) \quad (2)$$

where the expression $FEEL(P_j,a_s)$ represents the concept of affect or emotion (person P_j feels affect a_s), o_i is the object, event, or situation that causes affect a_s in P_j, the sign $\rightarrow$ represents the causal relation between o_i and a_s, P_A is the protagonist in *Borke's* stories, and the x and the question mark in ε_T signify that there is an unknown to be evaluated. Thus ε_T is a cognitive representation of the examiner's question, 'What affect (x) does situation o_i cause the main character (P_A) in the story to feel?' And the scheme φ_{FEEL} represents the child's knowledge that situation o_i causes a person P_j to feel affect a_s. (ε_T is set off by ellipses in expression 1 because representation of the problem is only one of several functions of the task executive in Constructive Operator Theory.)

According to this analysis, a correct response in the *Borke* task is the result of the coordination of ε_T and φ_{FEEL}. The subject, as it were, 'solves' for the unknown x in ε_T. Taken together, ε_T and φ_{FEEL} logically imply the correct response: as a result of o_i, P_A feels *affect* a_s. In Constructive Operator Theory, this act of coordination (or centration) is symbolized as follows:

$$\{M(\varepsilon_T, \varphi_{FEEL})\} \rightarrow R_T. \qquad (3)$$

Here the *M* indicates that the schemes enclosed within the parentheses are activated by the *M* operator, and R_T represents the correct task response as described above. If *e* is the amount of *M* power needed to activate the task executive ε_T, then the total *M* power required for a correct response is $e + 1$. In addition to the executive, one other scheme must be activated. Since $e + 1$ is the modal *M* power of 3- to 4-year-old children, this analysis is consistent with the results obtained by *Borke* [1971]: her interpersonal perception task is correctly solved by children aged 3½ years and older.

Analysis of the *Chandler* bystander task is more complex. In this task, children are shown three sets of pictures that tell a story involving a main character and a late-arriving bystander. Each story consists of eight pictures: In the first four the main character is depicted in a situation resulting in the arousal of some emotion. For example, a little girl is shown (a) accompanying her father to the airport, (b) watching an airplane take off, (c) climbing up on a fence to wave at the airplane, (d) returning home looking sad. The second four pictures depict the arrival of the bystander and the interaction of the bystander with the main character. In this example, (e) a postman arrives with a package for the little girl, (f) she opens it expectantly, (g) she finds a toy airplane inside, (h) the postman looks puzzled as the little girl starts crying. Children are asked to describe what is happening in each picture to make sure that they understand the point of the story: that the little girl is sad because the toy airplane reminds her of her father leaving. Then they are asked to look at the last four pictures again and describe what is happening in the story from the bystander's point of view: What does the postman think the little girl is feeling? And why does he think she feels that way? Children's responses to these questions are coded as egocentric if they attribute to the bystander knowledge of events which occurred before he arrived on the scene: if they say that the postman thinks the little girl is sad because her father left. According to *Chandler and Greenspan* [1972], such responses indicate that children have not clearly distinguished between their own point of view and that of the bystander. In contrast, children's responses are coded as nonegocentric if they recognize that the bystander does not know about events occurring in his absence. The most common nonegocentric response is that the postman 'doesn't know' why the little girl is sad 'because he wasn't there'. In this case, children clearly distinguish between what the bystander knows and what they know themselves.

The question once again is what children must know in order to give a correct (nonegocentric) response, and how that knowledge is represented schematically. According to this analysis, the following schemes are relevant:

$$\lambda_{THINK}: THINK(P_j,o_i) \equiv KNOW(P_j,o_i) \vee IMAG(P_j,o_i) \quad (4)$$
$$\lambda_{KNOW}: KNOW(P_j,o_i) \equiv DIR.KNOW(P_j,o_i) \vee IND.KNOW(P_j,o_i) \quad (5)$$
$$\pi_{RULE}: \sim(p \in S_T) \supset \sim p \quad (6)$$
$$\varepsilon_T: ..., THINK(P_B, x \xrightarrow{?} FEEL(P_A,a_s)), ... \quad (7)$$
$$\varphi_{FEEL}: (o_a \wedge o_b) \rightarrow FEEL(P_A,a_s) \quad (8)$$
$$\varphi_{DIR}: \sim(DIR.KNOW(P_B,o_a) \in S_T) \quad (9)$$
$$\varphi_{IND}: \sim(IND.KNOW(P_B,o_a) \in S_T) \quad (10)$$

where the expressions $THINK(P_j,o_i)$, $KNOW(P_j,o_i)$, and $IMAG(P_j,o_i)$ represent the concepts of thinking (person P_j thinks of object o_i), knowing (P_j knows o_i), and imagination (P_j imagines o_i), respectively, and the logical symbols $\equiv$, $\vee$, $\wedge$, $\sim$, $\in$, and $\supset$ represent semantic equivalence, disjunction, conjunction, negation, inclusion, and implication, in that order.

Taken one by one, these schemes may be evaluated as follows: λ_{THINK} represents children's understanding that what a person (P_j) thinks about something (o_i) may be the result of knowledge (thinking something with reason to believe that it is the case) or imagination (thinking something without reason to believe that it is the case);

λ_{KNOW} represents the fact that knowledge may be of two kinds, direct, perceived knowledge or indirect, communicated knowledge; π_{RULE} is a pragmatic, contextual rule to the effect that all relevant information has been presented by the examiner - specifically, π_{RULE} states that if a proposition (p) is not included in the set of propositions (S_T) communicated by the examiner as being relevant to the task, then p is not the case; ε_T is the task executive which includes a cognitive representation of the examiner's question, 'What (x) does the postman (P_B) think caused the little girl (P_A) to feel sad (a_s)? φ_{FEEL} represents the fact that the little girl (P_A) feels sad (a_s) because she was reminded (o_b) that her father left (o_a); φ_{DIR} represents the recognition that the postman (P_B) has no direct knowledge of the father's leaving (o_a); and φ_{IND} represents the recognition that he likewise has no indirect knowledge of that event.

The common nonegocentric response R_T, that the postman does not know why the little girl is sad, is generated as follows:

$$\{\lambda_{THINK}, \lambda_{KNOW}, \pi_{RULE}, M(\varepsilon_T, \varphi_{FEEL}, \varphi_{DIR}, \varphi_{IND})\} \rightarrow R_T. \quad (11)$$

Since λ_{THINK}, λ_{KNOW}, and π_{RULE} represent overlearned habits which do not include information unique to the task at hand, they do not need to be activated by *M* power. This is why they are outside the parentheses following the *M* in expression 11. The schemes inside the parentheses, however, all pertain directly to the task, are not overlearned, and therefore must be activated by *M* power. As indicated in this expression, the amount of *M* power necessary to generate R_T is $e + 3$. Since this is the modal *M* power of children aged 7–8 years, the present analysis agrees with the results obtained by *Chandler and Greenspan* [1972]: that children begin to give nonegocentric responses on the bystander task at about this age.

Expression 11 also demonstrates why children with an *M* power of less than $e + 3$ generate egocentric responses in the bystander task. Such children cannot activate φ_{FEEL}, φ_{DIR}, and φ_{IND} simultaneously. Generally, either φ_{DIR} or φ_{IND} (or both) are not activated so that children's responses are entirely a function of φ_{FEEL}. In response to the examiner's question, 'Why does the postman think the little girl is sad?', children reply, 'Because her father left', or 'Because the toy airplane reminds her that her father left'. This is simply a verbalization of the information contained in φ_{FEEL}. If children are asked how the postman knows this, they often reply, 'Because he was there', or 'Because someone told him' despite the fact that the stories contain no such information. These responses indicate that either φ_{DIR} or φ_{IND} has not been taken into account.

One other type of response to the bystander task, the 'probabilistic' response, also needs to be considered. Children sometimes say that the postman *might* think the little girl is sad because her father left her. *Chandler* [undated] considers this one of several types of borderline or transitional egocentric/nonegocentric responses: children giving such responses state the possibility that the bystander's perspective may be the same as their own, but the use of probabilistic language indicates some doubt that this is really the case. The present analysis suggests that an *M* power of $e + 3$ would likely be necessary even for doubt to exist that the two perspectives differ. The probabilistic response may indeed be transitional, characteristic of children who have only recently acquired *M* power of $e + 3$. Such children may realize that the bystander does not really known what made the main character sad, but lack confidence in their reasoning. Alternatively, they may realize that the bystander does not know, but in attempting to construct what he might imagine, they are swayed by their own knowledge of these events. In either case, if is predicted that *M* power of $e + 3$ is also a necessary but not sufficient condition for a probabilistic response of the type described.

This analysis suggests that both *Borke* and *Chandler* are correct in their interpretations of their respective tasks. If 'cognitive difficulty' is interpreted in terms of *M* demand, then *Borke* is correct in saying that the *Chandler* task (with *M* demand of $e + 3$) is more difficult than her own ($e + 1$). But the analysis also supports *Chandler's* assertion that children are unable to distinguish their own perspective from that of others before approximately the age of 7 years: only children with *M* power of a least $e + 3$ are able to construct what the bystander knows about events in the story apart from what they know themselves. To say that the two tasks differ in *M* demand is not to say that the difference between them is merely quantitative. It is a quantitative difference that is also qualitative. The ability of older children to coordinate more schemes makes a different type of thinking possible. The differences between *Borke* and *Chandler* reduce to different interpretations of the meaning of 'egocentrism'. If, following *Borke*, 'egocentrism' is taken to be an inability to comprehend the thoughts or feelings of other persons, then it is surely the case that even young children are not egocentric. But if egocentrism is interpreted, following *Chandler and Greenspan*, as the inability to distinguish one's own perspective from that of another when the two perspectives are different, then egocentrism does characterize the thinking of most children under the age of 7 years. This second interpretation seems to be closer to *Piaget's* original use of the term.

An Empirical Test

The major prediction of this analysis of the bystander task is that an *M* power of $e + 3$ is a necessary but not sufficient condition for nonegocentric or probabilistic responses of the types described. Given the known relation between age and *M* power, this prediction was seen to be consistent with the results obtained by *Chandler and Greenspan* [1972]. Since the correlation between age and *M* power is not perfect, a stronger test would be obtained by measuring *M* power directly. In the present study, *M* power was assessed with the Backward Digit Span subtest from the Wechsler Intelligence Scale for Children (WISC). It was predicted that only children who can reverse at least three digits (M power $\geqq e + 3$) will demonstrate nonegocentric responses on the *Chandler* bystander task.

20 girls and 20 boys between the ages of 4 years 1 month and 8 years 4 months (mean = 6–0) participated. This number included 5 4-year-olds, 10 5-year-olds, 11 6-year-olds, 9 7-year-olds, and 5 8-year-olds. The two major variables were the number of digits reversed on the Backward Digit Span subtest from the WISC [*Wechsler*, 1974] and coded responses on the *Chandler* bystander role-taking task [*Chandler*, undated]. The highest number of digits reversed on at least one of two trials in the standard WISC Backward Digit Span subtest was taken as an estimate of *M* power. For purposes of comparison, the Forward Digit Span subtest of the WISC was also administered.

The *Chandler* bystander task was administered according to the standard procedure [*Chandler*, undated]. Three stories were used: Postman, Sand Castle, and Bakery. For each story, children were asked to describe what was happening in each of the eight accompanying pictures. Children were questioned until they understood the antecedent event, the hero's affective reaction, and the relation between the two. Then children were instructed to return to the point at which the bystander entered the story and to recount the rest of the story from the bystander's point of view. Children were asked how the bystander thinks the protagonist feels in the last picture and why he thinks he or she feels that way. If it was unclear whether or not children realized that the bystander did not know why the main character felt as she or he did, additional questions were asked.

An initial effort to code children's responses according to *Chandler's* original categories indicated that several of his categories were not used by any children in this sample and that the responses of some of the youngest children did not fit into any of his categories. Therefore, an alternative coding scheme was added which included the following classes of responses.

Nonegocentric. Child clearly states that the bystander does not know why the protagonist feels the way he or she does.

Probabilistic. The child uses probabilistic language in attributing privileged information to the bystander. Example: 'The mailman *might* think that the little girl is sad because the toy airplane reminds her that her father left.'

Egocentric. The child clearly attributes to the bystander knowledge of events occurring before his entrance into the story.

Noncomprehending. The child insists that she or he does not know what the bystander thinks, or gives some evidence of forgetting the antecedents of the protagonist's feelings. Example: 'She just felt sad'.

Unscorable. Child makes up novel reasons for the protagonist's feelings, and it is unclear whether or not he or she realizes that the bystander does not know the true reason. Example: 'She's sad because she got an airplane, and she wanted a doll'. Both the oldest and youngest children sometimes gave responses of this type: older children gave responses of this type because they realized that the bystander did not know the true reason for the protagonist's feelings and went on to give a plausible alternative, while younger children gave this kind of response most likely because they had forgotten the true reason. Responses were considered unscorable when there was no additional information to distinguish between these two ways of arriving at the same response. Also considered unscorable were cases in which children gave both egocentric and nonegocentric responses or simply restated the story.

From the scores for individual stories, an overall perspective-taking score was derived in the following way: if the child did not obtain the same score on all three stories, then the most frequent score (that obtained on two of the three stories) was taken[2]. 2 children who had 'unscorable' responses on all three stories were eliminated from the study and replaced with 2 others. Overall scores were highly correlated with scores on the individual stories: r = 0.76 with Postman, r = 0.97 with Sand Castle, and r = 0.95 with Bakery. Inter-rater reliability was also high, with two independent raters agreeing on 90% of their overall scores. The Peabody Picture Vocabulary Test [*Dunn*, 1965] was also administered as a measure of verbal IQ and mental age.

As indicated in table I, the major prediction of the present analysis was supported: only children who were able to reverse at least three digits [i.e., whose estimated *M* power was at least $e + 3$] gave probabilistic or nonegocentric responses on the *Chandler* task. By the Empty Cells Test[3], the probability that zero observations should fall inside the predicted empty cells (enclosed by the rectangle in table I) is statistically significant ($p = 0.024$). Table II indicates that this effect is not solely a

[2] In view of the hypothesis that nonegocentric responses would require *M* power of $e + 3$, it was important to determine whether any children with 'egocentric' overall scores nevertheless gave a 'nonegocentric' response on at least one story. There were 2 such children, both with *M* power of $e + 2$. Their nonegocentric answers were both given to the Postman story and were advanced with some hesitation. In the Postman story, the bystander has a clearly puzzled expression in the last picture, and nonegocentric responses might have been based on his expression alone. Given this possibility, it seemed justified to base these children's overall scores on their egocentric responses to the other two stories according to the rule given in the text. In future studies, ambiguity could be avoided by asking children *why* the bystander does not know the reason for the protagonist's reaction.

[3] The Empty Cells Test was introduced by *de Ribaupierre and Pascual-Leone* [1979] in order to test the hypothesis that a particular level of one ordinal variable is a necessary but not sufficient condition for a particular level of another ordinal variable. The a priori probability that an observation will fall within the predicted empty cells is determined from the marginal frequencies. In table I, this probability is:

$$\frac{(4+9)}{40} \times \frac{(6+5)}{40} = 0.089.$$

The likelihood of the obtained distribution of observation is determined from the binominal formula. In table I, the likelihood that 0 of 40 observations fall in the predicted empty cells given the a priori probability of 0.089 is: $(1 - 0.089)^{40} = 0.024$.

Table I. Cross-classification of children by estimated *M* power and bystander task scores (with predicted empty cells enclosed by rectangle)

M power[a]	Bystander task scores				
	noncompre-hending	ego-centric	probabi-listic	nonego-centric	total
$\leqq e+1$	3	3	0	0	6
$e+2$	0	5	0	0	5
$e+3$	0	13	2	7	22
$\geqq e+4$	0	3	2	2	7
Total	3	24	4	9	40

[a] Estimated from backward digit span.

Table II. Cross-classification of children by age and bystander task scores

Age years	Bystander task scores				
	noncompre-hending	ego-centric	probabi-listic	nonego-centric	total
4	3	2	0	0	5
5	0	9	0	1	10
6	0	7	1	3	11
7	0	5	2	2	9
8	0	1	1	3	5
Total	3	24	4	9	40

function of age. Five 5- and 6-year-olds gave nonegocentric or probabilistic responses on the bystander task, but these were all children who had successfully reversed at least three digits. Thus, more specific predictions regarding children's bystander scores could be made using estimates of *M* power as compared to age alone.

Linear relations between variables are presented in table III. Zero-order correlations indicate that bystander scores are related to all other cognitive variables, but some of these relations may be attributed to

Table III. Intercorrelations of variables[a]

		Variable				
		2	3	4	5	6
1.	Age	0.55***	0.61***	0.32*	0.11	0.77***
2.	Bystander task		0.53***	0.41**	0.46**	0.65***
3.	Digits backward	0.30		0.64***	0.33*	0.60***
4.	Digits forward	0.29	0.54***		0.15	0.34*
5.	Peabody IQ	0.26	0.34*	0.12		0.65***
6.	Peabody Mental Age	0.34*	0.34*	0.19	0.90***	

[a] Zero-order correlations are presented above the diagonal and first-order partial correlations with age partialled out below the diagonal (n = 40).

* $p < 0.05$; ** $p < 0.01$; *** $p < 0.001$.

age: with age partialled out, only Peabody Mental Age remained correlated with perspective taking. Backward Digit Span is correlated with other cognitive measures, even with age partialled out. The mean Peabody IQ for the sample was 118 (SD = 10.4), suggesting that these children as a group were somewhat advanced for their ages. Sex differences were not found on any of the variables.

Discussion

The major hypothesis of this analysis of the *Chandler* bystander task, that an *M* power of at least $e + 3$ is a necessary condition for nonegocentric or probabilistic responses on this task, was supported by the data. As indicated in table I, not a single subject performed contrary to this expectation. None of the 11 children with *M* power of $e + 2$ or less gave probabilistic or nonegocentric responses on the bystander task, and none of the 13 children who did give such responses had an *M* power of less than $e + 3$. The remaining 16 children had *M* power of $e + 3$ or more but still gave egocentric responses, suggesting that although $e + 3$ may be necessary for nonegocentric and probabilistic responses, it is not a sufficient condition for them.

One obvious question is why these 16 children continued to give egocentric responses even though they possessed sufficient capacity for nonegocentric solutions. The foregoing task analysis suggests several possibilities. First, a typical nonegocentric response on the bystander task is seen to rest on certain linguistic prerequisites. Children's responses might be affected if they have an atypical understanding of 'thinking' and 'knowing'. Second, the pragmatic metarule πRULE, to the effect that all relevant information has been presented, is seen as functioning to prevent confabulatory egocentric responses. ('The postman knows why the little girl is sad because he was there', or 'because someone told him'). If children have not acquired this metarule from the practical experience of being questioned by adults, they might continue to give such responses. Third, the analysis indicates that a scheme such as φFEEL representing the causality involved in emotional reactions is also necessary. The fact that understanding emotional causality is prerequisite to nonegocentric solutions of the *Chandler* task has been demonstrated by *Edelstein* et al. [1980], and similar results were reported by *Gove and Keating* [1979].

A fourth possibility is that the bystander task presents children with what *Pascual-Leone* [1970] calls 'misleading cues'. These are perceptual or linguistic cues which tend to direct a subject's attention away from a correct solution to a problem in question. According to *Pascual-Leone*, field independence is a measure of the degree to which subjects can resist such misleading cues. The bystander task might present children with a misleading cue if from previous experience they have acquired the habit of equating a sentence of the form, '*A* thinks that *P*', with the subordinate clause, '*P*'. This might cause them to misrepresent the examiner's question, 'Why does the Postman think the little girl is sad?' as 'Why is the little girl sad?' To the extent that this occurs, measures of field independence should discriminate egocentric and nonegocentric responders from among children who have sufficient *M* power for nonegocentric solutions.

The present analysis clarifies several issues in the understanding of perspective taking. Rather than a force encapsulating children within their own point of view, 'egocentrism' is seen as a kind of default option elicited when the cognitive demand of a perspective-taking task exceeds available capacity. Young children are not held to be 'egocentric' in the sense of being unable to understand another person's feelings [*Borke*, 1971, 1978]. With a scheme such as φFEEL, even very young children should be capable of 'reading off' the affective quality of situations and events [*Gove and Keating*, 1979], thereby anticipating the emotional reactions of others. Below the age of 7 or 8 years, however, children are likely to give egocentric responses on tasks like the bystander task which require them to construct a perspective different from their own [*Chandler and Greenspan*,1972]. On the bystander task at least, nonegocentric responses require the coordination of three independent schemes. Here 'egocentrism' serves a purely descriptive function in labelling the responses of children to a particular task; it does not also purport to explain those responses.

Another implication of the analysis is that perspective taking is not a unitary construct [*Kurdek and Rodgon*, 1975; *Kurdek*, 1977; *Rubin*, 1973,1978]. All of the schemes represented in expression 11 (except πRULE) pertain either to the specific content of the task or to the language in which this content is communicated. None of these schemes represent any general perspective-taking construct. Instead, perspective taking is conceived as a novel performance [*Chapman*, 1981; *Pascual-Leone*, 1976] constructed from relevant schemes already possessed by the child. Accordingly, there is no reason to expect different perspective-taking tasks to correlate highly, unless task analysis shows them to have the same *M* demand or to involve similar schemes.

As for the importance of decentration in perspective taking, this is explicated by the *M* operator construct itself. Young children tend to center on one or two aspects of a task because they only have *M* power sufficient to activate one or two schemes at a time. Conversely, decentration is the growing ability to coordinate more schemes at once. Constructive operator theory also explicates the idea that perspective taking involves a process of *simultaneous synthesis* [*Kurdek*, 1977; *Urberg and Docherty*, 1976]. According to the *M* operator model, performance on perspective-taking and many other cognitive tasks results from the coordination (or 'synthesis') of simultaneously activated schemes. The present approach differs from previous accounts of perspective taking in attempting to specify in a precise way the cognitive operations involved, and for this reason it deserves further consideration.

Summary

An analysis of the *Chandler* bystander perspective-taking task is presented, based on *Pascual-Leone's* Theory of Constructive Operators. According to this analysis, a nonegocentric response on this task is the result of the simultaneous activation and coordination of three independent schemes by the *M* operator. Data from 40 children between 4 and 8 years support this hypothesis: only children with *M* power sufficient to coordinate at least three independent schemes, as estimated from backward digit span performance, were also capable of nonegocentric (or probabilistic) responses on the *Chandler* task. It is concluded that perspective taking is not a unitary construct, but a novel performance produced by.the coordination of several task-specific schemes.

References

Borke, H.: Interpersonal perception of young children. Devl Psychol. *5:* -269 (1971).

Borke, H.: Chandler and Greenspan's 'Ersatz egocentrism': a rejoinder. Devl Psychol. *7:* 107–109 (1972).

Borke, H.: The development of empathy in Chinese and American children between three and six years of age: a cross-culture study. Devl Psychol. *9:* 102–108 (1973).

Borke, H.: Piaget's view of social interaction and the theoretical construct of empathy; in Siegel, Brainerd, Alternatives to Piaget: .critical essays on the theory, pp. 29–42 (Academic Press, New York 1978).

Borke, H.: Interpersonal awareness test. Carnegie-Mellon University (undated).

Case, R.: Structures and strictures: some functional limitations on the course of cognitive growth. Cognitive Psychol. *6:* 544–573 (1974).

Chandler, M.J.: Social cognition: a selective review of current research; in Overton, Gallagher, Knowledge and development, vol. I: Advances in research and theory, pp. 93–147 (Plenum Press, New York 1977).

Chandler, M.J.: Manual for administration and scoring of bystander cartoon sequences. University of Rochester (undated).

Chandler, M.J.; Greenspan, S.: Ersatz egocentrism: a reply to H. Borke. Devl Psychol. *7:* 104–106 (1972).

Chapman, M.: Pascual-Leone's theory of constructive operators: an introduction. Hum. Dev. *24:* 145–155 (1981).

Dunn, L.M.: Peabody picture vocabulary test (American Guidance Service, Circle Pines, Minn., 1965).

Edelstein, W.; Keller, M.; Wahlen, K.: Structure and content in social cognition: a logical and empirical analysis. Paper presented at the Southeastern Conference on Human Development, Alexandria, Va. (1980).

Feffer, M.H.: The cognitive implications of role-taking behavior. J. Personality *27:* 152–168 (1959).

Feffer, M.H.: Developmental analysis of interpersonal behavior. Psychol. Rev. *77:* 197–214 (1970).

Feffer, M. H.; Gourevitch, V.: Cognitive aspects of role-taking in children. J. Personality *28:* 383–396 (1960).

Flavell, J.H.; Botkin, P.T.; Fry, C.L.; Wright, S.W.; Jarvis, P.E.: The development of role-taking and communication skills in children (Wiley, New York 1968).

Gove, F.L.; Keating, D.P.: Empathic role-taking precursors. Devl Psychol. *15:* 594–600 (1979).

Kurdek, L.A.: Structural components and intellectual correlates of cognitive perspective taking in first- through fourth-grade children. Child Dev. *48:* 1503–1511 (1977).

Kurdek, L.A.; Rodgon, M.M.: Perceptual, cognitive and affective perspective taking in kindergarten through sixth grade children. Devl Psychol. *11:*643–650 (1975).

Looft, W.R.: Egocentrism and social interaction across the life span. Psychol. Bull. *78:* 73–92 (1972).

Mossler, D.G.; Marvin, R.S.; Greenberg, M.T.: Conceptual perspective taking in 2- to 6-year-old children. Devl Psychol. *12:*85–86 (1976).

Pascual-Leone, J.: A mathematical model for the transition rule in Piaget's developmental stages. Acta psychol. *32:*301–345 (1970).

Pascual-Leone, J.: A view of cognition from a formalist's perspective; in Riegel, Meacham, The developing individual in a changing world. vol. 1, pp. 89–106 (Mouton, The Hague 1976).

Piaget, J.: The psychology of intelligence (Harcourt, Brace, New York 1950).

Piaget, J., Inhelder, B.: The child's conception of space (Norton, New York 1967).

Ribaupierre, A. de; Pascual-Leone, J.: Formal operations and *M* power. A neo-Piagetian investigation. New Direct. Child Dev. *5:* 1–43 (1979).

Rubin, K.H.: Egocentrism in childhood: a unitary construct? Child Dev. *44:* 102–110 (1973).

Rubin, K.H.: Role taking in childhood: some methodological considerations. Child Dev. *49:*428–433 (1978).

Selman, R.L.; Byrne, D.F.: A structural-developmental analysis of levels of role taking in middle childhood. Child Dev. *45:*803–806 (1974).

Urberg, K.A.; Docherty, E.M.: Development of role-taking skills in young children. Devl. Psychol. *12:*198–203 (1976).

Wechsler, D.: Wechsler Intelligence Scale for Children revised (Psychological Corp., New York 1974).

Contr. hum. Dev., vol. 5, pp. 64–87 (Karger, Basel 1981)

Formal Reasoning and Identity Formation: A Reconceptualization

Michael D. Berzonsky, Craig R. Barclay[1]

State University of New York College at Cortland, Cortland, N.Y., USA

One of the fundamental issues in developmental psychology focuses on the hypothetical relationship between a person's level of cognitive competence and observed behavior. An area where this problem has received increasing attention is in personality development. More specifically, developmental psychologists have been interested in the relationship between the development of formal-operational thinking and identity formation [*Inhelder and Piaget,* 1958; *Marcia,* 1980]. However, the available data generally fail to support this proposed relationship [e.g., *Berzonsky* et al., 1975; *Cauble,* 1976]. Moreover, the argument has been made [cf. *Blasi and Hoeffel,* 1974; *Broughton,* 1977] that, theoretically, one should not expect to find a correlation between the personality changes involved in identity formation and formal-operational reasoning.

Our purpose is to suggest that formal-operational reasoning can be conceptualized as a set of problem-solving strategies that can be applied to the personal problems and crises involved in identity formation. We attempt to show how this conceptualization is compatible with recent findings in social psychology, where adults generally are unable to verbalize the basis on which they make decisions [*Nisbett and Ross,* 1980; *Nisbett and Wilson,* 1977]. Our conclusions point to areas in which empirical verification may be sought.

[1] Gratitude is expressed to *William Hoyer, Robert Lehr, James Marcia,* and two anonymous reviewers for their thoughtful reactions to earlier versions of this chapter.

Formal Reasoning and Identity Formation

According to *Erikson's* [1959,1968] theory of personality development, adolescence is a time for intensive self-examination. In order to achieve a sense of identity or self-definition, youth must consider, examine, and test a variety of beliefs, aspirations, and adult roles. It is important to stress that Erikson distinguishes between having an identity and the process of personally achieving or forming an identity. Some youth, for instance, do not experience an extended period of self-testing and examination; they basically become what others expect them to be. The process of identity achievement, in contrast, presupposes a 'moratorium' period during which self-examination and role-experimentation occurs. While this process is not exclusively cognitive in nature, relatively accurate self-insight and a concern with inner [personal] truth as well as reality testing are said to be associated with identity achievement [*Erikson,* 1964]. *Erikson* [1964, 1968] has speculated that formal reasoning, as described by *Inhelder and Piaget* [1958], may play a role in this process.

Inhelder and Piaget [1958] have, likewise, theorized that an empirical relationship should be found between formal-operational thinking and identity formation. In order to consider and assume adult roles, *Inhelder and Piaget* [1958] argued, the adolescent has to go beyond the reality of the present and construct a personal theory about possibilities in the future. As they write:

> ... the child has no powers of reflection – i.e., no second-order thoughts which deal critically with his (or her) own thinking. No theory can be built without such reflection.
>
> In contrast, the adolescent is able to analyze his (or her) own thinking and construct theories ... From the functional standpoint, his (or her) systems are significant in that they furnish the cognitive and evaluative bases for the assumption of adult roles ... [p. 340].

In order for adolescents to go beyond immediate reality, construct personal theories, and deal with ideological issues, two aspects of formal reasoning are said to be critical: (1) second-order operations or thinking about thought, and (2) a reversal of reality and possibility.

The Piagetian description of formal reasoners – viz., they analyze, reflect upon, and deal critically with their own thinking – suggests activities and knowledge that are metacognitive in nature [cf. *Moshman,* 1979]. This same metacognitive theme was recently underscored by *Karmiloff-Smith and Inhelder* [1974/75] who noted that '... the formal operational child was frequently capable of attempting to test hypotheses and verify theories by deliberately seeking counter examples' [p. 208]. They found that a concrete reasoner, in contrast, employed *implicit theories* and was *unable* '... to conceptualize explicitly on what he (or she) is doing and why' [p. 209]. Our use of the term metacognitive here, seems to imply more than just thinking about cognitive phenomena [cf. *Brown and DeLoache,* 1978; *Flavell,* 1979]. The Piagetian description of formal reasoning implies an understanding (to some extent at least) of the constructive, relativistic, and theoretical nature of knowing which, in turn, results in deliberate attempts to logically examine and empirically verify (e.g., control variables, seek disconfirming evidence, etc.) personal hypotheses. Thinking about the process of thinking as well as thinking about thoughts (cognitive products) is said to occur, and this reasoning is purportedly applied to both personal life plans (identity issues) and physics-type problems (e.g., a pendulum, chemical combinations, etc.).

The majority of recent studies of Eriksonian identity formation have employed *Marcia's* [1966] identity-status paradigm [cf. *Bourne,* 1978a, b]. In his operationalization of Erikson's rather broad conceptualizations, *Marcia* [1966] focused on two criteria: the presence or absence of an identity crisis, and the presence or absence of firm personal commitments. It is important to realize that a *crisis* in *Marcia's* scheme pertains to an active decision-making period in one's life. That is to say, more than confusion and stress is involved; the subject must actively be attempting (or have attempted) to deal with and resolve identity questions and concerns. An identity-status interview is used in order to ascertain a subject's prior (or present) crisis experiences and his or her current commitments. Of the four status classifications that can be made, two indicate the presence of a firm identity: achievers and foreclosers. These two statuses differ from each other on the crisis dimension. Achievers have reportedly 'formed' their own commitments through role experimentation and personal decision making. Foreclosers, in contrast, have more passively (without crisis) adopted the values, goals, and standards prescribed for them by others, especially their parents. The two uncommitted status classifications are moratoriums (presently engaged in an active attempt to resolve a crisis) and diffusions (no present crisis or commitment). Reviews of research employing *Marcia's* identity-status classifications are presented by *Berzonsky* [1981], *Bourne* [1978a,b] and *Marcia* [1980].

Marcia's identity-status paradigm has been used in some recent attempts to investigate the empirical relationship between formal reasoning and the experiencing of identity crises. For instance, *Berzonsky* et al. [1975] hypothesized a undirectional relationship; that is, while affective factors such as guilt, anxiety, or indifference may prevent formal reasoners from constructing and examining theories about their personal lives, those individuals who have experienced such personal crises about their identities would necessarily have to be formal reasoners. *Marcia's* [1966] identity-status interview was administered to 60 undergraduates. Two measures of formal reasoning were also administered: a test of syllogistic logic and a concept attainment task that required the systematic exclusion of irrelevant variables. As expected, a number of formal reasoners had not had identity crises. Contrary to prediction, a number of identity-crisis subjects - as assessed by *Marcia's* [1966] measure - were not classified as formal reasoners. Other studies using *Marcia's* status paradigm have reported similar findings [*Cauble*, 1976; *Wagner*, 1976]. In a recent investigation, *Rowe and Marcia* [1980] found that all of the subjects who had experienced and resolved a personal identity crisis were formal operational as assessed by *Inhelder and Piaget's* [1958] balance-beam and chemical-combinations problems. However, only 26 subjects were included in the study and only 3 subjects had achieved an identity.

In general these investigations offer little support for the hypothesized relationship between formal reasoning and identity formation. Of course, one could question the specific tasks used to operationalize the two theoretical constructs. It may be that the specific measures that have been employed have not tapped the processes of theoretical interest. In a recent review, however, *Blasi and Hoeffel* [1974] have questioned the theoretical link between formal reasoning and identity formation.

The *Blasi and Hoeffel* [1974] Position

In their theoretical review, *Blasi and Hoeffel* [1974] emphasize three key issues. Their first point is empirical: considerable evidence suggests that most adolescents and even adults do not employ fully consolidated formal reasoning. If one were to assume that dealing with identity crises (as defined above) is a universal phenomenon - a contentious assumption as we argue below – then these data questions '... the necessary requirement of formal operations for adolescent personality development' [*Blasi and Hoeffel*, 1974, p. 349].

A second issue raised by *Blasi and Hoeffel* [1974] is that even in theory one should not expect to find individuals who have achieved an identity via formal reasoning. They note that the realm of possibility involved in the types of physics problems on which *Piaget's* theory is based (pendulum, communicating vessels, shadow projection, etc.) may be quite different than that which is relevant to one's personal development. Physics problems involve an equilibrated system of logically consistent and experimentally-transformable variables or possibilities. The realm of psychological possibility, relevant to the development of personal identity, tends to be open ended and less amenable to direct experimental verification.

> Thus, there seems to be a type of possibility which is not derived from rigidly compensated systems, not because the knower is not sufficiently developed to appreciate such systems – which may also be the case – but because the reality to which possibility is applied has different properties than physical reality and because the knower has, within it, a very different position than he has vis-à-vis physical reality [pp. 353–354].

In essence, they argue that *Piaget's* view of the adolescent as a 'scientist' may be inappropriate when it comes to personal problems and decision making.

Finally, *Blasi and Hoeffel* [1974] argue – correctly we think – that most of us can get along quite well in our everyday personal living without using formal reasoning. For example, concrete reasoners with 'rich and varied experiences' could undergo and resolve identity crises in which they personally questioned and examined factual (concrete) instead of hypothetical (formal) alternatives and possibilities. Such individuals, if given *Marcia's* [1966] identity-status interview, would be classified as having had an identity crisis. This line of reasoning provides a possible explanation as to why some investigations [*Berzonsky* et al., 1975; *Cauble*, 1976] have not found a relationship betwen identity development – as assessed by *Marcia's* measure – and formal reasoning performance. *Marcia's* [1966] interview technique does not discriminate individuals who have considered a broad range of theoretically possible alternatives from those who have dealt exclusively with a more restricted range of factual ones. In the following sections we critically examine each of these three points.

Formal Reasoning: Mediation or Production Deficiency?

As cited above, research indicates that many late adolescents and adults [*Berzonsky,* 1978; *Labouvie-Vief and Chandler,* 1978] as well as a majority of 11- to 14-year-olds do not spontaneously employ formal operational thinking. While acknowledging that there are several interpretations of these data, *Blasi and Hoeffel* [1974] argue the position that formal operations are *not* necessary for personality development in adolescence. In this section we take issue with the position that late adolescents or adults (even many normal teenagers) lack the structural competence to solve formal-reasoning problems, but agree with *Blasi and Hoeffel* [1974] that formal reasoning generally is not applied to problems associated with personal development and identity formation. The conditions under which exceptions may be observed are discussed.

The position taken here is that formal-reasoning competence is not evidenced by adolescents in many situations because they have not had certain experiences with the assessment tasks (or similar ones). Most adults and adolescents are not 'mediationally deficient' [*Reese,* 1962]; they do *not* lack the structural competence that underlies formal reasoning. Instead, in many cases, adolescents who do not use formal reasoning either have not acquired the strategies that are required, or they fail to produce available strategies in relevant situations. We are suggesting that much of the available data on formal reasoning reflects 'production deficiencies' [*Flavell et al.* 1966; *Keeney et al* 1967] that can be attenuated through relatively *short-term* intervention efforts.

Case [1974], for example, has demonstrated that intelligent, field-independent 7- to 8-year-old children can acquire a general scheme or strategy for systematically controlling and testing variables – an integral aspect of formal reasoning as assessed by *Inhelder and Piaget's* [1958] bending-rods problem. Likewise, *Scardamalia* [1977] has demonstrated that 8- to 10-year-olds can acquire a general strategy for solving combinatorial reasoning tasks consisting of 3 or 4 variables. Other evidence [*Siegler,* 1976, 1978] suggests that with appropriate experiences and instruction, many elementary school-aged children are capable of solving tasks used to assess formal reasoning [cf. *Case*, 1978].

If young children can acquire formal-reasoning strategies with limited instruction, why is it that teenagers and even adults typically fail to solve formal-reasoning problems? As suggested above they generally are capable of thinking formally but they fail to realize that such reasoning is required for, or applicable to particular problems. Consider the illustrative example offered by *Danner and Day* [1977]. Three tasks involving the systematic control of variables were given to 10-, 13-, and 17-year-old subjects: 20 subjects per age. The first task, presented under standard open-ended instructional procedures, produced marked age-related effects. No 10-year-olds, but nine (45%) 13- and eleven (55%) 17-year-olds were classified as formal reasoners. Had *Danner and Day* [1977] concluded their investigation at this point their results would have been consistent with the conclusions cited by *Blasi and Hoeffel* [1974]; that is, the majority of 11- to 14-year-olds do not reason formally nor do all late adolescents. However, *Danner and Day* [1977] introduced a series of prompts on Task 1 immediately after the subjects indicated that they had finished solving the problem on their own. These prompts highlighted the variables that were involved and a general rule or strategy for dealing with the problem. When Task 2 was presented *without prompting*, 70% of the 13-year-olds and 80% of the 17-year-olds were classified as formal reasoners. These percentages rose to 85 and 95%, respectively, on Task 3 following additional prompting on Task 2. Only 25% of the 10-year-olds were classified as formal reasoners on the third problem in spite of the fact that they had received the prompts for Tasks 1 and 2. *Danner and Day* [1977] concluded that the prompts served to clarify the task demands. Thus, those individuals who already possessed the appropriate strategies could be easily induced to employ them even though they did not spontaneously do so when the first task was presented in an open-ended fashion. This sort of prompting, however, apparently did not enable the 10-year-olds to acquire the 'control of variables' strategy. More systematic experiences similar to those used by *Case* [1974] may be needed before preadolescents evidence formal-reasoning performance. A second experiment by *Danner and Day* [1977] replicated this effect with twenty 17-year-olds (100% were classified as formal reasoners on Task 3) and demonstrated that practice per se (without prompts) resulted in negligible improvement. Additional evidence for the availability of formal-reasoning strategies is provided by *Stone and Day* [1978, 1980].

Formal-Reasoning Strategies

The reader may be aware that the conceptualization of formal reasoning implied in the research reviewed above [*Case*, 1974; *Danner and Day*, 1977; *Siegler*, 1978] diverges from the traditional Piagetian theoretical account of qualitatively emerging logical structures. Accordingly, one could ask: Were the subjects in the aforementioned experiments structurally at the stage of formal operations? Two points must be considered before we attempt to answer this question. First, the logical coherence of Piaget's structural theory has been criticized [cf. *Ennis*, 1975]. Second, and most important, even if Piaget's structural theory is internally consistent, we do not directly observe mental structures. Therefore, empirical investigators of formal reasoning must make inferences about logical structures (or whatever developmental mechanism is postulated) from observed behavior. Regarding this issue, the Piagetian account holds that correct responding on tasks that allegedly require formal operations is not a sufficient condition for inferring structural competence; the temporal stability and generalizability of the response patterns also have to be considered [*Piaget*, 1964]. However, how much stability (one's entire life span?) and generalizability are necessary before we conclude that the individual is formal operational? *Piaget's* original asumption of a content-free widely generalizable manner of responding is certainly not met in the experiments reviewed above. (In *Case's* [1974] investigation, for example, instruction on controlling variables did not lead to improved performance on tasks requiring the generation of combinations.) However, this original assumption, as *Piaget* [1972] himself has noted, is not met in investigations of formal reasoning that has 'spontaneously' developed [cf. *Berzonsky*, 1978; *Blasi and Hoeffel*,1974; *Martorano*, 1977].

The characterization of formal reasoning presented here, and implied in the research reviewed above, is that a formal reasoner is someone who can successfully employ a set of problem-solving strategies – hypothesis generation, combinatorial reasoning, hypothetico-deductive reasoning, controlling variables, and so on. While this account is certainly compatible with *Piaget's* structural view of formal-operational schemes [*Inhelder and Piaget,* 1958], it appears that Piagetian theory may have underemphasized the role that *specific* experience (especially, planned instruction) may play in the acquisition or development of these strategies. For instance, while Piagetian theory does acknowledge that an organism X environment interaction is involved in cognitive development, a distinction is made between the effects that specific versus general experiences have on structural development [cf. *Piaget* 1964]. Accordingly, a reading of *Piaget* would not lead one to predict that the *specific* instructional experiences provided to elementary-school children in, say, the *Case* [1974] or *Siegler* [1976] studies would have had the effects that were obtained. As *Case* [1974] notes, however, Piagetian theory can always provide a post hoc account of positive findings: Children who benefit from specific instruction are actually consolidating transitional structures that had spontaneously developed from previous general experiences.

In summary, a formal reasoner is someone who can successfully apply strategic behaviors when solving problems. The development of these strategies results from problem-solving experiences (that may be general or specific in nature). In addition, successful formal-reasoning requires knowledge about the different situations (tasks) to which the strategies can be applied and a motivation to solve a given problem. This does not necessarily imply that there are no organismic capacity limitations that affect the acquisition and/or application of formal-reasoning strategies. For instance, *Scardamalia* [1977] found that 100% (15/15) of a group of 10- to 12-year-olds were able successfully to employ a combinatorial strategy on a 3-variable problem (87% were also successful on a 4-variable task). However, all of these same subjects failed when task complexity was increased to 7 variables and only 1 passed a 6-variable problem [cf. *de Ribaupierre and Pascual-Leone,* 1979]. Also, we would not expect individuals of all ages (say, infants, to take the extreme) necessarily to benefit equally from the training methods employed above. Such limitations may be due to intra- and/or interindividual differences in Piagetian structural development, but they may also result from other factors: e.g., differences in information-processing capacity or the efficiency with which available mental resources are allocated [*Kahneman,* 1973].

Based on the research cited above, we would expect that most normal late adolescents and adults would be capable of formal reasoning in the Piagetian sense (in some cases relatively short-term instruction may be necessary). The likelihood that these strategies would be actually produced or utilized on relevant problems would depend, in part at least, upon: (a) the similarity of new problems to ones that have been previously solved (*Piaget,* [1972] also suggests this possibility); (b) the subject's understanding of the task demands; and (c) the previous consequences that have been experienced in comparable situations when the subject did not operate in a formal manner.

We contend that formal-reasoning strategies can (but not necessarily will) be used to solve problems of a personal as well as physical nature. As *Blasi and Hoeffel* [1974] point out, the nature and range of possibilities operating within these realms may differ. However, psychologists operating within different metaphysical world views (e.g., mechanistic versus organismic or dialectical models) are confronted with an analogous distinction [*Berzonsky,* 1981; *Reese and Overton,* 1970; *Riegel,* 1976]. Put differently, manipulative designs can more readily be utilized to answer questions when it is assumed that external forces or efficient causes are the determinants of behavior. However, when formal causes, i.e., developing skills, characteristics, or structures, are assumed to play a role in influencing behavior, it becomes more difficult to employ truly experimental designs: there are many manipulations that one would not want to perform as well as ones that are very difficult or infeasible to carry out.

In a seminal article, *Cronbach* [1957] made a similar distinction in pointing out that there are two disciplines of scientific psychology: experimental and correlational. In order to verify their hypotheses and make decisions about causation, experimentalists create the effects that they observe via the controlled and systematic manipulation of variables. This is the approach one would use on a Piagetian-type physics problem.

Correlational psychologists, likewise, attempt to verify their hypotheses and obtain empirical evidence to support their theoretical explanations. In order to do this, however, correlationists observe and organize data that result from manipulations over which they do not exert systematic control (e.g., nature, normal circumstances, etc.). The systematic manipulation of potentially relevant variables involved in many personal problems also may be infeasible, undesirable, or virtually impossible. Hence, individuals who use formal-reasoning strategies when dealing with personal problems may still operate in a 'scientific' fashion, but their approach may tend to be more correlational than experimental [cf. e.g., *Erwin and Kuhn*, 1979; *Kelley, 1973; Kuhn and Brannock*, 1977; *Kuhn and Phelps*, 1979]. Let us now consider how formal strategies might be used to deal with identity crises.

Identity, Personal Theories, and Formal Reasoning

Epstein [1973] has proposed the notion that a self-concept or sense of identity is actually a personal or informal theory that an individual has formed about himself or herself.

> It is a theory that the individual has unwittingly constructed about himself as an experiencing, functioning individual . . . Accordingly, there are major postulate systems for the *nature of the world, for the nature of the self, and for their interactions* . . . Two other basic functions . . . are to *facilitate the maintenance of self-esteem*, and *to organize the data of experience in a manner that can be coped with effectively* [p. 407].

Our personal self-theory or sense of identity involves the concepts, assumptions, and principles that we, over our lifetime, have come to hold about ourselves. (The reader should recall from our previous discussion, that an individual may have an identity or self-theory without having personally achieved it in the Eriksonian sense.) The functional effectiveness of a self-theory – the extend to which it can be used to solve problems and integrate information – should depend upon its testability, internal consistency, and empirical validity [*Epstein*, 1973]. The structure and function of formal and personal theories are analogous and, thus, similar criteria may be applied in assessing both types of theories [cf. *Epstein*, 1973].

While all individuals form personal theories about themselves, everyone is not equally cognizant of this effort. In the literature on identity formation, as we saw earlier, one finds committed foreclosers who have not personally considered why they hold the values and goals that they do. It is unlikely that formal-reasoning strategies were employed when they adopted their identity or self-theory from others.

Consistent with *Blasi and Hoeffel's* [1974] position, therefore, formal-reasoning strategies would not be necessary for personality development. A sense of identity or a theory about oneself can be acquired somewhat 'mindlessly' from others; explicit theoretical thinking and formal reasoning is not needed in order to assume socially-ascribed roles. This process, moreover, does not have to be limited to *one* socially determined option – a 'multiple-choice' sort of foreclosure may occur by concretely selecting from options and alternatives that are actually available. However, those individuals who actively attempt to resolve identity issues, consider alternatives, and make personal commitments (viz., achievers and moratoriums) may employ formal-reasoning strategies in the process of achieving a personal identity.

Also, there is evidence that suggests that, subsequent to the achievement or adoption of their identity, the status types may differ in the manner in which they deal with problems and make decisions. For instance, foreclosers have consistently been found to score the highest on measures of authoritarianism [*Marcia,* 1980]. Other studies indicate that foreclosers may tend to become inflexible and 'constricted' when stressed [cf. *Bourne,* 1978b; *Marcia,* 1966, 1980]; are classified as 'externals' on locus-of-control measures [*Adams & Shea,* 1979; *Marcia,* 1980]; and are relatively unrealistic when appraising their successes or failures on a task [*Marcia,* 1966]. These findings suggest that foreclosers may be relatively 'closed' to information that is incongruous with their self-theories. Also, the self-theories held by foreclosers are more likely to be *implicit* rather than explicit. In other words, while they employ personal theories to solve problems and integrate information (cf. *Epstein's* [1973] quote above), it is unlikely that they are explicitly aware that they are operating in a theoretical fashion. Therefore, foreclosers would not tend to utilize formal-reasoning strategies in order to attempt to verify the hypotheses (or theoretical principles) upon which their decisions and problem solutions are based.

In contrast to the picture of the foreclosers presented above, *achievers* give the impression of being relatively 'open' to new information, flexible, and realistic [see reviews by *Berzonsky,* 1981; *Bourne,* 1978a, b; *Marcia,* 1980] Since these individuals have experienced a period of active decision making, role experimentation, and self-examination, they are apt to hold relatively explicit self-theories. Consequently, the use of formal-reasoning strategies to verify personal decisions and ideas should be most apparent in a group of achievers.

One point should be added. If it is true that achievers employ formal-reasoning strategies when they first cope with identity crises, there is no reason to assume that they will necessarily continue to use this 'open' flexible approach to personal problem solving throughout their lives. *Marcia* [1976], for instance, in a 6-year longitudinal study, found that the majority (57%) of the subjects who had been classified as achievers and moratoriums in their early twenties, gave *little* indication of being 'open' alternative-considering individuals in their late twenties. However, marked consistency was apparent for those individuals who had been classified as being foreclosers in late adolescence (78% were classified as foreclosures or foreclosure/diffusions 6 years later). Since the reliability of status classifications over time has not been ascertained, one should be cautious when interpreting these findings. They are, however, consistent with other results that suggest intraindividual increases in inflexibility and rigidity over the life span [cf. *Neugarten,* 1977]. What is of interest, however, is that these findings suggest that there may be *inter* individual differences in this intraindividual trend.

If we were to assume that our position is valid, does it imply that achievers who use (or at least have used) formal-reasoning strategies are more effective in their personal lives than foreclosers who do not? No, not necessarily. If an individual were living in a relatively stable environment - say, what *Mead* [1970] refers to as a postfigurative culture - a foreclosed identity would be adaptive. Adults who have already lived in the society know what a youth will have to be able to do and what she or he should value in order to be an effective adult. Consequently, by adopting a socially ascribed identity and using it as a basis for future decisions and coping, the individual should be able to get by quite well.

However, individuals living in a rapidly changing environment, what *Mead* [1970] calls a prefigurative culture, will find that rules and expectations tend to change as they age. In such situations, the specific beliefs and problem solutions held by members of previous generations are less apt to be relevant to contemporary problems and crises. Hence, individuals who use formal-reasoning strategies as they attempt to adapt to new demands, will appear to have an advantage over their more inflexible-foreclosed counterparts. Here we are distinguishing between *product* (what one does and believes) and *process* (why one believes and does things). The specific decisions and choices made by foreclosers and achievers may be the same. Their reasons for doing so, however, would be important considerations when (if?) they have to deal with changing conditions and contradictory feedback.

Let us consider interpersonal relationships. At least some research [*Kacerguis and Adams,* 1980; *Orlofsky et al.* 1973] suggests that achievers may be more likely than foreclosers to establish close interpersonal relationships in which honest self-disclosure occurs (cf., however, *Hodgson and Fischer* [1979]). By exchanging information in an open fashion, one is apt eventually to detect inconsistencies and contradictions in the content of his or her views. Achievers who have presumably gone through a period of seeking information and making commitments in a relativistic world (a context of hypothetical and factual possibilities), should be better able to accommodate their self-theories to discrepant information than their foreclosed counterparts. This is not to say that whimsical and capricious change will occur. However, the information base that is available should increase as individuals age. Decisions and choices made in adolescence and early adulthood, therefore, should be modified and revised in light of new information, assuming that the individuals continue to verify their decisions and remain 'open' to new information. Foreclosers would be relatively more apt to close themselves off from (i.e., repress or deny) discrepant information in order to defend against the need to revise beliefs and aspirations (*Faught* et al. [1977] present an interesting computer simulation example of how this step in information processing may occur).

The reader may detect a parallel between our account of life span self-theory or identity development and the progress of scientific theories explicated by *Kuhn* [1970]. Scientific theories and personal theories necessarily must be formulated from the information that is presently available. If the theory is open to new information and if it is testable, discrepancies and inconsistencies – *Kuhn's* [1970] anomalies – will eventually be detected and revision or Piagetian-type accommodation will be necessitated. Perhaps identity crises are the personal theory analogue of a Kuhnian scientific revolution? If so, one would not necessarily achieve an identity in adolescence and maintain it intact the rest of his or her life. Perhaps *Marcia's* identity statuses could better be conceptualized as styles of dealing with the crises and problems encountered throughout one's life span (including adolescence). For instance, some individuals may be 'open' to new information and they may tend to use formal verification strategies. Others may be more apt to deal with personal problems in a more inflexible closed or, perhaps, avoiding fashion [cf. *Berzonsky*, 1981; *Cytrynbaum* et al., 1980; *Egli and Fleck*, 1980; *Whitbourne and Weinstock*, 1979].

Some similar notions are presented by *Greenwald* [1980] who likened the self-theory to a totalitarian society as well as a formal scientific theory. *Greenwald* [1980] makes the point that we not only integrate information into our self-theories, we are the historians of our own lives, and revisionists at that! Three cognitive biases influence this revisionary activity, according to *Greenwald* [1980]: (a) *egocentricity* (the observer is the center of the universe); (b) *beneffectance* (we tend to deny responsibility for our failures but accept credit for our successes); and (c) a *confirmation bias* (we are inclined to seek information – in the environment or our memory – that is apt to validate rather than invalidate our views). *Greenwald's* [1980] account (which is well documented and thoroughly developed) seems to correspond more closely to the description of a forecloser than an achiever. If he is correct in his view that these cognitive biases are operative in all individuals or knowledge systems, the use of formal-reasoning strategies would provide a means of at least partially correcting for their influence. Again, we are talking about individual differences in the extent to which this would occur. We are not implying that some (and certainly not all) people are totally objective while others are completely subjective. Those individuals who are interested in verifying their views and decisions and in attempting to correct for their own cognitive biases should be found to employ formal-reasoning strategies in their personal life: they generate alternate possibilities and explanations; perform logical analyses; make hypothetical deductions about the empirical implications and consequences of implementing various options; and seek evidence that might disconfirm those predictions.

When Will Formal Strategies be Applied to Personal Problems?

We have argued that formal strategies may be within the competency of most normal 17- to 18-year-olds and that such strategies may be used to solve personal crises. Under what conditions would we expect this to happen? One of the major considerations should be the prior *consequences* that were involved when one did not function in a formal fashion.

In this search for cognitive universals, *Piaget* [1950] has stressed the role that general physical experience plays in cognitive development. Since development through the stage of concrete operations appears to be almost a universal occurrence – at least most normal 21-

year-olds are able to solve the basic conservation of quantity, class inclusion, and seriation problems used to operationalize concrete operations [cf. *Berzonsky,* 1978] – one could argue that the physical world in which human beings live provides negative consequences when one fails to develop these operations (cf. however, *Jordan* [1972] and *Segalowitz* [1980]). For instance, free falling from an 11-story building would have certain physical consequences regardless of the culture in which it occurred. In a less extreme fashion, the nature of the real physical world may limit the sorts of cognitive structures and operations that we construct [cf. *Neisser,* 1976].

The social world in which we live may provide certain consequences that are more variable than those imposed by physical reality [cf. e.g. *Cole and Scribner,* 1974]. A 10-year-old boy in a suburban Chicago school hears snickers and giggles when he says that stones, the moon, and volcanoes are alive, whereas the 10-year-old in a primitive culture may receive confirmation for the same utterance. Perhaps this is one explanation as to why the use of Piagetian formal reasoning and participation in formal educational settings have been found to be related [*Berzonsky,* 1981]. Specifically, formal instruction may provide a set of problems, demands, and consequences that differ from those encountered in everyday living. Knowing what to do and how to do it (concrete operations) will typically suffice in everyday life; formalized instruction is more apt to focus additionally on the theoretical *why* that underlies what is being taught (i.e., fundamental concepts, assumptions, and explanatory principles). In everyday life, however, the issue as to why something 'works' usually is not a primary consideration, although malfunctions may focus attention on underlying causal structures.

Identity formation, at least as described by *Erikson* [1968] and *Marcia's* [1966] identity-status paradigm, appears to deal with personal issues and problems that do not necessarily produce the sorts of physical or social consequences described above. For instance, while identity is achieved in a psycho*social* context, it is the forecloser who adheres most closely to the expectations of significant others. The achiever uses social feedback, but anyone who takes a firm stand is bound to receive negative as well as positive social consequences. Thus, someone who focuses more on personal uniqueness and individuality, rather than the specific expectations of others, will tend to be concerned with maintaining a sense of personal truthfulness to oneself (this may be a 'feeling' of knowing what is true for oneself as well as more explicit cognitive awareness).

Kohlberg [1973] seems to be making a similar distinction when he discusses the conditions under which an individual may adopt a principled moral stance. Conventional morality, he contends, will develop as an individual interacts within social systems and gains experience taking various social roles; there are social consequences involved. However, these same sorts of experiences may not result in principled morality: 'Principled morality, however, is not a more adequate perception of what the social system *is*; rather, it is a postulation of principles to which the society and the self *ought to be commited'* [p. 194].

Consequently, the need to assess the validity, internal consistency, and truth of one's personally held principles, goals, and values seems to come from within rather than without; a need for personal integrity in the common sense meaning of the word may be involved. A sense of self-efficacy [*Bandura,* 1977] that is also reality-based may be necessary in order for individuals to undertake this sort of self-assessment or self-monitoring. The use of formal-reasoning strategies to assess the validity of one's personal commitments, therefore, will vary considerably between individuals. In fact, some recent work in social psychology suggests that individuals may be unaware of factors influencing their personal decisions.

Does Everyone Tell More Than They Know?

Nisbett and Ross [1980] and *Nisbett and Wilson* [1977] recently have amassed a variety of experimental evidence indicating that individuals are typically unaware of the process by which they make decisions [cf. also, *Langer* et al., 1978; *Langer and Imber,* 1979]. For example, they have demonstrated that an individual's evaluation of the quality of an article of clothing is influenced by its position in an array of items. When subjects were asked to compare, say, two identical negligees, the one on the right was most apt to be judged as superior in quality [*Nisbett and Wilson,* 1977]. However, the subjects did not spontaneously report that position influenced their decision. In fact, they tended somewhat vehemently to deny the importance of position when the possibility was suggested. The data reviewed by these authors indicated numerous situations where subjects do not accurately identify the stimuli that influenced a response, do not report that they responded in a particular fashion, and do not report that they changed their response when in fact they had [*Nisbett and Wilson,* 1977].

Nisbett and Ross's [1980] explanation of these findings parallels the position explicated above in that individuals have personal or implicit theories that they use to explain their experiences and behaviors. In the examples presented above, however, the subjects' personal theories provided inaccurate accounts of what actually happened in the experimental settings. This is not to imply that individuals will never correctly identify the factors involved in their decision making. Individuals should make correct assessments about situations, including their own behavior, when their personal theories coincide with what is actually happening [*Nisbett and Wilson,* 1977]. In other words, an observer who holds the same theory could look over a subject's shoulder (or be given a general description of the situation) and give as accurate an explanation of the subject's behavior as the subject does.

Nisbett and Ross's [1980] account reminds one of the foreclosed personality type described above, i.e., someone who is unaware that he or she is making inferences and constructing a version of truth. By adopting socially prescribed theories, roles, scripts, and the like, the forecloser may ordinarily be able to function effectively and efficiently. Of course, in a number of situations, as *Nisbett and Wilson* [1977] convincingly demonstrate, individuals are markedly inaccurate. Moreover, it is doubtful that such errors are restricted to laboratory settings. As *Nisbett and Ross* [1980] state: 'People, in short, do not suddenly assume a mantle of credulity or ignorance when they walk into the laboratory. On the contrary, there is reason to believe that they wear their Sunday best when they enter the psychologist's sanctum' [p. 252]. While real-life inferential errors may ordinarily have few severe consequences, '. . . it takes only a few such errors to seriously disrupt individual and collective social experiences' [*Nisbett and Ross,* 1980, p. 254].

Nisbett and Ross [1980] suggest that the first step in eliminating inferential errors would be to have individuals become aware of the inferential nature of their own thinking. They further suggest that rules of methodology, i.e., formal-reasoning strategies, could informally be applied to verify the inferences that one has drawn. (Slogans to serve as mnemonics are also offered: 'Okay, what do the other three cells look like?' 'You can lie with statistics, but a well-chosen example does the job better!' etc.)

Conclusions and Directions for Future Research

We have posited that formal-reasoning strategies are necessary in order to experience identity achievement as described by *Erikson* [1968]. Specifically, one must be aware of a context of alternatives and possibilities and then actively attempt to examine, consider and choose among them. In the present chapter, formal thinking is conceptualized as a set of strategies that *could* be used to solve personal as well as physical problems. Evidence suggests that these strategies are within the competence of normal late adolescents and adults and even, perhaps, some select younger children. However, ample evidence suggests that such strategies are *not* produced by all adolescents or even adults in potentially relevant situations.

Consistent with the position advanced by *Blasi and Hoeffel* [1974], the available data suggest that individuals do not necessarily use formal-reasoning strategies to solve personal crises and/or make individual decisions. It is doubtful, however, whether these individuals have undergone the process of identity achievement as explicated by *Erikson* [1968]. Instead, these individuals have seemingly foreclosed on socially provided roles, scripts, and values.

The position advanced in the present chapter is that individuals *could* use formal-reasoning strategies to deal with personal crises and those who have achieved an identity, in the Eriksonian sense, are most apt to have done so. If this is the case, it may be possible to demonstrate individual differences in the accuracy of self-reports obtained in experimental situations such as those reviewed by *Nisbett and Wilson* [1977]. While individuals in general may be unaware or foreclosed, some individuals should be more aware, i.e., more accurate in their self-assessments, than others. One could object that we cannot spend all our time verifying decisions and that the situation involving a comparison of two nightgowns (described above) simply was not worth the mental effort needed to re-examine the basis for their selection. (As *Nisbett and Wilson* [1977] indicated, a position efect was operating but subjects did not tend to report that this influenced them.) More ego-involving types of manipulations might be necessary to demonstrate the individual differences we predict: feedback that conflicts with the subject's responses; conditions that lead to attitude changes; information that contradicts basic beliefs, etc. Moreover, we do not predict that individual differences in the *accuracy* of self-reports will necessarily be obtained, only that differences will be found in the subjects' certainty about the reasons that underlie and the factors that influence their decisions and behaviors (especially when contradictory feedback is provided). It is this tentativeness that should lead to the relatively more frequent use of formal-verification strategies.

Most research on identity achievement has used *Marcia's* [1966] identity-status interview. Since this method does not distinguish between individuals who achieved an identity through concrete reasoning and those who use formal reasoning to achieve the same objective, one would not expect to find a reliable relationship between *Marcia's* status classifications and general measures of formal reasoning. One means of testing the aforementioned predictions, using *Marcia's* paradigm, would be to stratify status types on the basis of formal-reasoning performances: formal-achievers; concrete-achievers, etc.

These predictions do not necessarily imply that some individuals have direct introspective access to the cognitive processes governing their decisions and behavior. What this position implies is that individuals vary in the extent to which they have knowledge about the constructive and relativistic nature of their thinking and decisions. Also, individuals differ in the degree to which they deliberately attempt to use environmental feedback to verify the hypotheses that they hold and the inferences they draw.

While the present review has focused almost exclusively on the achiever and forecloser identity statuses, we do not contend that all individuals who use formal strategies will necessarily become (or be) identity achievers. For example, research suggests that at least some diffuse-like individuals may also actively monitor their behavior in order to create an impression deemed appropriate for a given situation [*Snyder*, 1979]. In contrast to the achiever who tends to ask 'Who am I and what would be most like me in this situation?', the so-called high self-monitor asks: 'Who does this situation expect me to be and how can I best do that?' [*Snyder*, 1979]. The ability of high self-monitors to adapt superficially or flexibly (depending on your perspective) from situation to situation is said to require '. . . deliberate and strategic attempts to create images appropriate to particular situational contexts, to appear to be the right person in the right place at the right time' [Snyder, 1979, p. 86].

Summary

In this theoretical chapter, formal reasoning is conceptualized as a set of strategic behaviors that can be used to solve problems of a physical and personal nature. Research evidence indicating that these strategies are within the structural competence of most normal 18-year-olds and specially trained elementary school children is presented. The question is raised as to why many adults and adolescents do not spontaneously utilize formal reasoning in relevant situations. It is argued that the deployment of formal reasoning depends, in part, upon problem familiarity, clarity of the problem demands, and the consequences that have been involved. Some predictions about the hypothetical relationship between formal reasoning and personal-identity formation and some suggestions for future research are offered.

References

Adams, G.R.; Shea, J.A.: The relationship between identity status, locus of control, and ego development. J. Yth Adolesc. *8:* 81–89 (1979).

Bandura, A.: Self-efficacy: toward a unifying theory of behavioral change. Psychol. Rev. *84:* 191–215 (1977).

Berzonsky, M.D.: Formal reasoning in adolescence: an alternate view. Adolescence *13:* 279–290 (1978).

Berzonsky, M.D.: Adolescent development (Macmillan, New York 1981).

Berzonsky, M.D.: Weiner, A.S.; Raphael, D.: Interdependence of formal reasoning. Devl Psychol. *11:* 258 (1975).

Blasi, A.; Hoeffel, E.C.: Adolescence and formal operations. Hum. Dev. *17:* 344–363 (1974).

Bourne, E.: The state of research on ego identity: a review and appraisal. Part. I. J. Yth Adolesc. *7:* 223–251 (1978a).

Bourne, E.: The state of research on ego identity: a review and appraisal. Part. II. J. Yth Adolesc. *7:* 371–392 (1978b).

Broughton, J.: 'Beyond formal operations': theoretical thought in adolescence. Teach. Coll. Rec. *79:* 87–97 (1977).

Brown, A.L.; DeLoache. J.S.: Skills, plans, and self-regulation: in Siegler, Children's thinking: What develops? pp. 3–35 (Erlbaum, New York 1978).

Case, R.: Structures and strictures: some functional limitations on the course of cognitive growth. Cognitive Psychol. *6:* 544–573 (1974).

Case, R.: Intellectual development from birth to adulthood: a neo-Piagetian approach: in Siegler, Children's thinking: What develops? pp. 37–71 (Erlbaum, New York 1978).

Cauble, M.A.: Formal operations, ego identity, and principled morality: Are they related? Devl Psychol. *12:*363–364 (1976).

Cole, M.; Scribner, S.: Culture and thought (Wiley, New York 1974).

Cronbach, L.J.: The two disciplines of scientific psychology. Psychol. *12:*671–684 (1957).

Cytrynbaum, S.; Blum, L.; Patrick, R.; Stein, J.; Wadner, D.; Wilk, C.: Midlife development: a personality and social systems perspective; in Poon, Aging in the 1980s: psychological issues, pp. 463–474 (American Psychological Association, Washington 1980).

Danner, F.W.; Day, M.C.: Eliciting formal operations. Child Dev. *48:*1600–1606 (1977).

Egli, D.; Fleck, J.R.: Ego integrity, identity status, and death perspective in late adulthood. Geront. Soc., San Diego 1980.

Ennis, R.H.: Children's ability to handle Piaget's propositional logic: a conceptual critique. Rev. educ. Res. *45:*1–41 (1975).

Epstein, S.: The self-concept revisited: or a theory of theory. Am. Psychol. *28:* 404–416 (1973).

Erikson, E.H.: Identity and the life cycle. Psychol. Issues *1:*monogr. No. 1 (1959).

Erikson, E.H.: Insight and responsibility (Norton, New York 1964).

Erikson, E.H.: Identity: youth and crisis (Norton, New York 1968).

Erwin, J.; Kuhn, D.: Development of children's understanding of the multiple determination underlying human behavior. Devl Psychol. *15:*352–353 (1979).

Faught, W.S.; Colby, K.M.; Parkison, R.C.: Inferences, affects, and intentions in a model of paranoia. Cognitive Psychol. *9:*153–187 (1977).

Flavell, J.H.: Metacognition and cognitive monitoring: a new area of cognitive-developmental inquiry. Am. Psychol. *34:*906–911 (1979).

Flavell, J.H.; Beach, D.R.; Chinsky, J.M.: Spontaneous verbal rehearsal in a memory task as a function of age. Child Dev. *37:*283–299 (1966).

Greenwald, A.G.: The totalitarian ego: fabrication and revision of personal history. Am. Psychol. *35:*603–618 (1980).

Hodgson, J.W.; Fischer, J.L.: Sex differences in identity and intimacy development in college youth. J. Yth Adolesc. *8:*37–50 (1979).

Inhelder, B.; Piaget, J.: The growth of logical thinking (Basic Books, New York 1958).

Jordan, N.: Is there an Achilles' heel in Piaget's theorizing? Hum. Dev. *15:* 379–382 (1972).

Kacerguis, M.A.; Adams, G.R.: Eriksonian stage resolution: the relationship between identity and intimacy. J. Yth Adolescence *9:*117–126 (1979).

Kahneman, D.: Attention and effort (Prentice Hall, Englewood Cliffs 1973).

Karmiloff-Smith, A.; Inhelder, B.: 'If you want to get ahead, get a theory'. Cognition *3:* 195–212 (1974/75).

Keeney, T.J.; Cannizzo, S.R.; Flavell, J.H.: Spontaneous and induced verbal rehersal in a recall task. Child Dev. *38:*953–966 (1967).

Kelley, H.H.: The process of causal attribution. Am. Psychol. *28:*107–128 (1973).

Kohlberg, L.: Continuities in childhood and adult moral development revisited; in Baltes, Schaie, Life-span developmental psychology: personality and socialization (Academic Press, New York 1973).

Kuhn, D.; Brannock, J.: Development of the isolation of variables scheme in experimental and 'natural experiment' contexts. Devl Psychol. *13:*9–14 (1977).

Kuhn, D.; Phelps, E.: A methodology for observing development of a formal reasoning strategy; in Kuhn, New directions for child development: intellectual development beyond childhood (Jossey-Bass, San Francisco 1979).

Kuhn, T.S.: The structure of scientific revolutions; 2nd ed. (University of Chicago Press, Chicago 1970).

Labouvie-Vief, G.; Chandler, M.J.: Cognitive development and life-span development theory: idealistic versus contextual perspectives, vol. 1; in Baltes, Life-span development and behavior, pp. 181–201 (Academic Press, New York 1978).

Langer, E.J.; Blank, A.; Chanowitz, B.: The mindlessness of ostensibly thoughtful action: the role of 'placebic' information in interpersonal interaction. J. Pers. soc. Psychol. *36:*635–642 (1978).

Langer, E.J.; Imber, L.G.: When practice makes imperfect: debilitating effects of overlearning. J. Pers. soc. Psychol. *37:*2014–2024 (1979).

Marcia, J.E.: Development and validation of Ego identity status. J. Pers. soc. Psychol. *3:* 551–558 (1966).

Marcia, J.E.: Identity six years after: a follow-up study. J. Yth Adolesc. *5:* 145–160 (1976).

Marcia, J.E.: Identity in adolescence; in Adelson, Handbook of adolescent psychology, pp. 159–187 (Wiley, New York 1980).

Martorano, S.C.: A developmental analysis of performance on Piaget's formal operational tasks. Devl Psychol. *13:*666–672 (1977).

Mead, M.: Culture and commitment: a study of the generation gap (Doubleday, New York 1970).

Moshman, D.: To really get ahead, get a metatheory; in Kuhn, New directions for child development: intellectual development beyond childhood, pp. 59–68 (Jossey-Bass, San Francisco 1979).

Neisser, U.: Cognition and reality (Freeman, San Francisco 1976).

Neugarten, B.L.: Personality and aging; in Birren, Schaie, Handbook of the psychology of aging, pp. 626–649 (Van Nostrand and Reinhold, New York 1977).

Nisbett, R.; Ross, L.: Human inference and shortcomings of social judgment (Prentice Hall, Englewood Cliffs 1980).

Nisbett, R.; Wilson, T.D.: Telling more than we know: verbal reports on mental processes. Psychol. Rev. *84:*231–259 (1977).

Orlofsky, J.L.; Marcia, J.E.; Lesser, I.M.: Ego identity status and the intimacy vs. crisis of young adulthood. J. Pers. soc. Psychol. *27:*211–219 (1973).

Piaget, J.: Psychology of intelligence (Kegan Paul, London 1950).

Piaget, J.: Development and learning; in Ripple, Rockcastle, Piaget rediscovered. pp. 7–19 (Cornell University Press, Ithaca 1964).

Piaget, J.: Intellectual evolution from adolescence to adulthood Hum. Dev. *15:* 1–2 (1972).

Reese, H.W.: Verbal mediation as a function of age level. Psychol. Bull. *59:* 502–509 (1962).

Reese, H.W.: Overton, W.F.: Models of development and theories of development; in Goulet, Baltes, Life-span developmental psychology: Research and theory (Academic Press, New York 1970).

Ribaupierre, A. de; Pascual-Leone, J.: Formal operations and M power: A neo-Piagetian investigation; in Kuhn, New directions for child development: intellectual development beyond childhood (Jossey-Bass, San Francisco 1979).

Riegel, K.F.: The dialectics of human development. Am. Psychol. *31:* 689–700 (1976).

Rowe, I.; Marcia, J.E.: Ego identity, formal operations, and moral development. J. Yth Adolesc. *9:* 87–99 (1980).

Scardamalia, M.: Information processing capacity and the problem of horizontal decalage: a demonstration using combinatorial reasoning tasks. Child Dev. *48:* 128–137 (1977).

Segalowitz, S.J.: Piaget's Achilles' heel: a safe soft spot? Dev. *23:* 137–140 (1980).

Siegler, R.S.: Three aspects of cognitive development. Cognitive Psychol. *4:* 481–520 (1976).

Siegler, R.S.: The origins of scientific thinking; in Siegler, Children's thinking: What develops? pp. 109–149 (Erlbaum, New York 1978).

Snyder, M.: Self-monitoring processes; in Berkowitz, Advances in experimental social psychology, vol. 12 (Academic Press, New York 1979).

Stone, C.A.; Day, M.C.: Levels of availability of a formal operations strategy. Child Dev. *49:* 1054–1065 (1978).

Stone, C.A.; Day, M.C.: Competence and performance models and the characterization of formal operational skills. Hum. Dev. *23:* 323–353 (1980).

Wagner, J.A.: A study of the relationship between formal operations and ego identity in adolescents (Doctoral dissertation, State University of New York at Buffalo, 1976). Diss. Abstr. Int. *37:* 2486-B-2487-B (1976).

Whitbourne, S.K.; Weinstock, C.S.: Adult development: the differentiation of experience (Holt, Rinehart & Winston, New York 1979).

Contr. hum. Dev., vol. 5, pp. 88–99 (Karger, Basel 1981)

Formal Operations and the Issue of Generalizability: The Analysis of Poetry by College Students[1]

Karen Hardy-Brown

University of Colorado, Boulder, Colo., USA

The cognitive developmental theories of *Jean Piaget* have commanded considerable attention from psychologists ever since their introduction into the scientific community. Describing the character and component features of formal operations, for example, has generated much research following the classic work by *Inhelder and Piaget* [1958]. Of central concern has been the verifiability of formal operations as a genuinely unitary, structural advance over concrete operational thought. *Inhelder and Piaget* argue that formal operational thinking is importantly characterized by a marked dissociation of form from content via an interrelated network of operations. This assertion suggests an inherent generalizability of such a network across many content areas and, hence, it is this particular aspect of the theory which has become the subject of much debate in recent years.

Research efforts at establishing descriptive parameters of formal thought have sought both to delineate the variables within formal operations and to arrive at satisfactory methods of assessing a subject's stage. Complicating the picture have been findings, such as by *Neimark* [1970] and *Martorano* [1973], which yielded low intercorrelations among certain tasks, and which could certainly be used to support a more multiform picture of the nature of formal ability than that proposed by Piaget. Studies in physics by *McKinnon* [1971] and *Renner and Lawson* [1973] found that, in general, college students performed

[1] This work was supported in part by NICHD research grant number HD-10333. Special thanks are due to *Debra Eisert* for her help in scoring the tests.

with surprisingly little consistency at the formal operational level. Others, however [*Bart*, 1971; *Berzonsky* et al., 1975], have suggested that Piaget's description of formal reasoning was meant to imply the generalizability within, but not between, certain cognitive domains (e.g., semantic, figural, symbolic, behavioral). *Piaget* [1972] himself had begun to turn his attention to the concept of 'aptitude' in attempting to understand and come to terms with the seeming compartmentalization of formal reasoning into only a few specific areas in the functioning of many adults. The role of aptitude, he argued, should be seen as one of a directing, not a causal, agent in regard to the appearance of formal reasoning.

In addition, *Kuhn* et al. [1977] argue that it is also to be expected that the relative instability of an emerging system of operations, along with the variable degrees of difficulty inherent to individual tasks, will certainly result in the nonuniformity of its applications to various domains in comparison with a consolidated network of formal structures. Thus, a formal orientation ought to be recognizable in the groping of an individual in a content area unfamiliar to him, as well as in the smoother and more articulated performance of the same subject in an area with which he has had considerable experience. It is possible that only the latter type of facile and polished performance has been taken as an indication of formal operational thinking in many studies.

The study described here is an attempt to add information and direction to the research efforts investigating Piaget's cognitive stage theory by exploring the nature of concrete and formal reasoning as it may be manifested in the interpretation and understanding of literary art. To date a few studies have strongly supported the possibility of a stepwise progression in various artistic domains such as children's drawing, improvisation [*Lazier* et al., 1971], aesthetic judgement [*Brunner*, 1974] and story-telling narrative [*Sutton-Smith*, 1975]. Other than *Billow* [1975], few studies have explicitly set out to examine thought processes within the literary arts in terms of cognitive skills comparable to scientific reasoning or operational thinking, however.

An important indication of formal manipulation of a literary work ought to involve the discrimination of the literal (or narrative) from the symbolic level. The ability to perceive and consistently discuss the symbolic level in a literary work requires the creation of hypotheses and propositions not given within the immediate empirical data (i.e., the story or poem), in the same way that a formal approach to a scientific problem begins with hypotheses and possibilities rather than limiting itself to a direct reorganization of the perceived data. A symbol invariably points beyond itself to implicate an idea or another concrete image which is not explicitly presented in the literary work. Thus, as in most formal operational tasks, the subject must manipulate 'data', in the form of hypotheses and ideas, which do not exist concretely in the situation before him, but must be created by him for the purpose of resolving the problem.

This study hypothesized that the analysis or interpretation of a poem would be dealt with differently by subjects who were capable of spontaneously considering a structured whole, or formal operational approach to problem solving (whether the problem be one of spatial proportionality or literary meaning). For example, it was anticipated that subject responses to the poems would be found to be categorizable into three general groupings in accordance with their performances on the formal operational tasks. Theoretically, one would expect concrete thinkers to focus upon literal objects or people, and on surface story line in a poem. Transitionally formal subjects might be expected to indicate acknowledgement of both the literal and symbolic levels, but not be capable of reconciling the two. Fully formal subjects ought to be able to successfully recognize and integrate the two levels in their responses.

More specifically, it was predicted that a formal approach to literature would involve: (a) the ability to approach a literary piece hypothetically by consideration of several alternative interpretations of symbolic meaning before drawing conclusions; (b) the ability to even perceive the symbolic level in a literary piece at all, and to be capable of apprehending and discussing the two levels separately, as well as appropriately synthesizing them when necessary, and (c) the capacity to perceive and bear in mind multiple combinations of elements within the poem, and to subsequently synthesize them in arriving at interpretations of poetic meaning.

The general aim of this investigation was to determine general Piagetian notions of what must constitute a formal reasoning orientation, and to apply these core characteristics of formal thought to the assessment of subject performance on: (a) a paper-and-pencil measure of traditional Piagetian tasks, and (b) the analysis of a literary work of art. It is suggested that the methodological problem of assessment would be alleviated by closer attention to the stated characteristics of concrete and formal operational thinking as first described by *Inhelder and Piaget* [1958], which would in turn guide the establishment of appropriate testing procedures. The establishment of comparable criteria for assessment across domains would mean that evidence for generalizability is obtained if significant agreement across areas is obtained.

Method

Subjects

44 college students ranging from sophomore to senior standing served as the subjects of this study. It was thought that college students – more likely to be relatively practiced in their formal reasoning than younger students – would provide more extensive and less hesitant interview material if, as *Gardner and Lohman* [1975] have suggested, sensitivity to aesthetic discriminations in literature is the latest to be developed among the various art forms. The sample was composed of both men and women from a wide variety of academic majors, and with considerable variability in the self-reported number of books read outside of school assignments.

Measures

All 44 subjects were tested for formal operational ability, and 30 subjects were recalled individually for the last half of the study based on their performance on a paper-and-pencil version of the Piagetian formal operations test devised by *Carol Tomlinson-Keasey and Tom Campbell* of the University of Nebraska.[2] The operational tasks included the chemicals task, the flexibility of rods task, a ratio problem (involving the conversion of kilometers to miles), and a proportional reasoning task. Each task score reflected the operational level of strategy used to solve the problem as well as correctness of response (effectively reducing the likelihood of inflated scores due to lucky guessing).

In order to provide a formal operational assessment which could be appropriately compared with the subject's performances on the literary tasks, scores from the four tasks were then averaged for each subject to arrive at a best estimate of overall operational ability accord-

[2] The test and complete scoring details may be obtained by writing to the author.

ing to a system adapted by *Toni E. Santmire*. This system divided the 30 subjects into three groups of 10 each based upon these averaged scores from the four formal operations tasks. Thus, the three operational groupings characterized the subjects as either concrete operational (C), as transitional between concrete and fully consistent formal operations (F_1), or as relatively stable in their formal reasoning ability (F_2). Reliability of the formal operational measures between the author and a second trained rater was estimated at 0.94. Inclusion of the transitional category was intended to provide a more accurate picture of formal reasoning and its development within the individual than a simple concrete-formal dichotomy. In addition, two subdivisions of formal thought are also described in the original report by *Inhelder and Piaget* [1958] on the development of formal reasoning.

Materials

Two poems were chosen for the literary task which would be roughly representative of two different types of structuring possible in communicating poetic meaning. These two selections are cited by *Rosenthal and Smith* [1973] as respectively exemplifying the two types of structuring: one type in which the attention of the reader is immediately directed to a salient and central element around which the poetic meaning of the work appears to revolve; and one type in which the poetic meaning of the work is more subtly diffused throughout several stylistic and figural aspects of the piece and must be arrived at relatively indirectly. The poem 'Eight O'Clock', by *A.E. Houseman,* may be said to exemplify the latter type of poetic structure; while 'Anecdote of the Jar', by *Wallace Stevens,* engages a poetic structuring of the former type as described by *Rosenthal and Smith* [1973].

Procedure

After the preliminary selection of 30 subjects to participate in the second half of the study (the formal operational tasks having been scored blindly), each subject was recalled individually for an interview session, lasting approximately 20 min, in which they were asked to respond to the task poems. The poems were presented to each subject one at a time for discussion, with 'Anecdote of the Jar' always appearing first. The interviewer tried to remain continually open to directions of discussion initiated by the individual and attempted to probe particularly for clarification of the subject's logical or illogical statements, but invariably opened discussion of each poem by asking the subject what he or she thought the poem was about. Subsequent questions by the interviewer were attempts to get the subject to say as much as possible about the poem while being careful not to 'lead' the subject into any particular directions or interpretations. This strategy thus imposed a loosely similar structure upon the interview situation for all subjects, and yet could allow for directions unpredicted by the researcher to be initiated by the individual subject and pursued further. This approach is in keeping with the clinical interview method employed by *Inhelder and Piaget* [1958] in their own investigations of formal reasoning.

Data Analyses

Lastly, the interview protocols were carefully reviewed for evidence of actual manifestation of the literary groupings suggested earlier. Close inspection of the protocols revealed the opportunity for a more differentiated categorization of response to 'Anecdote of the Jar' than was originally anticipated. Subject responses disclosed a range of ability to comprehend the symbolic level, and a sort of hierarchical categorizability of the responses reflecting increasing complexity of interpretation, and increasing integrative ability. The categories proceed from concrete to abstract interpretations of the poem's central figure (a jar), and from lesser to greater ability to suggest abstract, summarizing meanings for the poem.

A. Literal comprehension: (1) Appeared to perceive the jar in a very literal fashion, as just a jar, throughout the interview. Suggested no type of symbolic or abstracted meanings for the poem. (2) Insisted that the jar was a symbol, but could make no suggestions as to what it might symbolize nor made any attempt to suggest an overall meaning for the poem.

B. Mixed literal and symbolic comprehension: (1) Insisted that the jar was a symbol, and suggested some possibilities, but could not arrive at any sort of overall meaning or summary of what the poem was about. (2) Appeared to suggest that the jar was symbolic, and attempted to make summarizing statements as to the poem's meaning, but other comments made during the interview indicated that the subject was still perceiving the jar literally.

C. Consistent symbolic comprehension: (1) Indicated that the jar was symbolic and could suggest possibilities. Always made some sort of summarizing statement as to the poem's meaning. Tended to initially make a one-to-one transference of the jar to some other specific object or image which it was supposed to represent (e.g., a 'nuclear tower', or 'a person'). (2) Understood the jar to be symbolic, and did not need to specifically refer to the jar when asked what the poem was about (i.e., first reaction was a global abstraction of the poem's events). Nor did they initially 'translate' the jar into another specific image or object, but discussed the poem abstractly from the beginning.

For the purpose of statistical analysis the above literary categories were collapsed into the three overall categories of A, B, and C.

Subject responses to 'Eight O'Clock' indicated that the 'diffuseness' of meaning throughout the poetic structure, in contrast to the more focused arrangement of 'Anecdote of the Jar', made it more difficult to look beyond the narrative structure for a secondary level of meaning. Many students commented that it was merely a tale, albeit a very short one. Perhaps the most interesting phenomenon to arise from the interview material on this poem was the surprising variety of ways in which the subjects interpreted the identity of the subject (or experiencer of the action) of this poem, inasmuch as the subject is never explicitly named or identified in the poem itself. Analysis of the data on this point led to two sorts of categorization of responses. One sort yielded two groups based upon the correctness of their interpretation; that is, those who perceived that the 'he' of the poem referred to a man waiting to be hanged at dawn, and those who did not. It seemed plausible that arrival at a recognition of the identity of this entity implied a formal capacity to marshall the numerous individual clues throughout the text into a logical synthesis of what, or who, they might be referring to.

In addition to this categorization, a second one was arrived at based upon the subject's capacity to suggest summarizing statements of meaning for the poem. The categorization of this second dimension was divided into three levels according to the abstraction of the summarization as follows: (a) no summary attempted; (b) concrete summary suggested, in which an abstraction of meaning is attempted, but is still very concretely tied to the surface events of the poem and (c) abstract summary suggested, implicating larger classes of referents and action than the individual and specific referents of the surface story. Finally, whether or not the subjects appeared to be aware of the poet's personification of the clock (in 'Eight O'Clock') was noted and also compared by chi-square analysis to the operational groupings.

Table I. Chi-square tests for operational groupings and literary categories

	Operational level			Total
	C	F_1	F_2	
Literary categories of 'Anecdote of the Jar'				
A	5	2	1	8
B	4	5	1	10
C	1	3	8	12
Total	10	10	10	30
$\chi^2 = 12.47$, d.f. = 4, $p < 0.05$				
Indentity of 'he' in 'Eight O'Clock'				
Man executed	2	7	8	17
Other	8	3	2	13
Total	10	10	10	30
$\chi^2 = 8.49$, d.f. = 2, $p < 0.05$				
Statement of meaning of 'Eight O'Clock'				
No summary	5	2	1	8
Concrete summary	3	6	2	11
Abstract summary	2	2	7	11
Total	10	10	10	30
$\chi^2 = 10.47$, d.f. = 4, $p < 0.05$				

Results

In order to examine the particular associations between logical operational performance and performance on the literary categories, chi-square analysis were performed comparing operational groups and literary analyses categories, as is suggested by *McNemar* [1962] for use on categorical measures. The chi-square analyses of operational groupings and performance on the poetry revealed significant associations in all cases except for the relationship of operational standing to recognition of personification of the clock in 'Eight O'Clock' (table I). More importantly, the table reveals not only that the relationship between the two types of measures is a significant one, but that it is also in the theoretically predicted direction. It was not expected that concrete thinkers (C) would be capable of engaging in the literary analysis characterized by the highest literary categorization (C), nor that the fully formal subjects (F_2) would be likely to exhibit literary analysis as characterized by the lowest level of the literary categorization scheme (A). As may be seen, the composition of all of the cells of the three separate analyses for operational level and literary analysis presented in table I conform to the theoretically predicted loading of concrete operational thinkers into the 'A' literary categories and the fully formal thinkers into the 'C' literary categories. In addition, chi-square analysis of formal operational performance and academic major yielded no significance; nor did the relationship between the self-reported number of books read and performance on the literary tasks prove to be significant.

Discussion

Translation of formal operational criteria in the logico-mathematical realm into comparable analysis of subject responses in an artistic medium was necessary before attempting to address the question of the generalizability of formal operations. Evidence of an initially hypothetical stance to the question of the poem's meaning was assumed to be reflected in the multiplicity of interpretations offered by the subject, and in the flexibility of response exhibited when challenged upon a particular interpretation. The ability to simultaneously bear in mind multiple combinations of elements and to utilize them systematically in the resolution of the task problem was partially reflected in the capacity of the subject to reconcile conflicting words and phrases within the poem in arriving at an interpretation which would take into account the entire poem, and not just selectively cited lines.

The issue of the generalizability of formal operations is also the issue of whether or not the core characteristics of formal operational thought, as originally outlined by *Inhelder and Piaget* [1958] are indeed 'core' characteristics of an approach to problem solving: an approach which is an inevitable point (or period) of development in the course of cognitive growth. *Kuhn* et al. [1977] are persuaded that the logical operations as described by *Inhelder and Piaget* [1958] do represent a cognitive structuring which is somehow central to the formal thinker's system, and that they serve a unidirectional, 'informatory' role in the individual's subsequent efforts to master, comprehend, or produce mature thinking in other areas (such as moral judgment, or comprehension). That is, the emergence of the logical operational structure is prerequisite to certain levels of achievement in other areas (and, in essence, informs them), but it alone cannot guarantee or determine higher levels of functioning in these other domains; and hence, the role of experience is critical to the expression of formal operational ability. The research presented here contributes further evidence of the informatory relationship of the logical operations to other domains. These data are in general agreement with the findings of other investigators [*Cavior and Lombardi,* 1973; *McGhee,* 1971; *Kuhn* et al., 1977; *Miller* et al., 1970; *Tomlinson-Keasey and Keasey,* 1974] underscoring the importance of exploration within other developmental sequences in an effort to understand the role, and the possible centrality, of the logical operations in the progression of these domains.

This study has also demonstrated a means of effectively translating logical operational criteria from one domain to another, thereby making valid comparison of performance between domains possible. There has always been the problem of comparability of assessment techniques across content areas, and it is suggested that Piaget's own clinical interview approach is the most reasonable for the exploratory investigation of formal operational performance in any new content areas. Otherwise, there appears to be considerable danger of the investigator's incomplete knowledge of the kind of activity which typically engages the thinker in a particular area giving rise to inadequate assessment techniques for that area (such as when the terminology of a given discipline is simply plugged into formal logic problems in order to test for formal operational thinking 'in that discipline'). It seems clear that 'objective', noninterview formats for assessing formal operations within a given domain should be derived only after exploration of operational thinking in that domain via the more flexible and sensitive clinical interview approach. In addition, only a clinical interview approach is likely to be reasonably sensitive to variables such as the subject's prior familiarity with the testing area, as well as his motivation toward, or interest in, the area. Perhaps these variables are what ultimately constitute 'aptitude' as exhibited by the individual for a particular subject matter.

Summary

In an investigation of the relationship of the logical operations to other developmental sequences, 30 college students were assessed as to logical operational ability, and these results compared with their performance on a literary task of poetic interpretation. Operational performance criteria in the logico-mathematical realm were translated into comparable analysis of subject performance in a literary medium. The strong association obtained between logical operational performance and sophistication of poetic interpretation supports the theoretically predicted applicability of central, formal reasoning structures to various content areas.

References

Bart, W.M.: The factor structure of formal operations. Br. J. educ. Psychol. *41:* 70–77 (1971).

Berzonsky, M.D; Weiner, A.B.; Raphael, D.: Interdependence of formal reasoning. Devl Psychol. *11:*258 (1975).

Billow, R.M.: A cognitive developmental study of metaphor comprehension. Devl Psychol. *11:*415–423 (1975).

Brunner, C.: Aesthetic judgment. Criteria used to evaluate representational art at different ages; diss. Columbia University (1974).

Cavior, N.; Lombardi, D.A.: Developmental aspects of judgment of physical attractiveness in children. Devl Psychol. *8:*67–71 (1973).

Gardner, H.; Lohman, W.: Children's sensitivity to literary styles. Merrill-Palmer Q. *21:* 113–126 (1975).

Inhelder, B.; Piaget, J.: The growth of logical thinking from childhood to adolescence (Basic Books, New York 1958).

Kuhn, D.; Langer, J.; Kohlberg, L.; Haan, N.: The development of formal operations in logical and moral judgment. Genet. Psychol. Monogr. *95:*(1977).

Lazier, G.; Sutton-Smith, B.; Zahn, D.: A systematic analysis of developmental differences in dramatic improvisational behavior. Speech Monogr. *37:* 155–165 (1971).

Martorano, S.C.: The development of formal operations thinking. Paper presented at the Society for Research in Child Development, Philadelphia 1973.

McGhee, P.E.: The role of operational thinking in children's comprehension and appreciation of humor. Child Dev. *42:*733–744 (1971).

McKinnon, J.W.: Earth science, density, and the college freshman. J. geol. Educ. *19:*218 (1971).

McNemar, Q.: Psychological statistics; 3rd ed. (Wiley, New York 1962).

Miller, P.H.; Kessel, F.S.; Flavell, J.H.: Thinking about people thinking about people thinking about . . .: a study of social cognitive development. Child Dev. *41:*613–624 (1970).

Neimark, E.: A preliminary search for formal operations structures. J. gen. Psychol. *116:* 223–232 (1970).

Piaget, J.: Intellectual evolution from adolescence to adulthood. Hum. Dev. *15:* 1–12 (1972).

Renner, J.W.; Lawson, A.E.: Promoting intellectual development through science teaching. The Physics Teacher *11:* 273 (1973).

Rosenthal, M.L.; Smith, A.J.M.: Exploring poetry; 2nd ed. (Macmillan, New York 1973).

Sutton-Smith, B.: The importance of the story taker: an investigation of the imaginative life. Urban Rev. *8:* 82–95 (1975).

Tomlinson-Keasey, C.; Keasey, C.B.: The mediating role of cognitive development in moral judgment. Child Dev. *45:* 291–298 (1974).

Contr. hum. Dev., vol. 5, pp. 100–112 (Karger, Basel 1981)

Moral Reasoning and Moral Action: A Critical Analysis of Kohlberg's Theory of Moral Development

Walter E. Conn

Villanova University, Villanova, Pa., USA

The primary focus of Kohlberg's research and theorizing on moral development has not been on moral behavior, nor even on the content of moral judgments, but rather on the structure of reasoning behind moral judgments. Still, Kohlberg's work has not ignored the relationship between moral reasoning and moral action. In one of his most important recent articles, for example, *Kohlberg* [1976, p. 32], after asserting that 'just as there is a vertical sequence of steps in movement up from moral Stage 1 to moral Stage 2 to moral Stage 3, so there is a horizontal sequence of steps in movement from logic to social perception to moral judgment', immediately adds to this horizontal sequence the final step of moral behavior.

An examination of Kohlberg's position on the relationship between moral reasoning and moral behavior raises several problematic issues about Kohlberg's theory of moral development, especially about the nature of postconventional morality and universal ethical principles. Presupposing a basic familiarity with Kohlberg's six-stage structural theory of moral development[1] this chapter will explore some of the most important of these issues: (a) the relationship between conventional moral rules and postconventional ethical principles; (b) the rela-

[1] For a convenient summary statement of the theory, see *Kohlberg* [1976]; for critical assessment from various perspectives, consult *Kurtines and Greif* [1974], *Simpson* [1974], *Conn* [1975], *Philibert* [1975], *Gibbs* [1977] and *Gilligan* [1977]. Although Stage 6 has been dropped from *Kohlberg's* most recent scoring manual [1978] because of its statistical rarity (none of *Kohlberg's* original group of longitudinal subjects – now adults in their thirties – has reached it) and consequent lack of full empirical definition or confir-

tionship between moral judgment and ego-strength in moral action; (c) the relationship between the structure and content of moral judgment; and (d) the identity of knowledge and virtue in the principled moral subject.

Moral Rules and Ethical Principles

Although moral behavior has never been the focus of Kohlberg's research, his studies have included some interesting and occasionally provocative observations on the subject. A particularly important example is *Kohlberg's* assertion [1976, p. 32] that: 'To act in a morally high way requires a high stage of moral reasoning. One cannot follow moral principles (Stages 5 and 6) if one does not understand or believe in them'. On the face of it, the first part of this statement is highly questionable, if not simply false. The second part needs strong qualification.

First of all, high moral action is a matter of a responsible, even courageous, decision to follow or act in accord with a particular practical moral judgment. High or good practical moral judgments are those judgments which direct action toward the realization of value in concrete situations. There is simply no reason to assume that such a good practical moral judgment could not be made by a person of conventional Stage 3 or 4 moral reasoning. In fact, experience tells us that this happens all the time. As guides to value-creating action, good practical moral judgments are good by reason of their *content*. And in terms of content, postconventional moral reasoning, precisely as postconventional, adds nothing to moral judgment. As a guide to action, a good Stage 4 practical moral judgment will, in a given situation, be just as effective in directing action to the realization of value as a good Stage 6 judgment. In fact, it is not difficult to imagine a situation in which a person at a conventional stage could make and follow a better practical moral judgment than a given person of a postconventional stage. The

mation (Stage 6 data come mostly from interviews and writings of persons with serious philosophical training), *Kohlberg* does retain it in his theoretical position: 'Its use is speculative, to clarify the philosophic meaning of moral stages and their claim to adequacy' [1977, p. 195; also see *Hennessy,* 1979, pp. 218–221]. Definitions and characteristics of postconventional or principled moral reasoning apply, of course, to the firmly established Stage 5 (20% of the longitudinal subjects).

point here is not to deny that postconventional moral reasoning is preferable to conventional, but simply to assert that persons at conventional stages of moral reasoning can make excellent practical moral judgments and follow them out in action, and thus 'act in a morally high way'.

Of course, one can define 'acting in a morally high way' as acting in accord with postconventional moral reasoning, as the second part of Kohlberg's statement seems to suggest, but this would be simply gratuitous. The point of this second part seems obviously correct; one cannot follow principles one does not understand. In this case, the principles are self-chosen universal ethical principles. But just what does it mean to follow such principles? Responsible action follows practical moral judgments of conscience, which are made in the light of practical, substantive moral principles or rules. Until recent years the prohibition of abortion was a commonly recognized example of such a moral rule.

In contrast, universal ethical principles serve as second-order critical norms appealed to when first-order substantive moral principles or rules are called into question (see *Aiken,* 1962, pp. 65–87). On the question of abortion, for example, the relevant second-order ethical principle is the sanctity of life. To a large extent, the content of these second-order, or philosophical, ethical principles is vague or indeterminate, and it is precisely this vagueness or indeterminate character that gives them their power as formal, critical norms in terms of which the validity of substantive moral principles is assessed. But as they are indeterminate, these universal ethical principles are not directives of moral action, and so they cannot be 'followed'. Only practical moral judgments informed by substantive moral principles or rules can be 'followed'.

As characterized by Kohlberg, postconventional moral reasoning is philosophical, or *ethical* in the specific sense of critical reflection upon substantive moral principles. However, postconventional moral reasoning, precisely because it is the *moral* reasoning of a person engaged in making a practical moral judgment in a concrete situation, is not the detached, abstract *ethical* analysis of philosophers. Rather, the transition to postconventional moral reasoning involves a *transformation* of conventional moral reasoning which critically grounds or justifies its substantive moral principles or rules in terms of universal ethical principles. Persons of postconventional moral reasoning, then, do not follow formal, indeterminate universal ethical principles. They follow critically grounded substantive moral principles, or, rather, practical moral judgments informed by the latter principles or rules. Clearly, in a cultural and social situation like our own, in which an endless variety of conflicting moral values and principles compete on the open market, such *critically* grounded moral principles are no longer luxury items, but more and more are becoming necessary equipment for *consistent* performance in the struggle for authentic self-transcendence [see discussion of critical moral conversion in *Conn*, 1981, pp. 191–194]. Still, many persons of conventional moral reasoning do lead excellent moral lives by following practical moral judgments based on sound moral principles which they have accepted without critical questioning. To conclude: 'to act in a morally high way' does not require 'a high stage of moral reasoning' for the simple reason that the higher postconventional level of moral reasoning proposes no higher way of *acting* than does the conventional. The advantages of postconventional reasoning are of an important, but different kind.

Moral Action and Ego-Strength

Reference to 'responsible decision' brings us directly to the question of the relationship between moral reasoning and moral action. Continuing his discussion of moral behavior and postconventional ethical principles, *Kohlberg* [1976, p. 32] says: 'One can, however, reason in terms of such principles and not live up to them. A variety of factors determines whether a particular person will live up to his stage of moral reasoning in a particular situation, though moral stage is a good predictor of action in various experimental and naturalistic settings.'

In explicit contrast to superego-strength or moral habit interpretations, *Kohlberg* [1971b, p. 76; also see 1969, p. 396; 1964, pp. 389–392; 1968, p. 485] maintains that the most important of this 'variety of factors' is clearly ego-strength (ego-control, or will), which includes 'capacity to maintain attention, intelligent task performance, capacity to delay response, and capacity to delay gratification.' This interpretation of moral character 'implies that the major consistencies in moral conduct represent decision-making capacities rather than fixed behavior traits' [*Kohlberg*, 1964, p. 391]. In a certain sense, however, ego-strength or will is morally neutral, as indicated by cheating tests in which 'strong-willed' (high IQ, high attention) Stage 2 subjects cheated more than 'weak-willed' Stage 2 subjects, while 'strong-willed' Stage 4 subjects cheated less than their 'weak-willed' counterparts [*Kohlberg*, 1969, p. 396]. Ego-strength, in other words, works to translate into conduct whatever a person's stage of moral reasoning happens to be.

None of this is particularly surprising. What is surprising and problematic, in this context, is Kohlberg's claim that 'moral stage is a good predictor of action', when, as we have just seen, ego-strength is so influential for determining behavior within a given stage (Stage 2 subjects cheated more or less depending on the strength of their will).

Kohlberg's claim seems least problematic in connection with postconventional moral reasoning. Here relatively high percentages of experimental subjects or persons in real-life situations act in accord with what Kohlberg thinks postconventional judgment dictates: only 11% of principled college students cheated in an experiment (in contrast to 42% at lower levels); 80% of Stage 6 students participated in the Berkeley sit-in (as opposed to 50% at Stage 5 and 10% at Stages 3 and 4); 75% of the Stage 6 subjects quit or refused to shock the victim in Milgram's experiment (as opposed to 13% of subjects at lower stages). These figures and others like them lead *Kohlberg* [1971b, pp. 78–79] to assert that 'moral maturity in judgment and in action are closely related', that 'advance in moral judgment seems to correlate with more mature moral action'.

Of course there are obvious complications in this kind of conclusion. For here the issue is not the structure of reasoning, but the content of moral judgments; not whether action conforms to the person's own (presumably Stage 6) reasoning and judgment, but whether it conforms to what Kohlberg posits as an appropriate Stage 6 judgment. For example, in the Milgram experiment, Stage 5 moral reasoning did 'not clearly prescribe a decision', according to *Kohlberg* [1971b, pp. 78–79]. Obviously, Kohlberg must mean it did not clearly prescribe a decision to refuse to administer the shock, for 87% participation could appear to represent a rather clear decision. Only Stage 6 moral reasoning, says *Kohlberg* [1971b, p. 79], 'clearly defined the situation as one in which the experimenter did not have the moral right to ask them to inflict pain on another person'. Here Kohlberg appears to mean that a Stage 6 judgment would dictate a refusal to participate in the experiment. Whether or not he is correct, whether or not we agree with the judgment to refuse, is irrelevant for the moment. The point is that Kohlberg has, in this and other examples, identified a particular judgment of *content* with Stage 6 reasoning, which, like the other stages, was carefully defined only in *structural* terms, free of any content.

The general question this raises can be explored in the context of the Milgram example. What, for instance, are we to think of the 25% of Stage 6 subjects who continued with the experiment? Did they not reason at Stage 6 in this particular situation? Or did they indeed reason at Stage 6, but reach a judgment to continue with the experiment? Does Kohlberg's position admit this possibility? And what about their *decision* to continue? With the 75% who refused to participate, we can assume that their decision followed their judgment. Those who continued, however, might have judged that they should continue, and thus decided to follow their judgment. Or they might have judged that to continue would be morally wrong, but after an inner struggle decided to continue, pressured by 'human respect' or other situational factors.

In other words, in this case as in others, 'maturity of action' is being defined in terms of content. A person's action is measured not against his or her own judgment of what is the moral thing to do, but against an external standard: inflicting pain in an experimental situation is wrong; cheating on a test is wrong; 'sitting in' in support of free speech is right. Recently, in an interview, Kohlberg has said that Stage 6 reasoning could not possibly support capital punishment [*Hennessy*, 1979, p. 221].

There are several layers to the problem. First, as we have seen, Kohlberg sets up the question of moral behavior or action as the final step in a horizontal moral sequence, following logic, social perception, and moral judgment. But, although he states the problem in terms of the fact that one can 'reason in terms of such (postconventional) principles and not live up to them', his stress in discussing the facors determining 'whether a person will live up to his stage of reasoning in a particular situation' falls on moral judgment stage as a predictor of action. Kohlberg's reports, in other words, do not deal with the issue of consistency between what a person *judges* should be done in a particular situation and what that person actually *does*. For this question, one must know what the person actually *judged* to be the moral course of action. His reports do not supply this data. Kohlberg's research, rather, deals with the statistical issue of determining how often persons judged to be at a given stage, say Stage 6, will act in a way considered appropriate to that stage. So, for example, 75% of persons at Stage 6 refused to continue with Milgram's experiment; 25% continued. Since we do not know what the persons actually judged to be the right thing to do in this particular situation, we have no way of knowing how consistent their judgments and actions were. Since 25% of the Stage 6 subjects did not act according to Stage 6 reasoning, as Kohlberg sees it, he can conclude that factors (ego-strength, for example) not present in detached interview situations are operating in real moral situations. But are these factors affecting reasoning and judgments, i.e., is the 25% acting in accord with inadequate judgments? Or is it deliberation and decision that are being affected, i.e., is the 25% making the judgment that continued participation is morally wrong, but not following that judgment, not deciding to act in accord with that judgment? Kohlberg, unfortunately, does not provide data for an explicit distinction between judgment and decision. It is a crucial distinction, though, for our experience offers examples of instances when our reasoning and judgment were clouded or distorted, as well as times when we *knew* quite well what *ought* to be done, but did not do it. In the end, it seems that Kohlberg's writing on moral behavior is limited to showing that there is a positive correlation between moral reasoning as diagnosed in dilemma interviews and specified kinds of moral action in real-life situations.

Structure and Content of Moral Judgment: Justice

Some important questions regarding the nature of postconventional, principled reasoning have surfaced in this discussion about judgment and behavior. As we have noted, in order to attempt a correlation of moral reasoning stages with moral behavior, Kohlberg has designated certain types of behavior as characteristic of a given stage: cheating at Stage 2, for example, or 'sitting in' for free speech at Stage 6. He has, in other words, characterized stages of moral reasoning in terms of behavior content. In some cases this characterization may be simply statistical: most Stage 2 subjects cheat, for example. Regarding Stage 6, however, there is a definite normative tone to Kohlberg's statements. The subject in the Milgram experiment, he says, 'has to realize that the experimentor does not have the right to order another human being to be shocked' [*Hennessy,* 1979, p. 237].

Despite Kohlberg's structural approach, then, and despite his definition of moral judgments as precisely *moral* in the strictly *formal* terms of their being 'universal, inclusive, consistent, and based on objective, impersonal, or ideal grounds' [*Kohlberg*, 1968, p. 490], we find him identifying Stage 6 with particular concrete moral judgments. And this is quite deliberate, not the result of an inadvertent slip. For Kohlberg's position is that the development of the very structure of moral reasoning leads – in the limit of Stage 6 – to a moral orientation grounded in the central principle of justice. On this point, *Kohlberg* [1971b, pp. 62–63] is unambiguous: 'Our major and most controversial claim is that the only "true" (stage 6) moral principle is justice.' He explains this claim by asserting 'that human welfare is always the core of morality but that, at the principled level, welfare considerations subsumed under the heading "justice" take priority over other "principles" for considering welfare whenever there is conflict between the two, and that there is no strong "principle" for deciding between the various welfare alternatives other than justice' [*Kohlberg*, 1971b, p. 63].

At Stage 6, then, structure (or form) and content are one: justice. As *Kohlberg* [1971b, p. 60] says, his 'conception of moral principle implies that one cannot ultimately separate form and content in moral analysis'. While 'concern for welfare consequences' in some way characterizes each stage of moral reasoning [*Kohlberg*, 1971b, p. 63], only at Stage 6 are welfare concerns structured by the universal principle of justice: the equality of human rights and respect for the dignity of human beings as individual persons [*Kohlberg*, 1976, p. 35]. Empathy structured in any way short of this fundamental principle of justice was not effective, for example, as a reason for refusing to continue in the Milgram experiment.

Claiming that justice is a universal principle, Kohlberg takes a deliberate nonrelativist position. There is an objectivity to moral reasoning that goes beyond personal opinion. In fact, Kohlberg sees principled moral reasoning, especially Stage 6, as the developmental overcoming of the relativistic Stage 4½, which, though having perceived conventional morality as only one among many moralities and not absolutely 'given', still lacks objective grounding. With Stage 6, then, Kohlberg becomes something of an ethical theorist as well as a psychologist. Speaking about the Heinz dilemma, for example, Kohlberg [*Hennessy*, 1979, p. 223] says he 'would claim that in this situation it is universally morally right to steal the drug'[2]. By its very definition, then,

[2] For Kohlberg's attempt to explain the adequacy of Stage 6 philosophically as well as psychologically, see *Kohlberg* [1971a, 1973].

Stage 6 moral reasoning is objectively grounded in universal, principled justice. This is not to say that the moral principles of conventional morality may not be objective. The point, rather, is that, unlike conventional reasoning, postconventional principled reasoning is *intrinsically* objective. Persons at conventional stages may claim to – and sometimes clearly do – make moral judgments in terms of objective principles. But the objectivity here is in a sense 'accidental', dependent upon whether the moral principles borrowed from the 'given' morality happen to be objective. Conventional morality is a 'borrowed' morality, and whatever objectivity it possesses is also borrowed. In contrast, postconventional morality is the orientation of a person whose critically appropriated moral principles have been objectively grounded and justified in ethical reflection. Objectivity is a constitutive component of such a principled orientation.

Does the objectivity of Stage 6 moral reasoning preclude moral disagreement, then? Will persons reasoning at Stage 6 always agree on the morality of a given question? Some of Kohlberg's apodictic statements about capital punishment, as well as other issues we have noted, suggest a positive response. A different answer emerges, however, when we recall that Kohlberg's notion of principle, unlike the purely formal principle of Kantian morality [*Kohlberg*, 1971b, p. 60], integrates form and content, inasmuch as the basic moral values, the welfare concerns present throughout lower stages, are structured by the principle of justice at Stage 6. The answer to our questions, then, seems to be 'yes, in principle'. But what is true in principle is not necessarily so when principles are brought to bear on concrete, individual cases. And Kohlberg seems to be in clear agreement. For despite his insistence on universal principles, *Kohlberg* [1971b, pp. 60–61] at the same time very clearly states that his 'conception of principle implies a "situation ethic" in the sense that it reduces all moral obligation to the interests and claims of concrete individual persons in concrete situations'.

For Kohlberg, then (and this is a side of his thought which has not been taken into sufficient account), true principles are 'guides to perceiving and integrating all the morally relevant elements in concrete situations, . . . to the obligating elements in the situation, to the concrete human claims there' [*Kohlberg*, 1971b, pp. 60–61]. In his view, 'the case is always higher than the principle, a single human life is worth more than all the principles in philosophy to the man. Principles simply tell us how to resolve these concrete claims, when claims conflict in a situation, when it is one man's life against another's' [*Kohlberg*, 1971b, p. 61]. In contrast, the universality of principles used as rules of action is 'always purchased at the price of ignoring unique elements of human welfare and justice in the concrete situation' [*Kohlberg*, 1971b, p. 60]. Asserting that 'moral obligations are towards concrete other people in concrete situations', *Kohlberg* [1971b, p. 61] rejects the 'fallacy of treating a principle as elevated above the individual in the situation to which it applies'. Kohlberg's view is 'situational', then, in the sense that, while affirming the universality and objectivity of ethical principles as guides for dealing morally with concrete situations, he rejects the validity of principles understood as universal rules of action. Indeed, Kohlberg is the rare moral thinker who explicitly understands his position in terms of both natural law and situation ethics perspectives. He can do this because he understands natural law in terms of universal principles of justice [*Kohlberg*, 1974, p. 5]. And these are the ethical principles which guide us in concrete situations, directing the use of lower-level moral rules to the realization of the interests and claims of persons in those situations. The objectivity in question here, then, is a quality of ethical principles; this does not mean that every person of postconventional moral reasoning will judge a given situation in the same way. Despite his definitive statements about issues like capital punishment, Kohlberg's position on ethical principles clearly allows for moral disagreement about concrete situations, but not about justice as constitutive of fully ethical reasoning. Because moral judgment involves more than principles, individuals at Stage 6 will differ in specific judgments about what justice means in a given situation; objectivity means they will share a common orientation of reasoning structured by the universal principle of justice.

The Integrated Self: Judgment and Action

For Kohlberg, not only do form and content come together in postconventional moral reasoning, as the universal principle of justice structures welfare concerns, but moral reasoning itself becomes one with action. On the connection between moral judgment and moral action, *Kohlberg* not only points out that 'advance in moral judgment seems to correlate with more mature moral action' [1971b, p. 79], but goes so far as to assert with Plato that 'true knowledge of principles of justice does entail virtuous action' [1971b, p. 78]. Unlike mere opinion or conventional belief that some particular kind of act is wrong, judgments of principled moral reasoning, according to Kohlberg, will be followed. At Stage 6, Kohlberg seems to be saying, knowledge (of the universal principles of justice) is virtue.

Whatever degree of truth there is to this assertion, the possibility of action consistently conforming to judgment would appear to lie in the affective and cognitive integration of the whole self. To the degree that action consistently follows judgment, it follows not the judgment of merely conceptual knowing but the judgment made within a symbolic pattern of knowing in which the affective and cognitive are integrated as one [see *Conn*, 1977, pp. 194–205]. In this symbolic pattern feeling, knowing, loving, and deciding all work together in an undifferentiated personal unity to bring forth action. Here ego-strength is not something alongside moral judgment, but is so deeply interwoven with it that to judge is to decide is to act. Reflective ethical analysis may play an important auxiliary role, but the fundamental power of the symbolic pattern comes from the center of the person where the affective and cognitive dimensions speak with one voice. All of this is not to say that the symbolic pattern is found exclusively at postconventional stages, nor that it is always true. Neither is the case. Love, after all, is sometimes blind. But when persons are able to respond to the values in a situation symbolically, as full persons, their judgments and their actions will be as one. Of course this is not our universal experience.

Kohlberg's point is that persons of principled reasoning are able to respond in this fashion more frequently than others, because, it seems, postconventional persons reason with self-chosen principles – not with borrowed moral rules, but with principles which have been personally appropriated and become identified with them in such a way that what one judges *should* be done is what one *wants* to do. Personal moral judgments of principle, and not other situational factors, dominate the decision-making process. In this sense, *Kohlberg* [1971b, p. 80] says, the basic virtue may be called "autonomy" as well as "justice". This is possible because principled moral reasoning has its source in and flows from the integrated affective-cognitive core of the personal subject. It does not merely represent what the subject *thinks*, but expresses who the subject *is*. And in one important sense, to talk about who the personal subject is, is to talk about conscience in the most concrete sense of character.

Summary

A critical discussion of Kohlberg's position on the relationship between moral reasoning and moral action raises several problematic issues about his theory of moral development, especially about the nature of postconventional morality and universal ethical principles. This chapter offers a unified theoretical approach to some of the most important of these issues in Kohlberg's writings: (a) the relationship between conventional moral rules and postconventional ethical principles; (b) the relationship between moral judgment and ego-strength in moral action; (c) the relationship between the structure and content of moral judgment; and (d) the identity of knowledge and virtue in the principled moral subject.

References

Aiken, H.D.: Reason and conduct (Knopf, New York 1962).

Conn, W.E.: Postconventional morality: an exposition and critique of Lawrence Kohlberg's analysis of moral development in the adolescent and adult. Lumen Vitae *30*: 213–230 (1975).

Conn, W.E.: Moral development as self-transcendence. Horizons *4*: 189–205 (1977).

Conn, W.E.: Conscience: development and self-transcendence (Religious Education Press, Birmingham, Ala 1981).

Gibbs, J.C.: Kohlberg's stages of moral development: a constructive critique. Harv. educ. Rev. *47*: 43–61 (1977).

Gilligan, C.: In a different voice: women's conception of self and morality. Harv. educ. Rev. *47*: 481–517 (1977).

Hennessy, T.C.: An interview with Lawrence Kohlberg; in Hennessy, Value/moral education: the schools and the teachers, pp. 211–242 (Paulist Press, New York 1979).

Kohlberg, L.: Development of moral character and moral ideology; in Hoffman, Hoffman, Review of child development research, vol. 1, pp. 383–431 (Russell Sage Foundation, New York 1964).

Kohlberg, L.: Moral development; in Sills, International encyclopedia of the social sciences, vol. 10, pp. 483–494 (Macmillan and Free Press, New York 1968).

Kohlberg, L.: Stage and sequence: the cognitive-developmental approach to socialization; in Goslin, Handbook of socialization theory and research, pp. 347–480 (Rand McNally, Chicago 1969).

Kohlberg, L.: From is to ought: how to commit the naturalistic fallacy and get away with it in the study of moral development; in Mischel, Cognitive development and epistemology, pp. 151–235 (Academic Press, New York 1971a).

Kohlberg, L.: Stages of moral development as a basis for moral education; in Beck, Crittenden, Sullivan, Moral education: interdisciplinary approaches, pp. 23–92 (Newman Press, New York 1971b).

Kohlberg, L.: The claim to moral adequacy of a highest stage of moral judgment. J. Phil. *70:* 630–646 (1973).

Kohlberg, L.: Education, moral development and faith. J. moral Educ. *4:* 5–16 (1974).

Kohlberg, L.: Moral stages and moralization: the cognitive-developmental approach; in Lickona, Moral development and behavior, pp. 31–53 (Holt, Rinehart & Winston, New York 1976).

Kohlberg, L.: The implications of moral stages for adult education. Relig. Educ. *72:* 183–201 (1977).

Kurtines, W.; Greif, E.C.: The development of moral thought: review and evaluation of Kohlberg's approach. Psychol. Bull. *81:* 453–470 (1974).

Philibert, P.J.: Lawrence Kohlberg's use of virtue in his theory of moral development. Int. phil. Q. *15:* 455–497 (1975).

Simpson, E.L.: Moral development research: a case study of scientific cultural bias. Hum. Dev. *17:* 81–106 (1974).

Contr. hum. Dev., vol. 5, pp. 113–130 (Karger, Basel 1981)

The Influence of Family Interaction on Moral Development: A Sociological Perspective

Thorolfur Thorlindsson, Stephen G. Wieting[1]

University of Iceland, Reykjavik, Iceland; University of Iowa, Iowa City, Iowa, USA

In 1932, *Piaget* in *The Moral Judgment of the Child* addressed an enduring problem comprised of philosophical, political, and human developmental facets by describing two kinds of moralities: the morality of constraint and the morality of reciprocity. Since that time, attention to the various facets of this problem has been energetic and voluminous, though the weight of attention to the several facets has been notably uneven. The efforts of *Kohlberg* and his associates in measuring and describing elements of the cognitive developmental features of morality are sizable [*Kohlberg*, 1963, 1969, 1973, 1976; *Kohlberg and Gilligan*, 1971]. Though attention to philosophical and political issues has been modest, recent work by *Rawls* [1971] on theory (and the large amount of interest his ideas have stirred) has brought into current forums topics introduced long ago by *Piaget*. The facet addressed by this paper – and one it is felt which has long been underdeveloped empirically and theoretically – is the matter of social influences on moral development. *Piaget* conveyed his recognition of the influence of family and peers, for example, but did not develop these points in the 1932 statement. Within the *Kohlberg* tradition, in fact, the awareness of the need for clarifying the role of social factors is becoming prominent.

[1] We want to thank *Wolfgang Edelstein* for his helpful suggestions on an earlier draft of this paper. We would also like to thank *Gudridur Sigurdardottir, Kristin Magnusdottir, Palina Dora Petursdottir, Alfheidur B. Einarsdottir,* and *Runar Brynjolfsson* for their assistance. The work reported in this chapter was supported in part by a grant from the Icelandic National Science Foundation.

The discussion below begins by developing a conceptual basis for talking of one kind of social influence, that of the family. This is done by proceeding in terms of an important distinction made in the moral development literature (conventional versus principled morality) [*Kohlberg and Gilligan*, 1971; *Kohlberg*, 1973; *Gibbs*, 1977, 1979]; and then by tying the theoretical lead that *Piaget* does provide to an available, developing theory of family socialization [particularly, the work of *Bernstein*, 1971]. Secondly, the methodological steps undertaken in this project are described. Even though the research literature elaborating on aspects of *Kohlberg's* theory is becoming common in the United States, there remain relatively few instances [notable exceptions including *Kohlberg* himself, e.g., 1973] where comparable research has been conducted in other than United States settings, implying necessary constraints on the generality of the conceptions. This study, done in Iceland, intends to add to this needed generality. Results are presented in a third section. Finally, implications of the findings for the several facets of *Piaget's* morality of constraint/morality of reciprocity are explored.

Background for Consideration of Family Influence

The Conventional-Principled Morality Distinction

For several reasons we have chosen to focus in this chapter on the conventional-principled morality distinction. The conventional-principled morality distinction has been given special attention because of its social-political implications. *Rest* [*Rest* et al., 1974] has pointed out that the functioning of modern democracy presupposes principled moral judgment. Further, from the perspective of the individual, the shift from the conventional to the principled level has special importance. *Erikson* [1978], *Fromm* [1955], and others have pointed out how ideology comes to play a central role in personality organization as the individual shifts away from a conformist, other-directed orientation to a more autonomous orientation.

The distinction between the level of conventional and principled morality has recently received considerable attention as well from theorists [*Gibbs*, 1977, 1979; *Flavell*, 1970] who have argued that the Piagetian ontogenetic stage model can only be applied to the first four stages of moral development. *Gibbs* maintains that if the two stages of the principled morality level are included in the structuralists' standard stage sequence model, the model fails to meet some of the major criteria characterizing the genetic structuralist development.

Gibbs has argued for a two-phase model of moral development which emphasizes the distinction between standard child development of a Piagetian genetic structuralist nature and 'existential' adult development (that is, in *Gibbs's* formulation, reflective morality, in which the individual makes moral options the objects of contemplation). According to *Gibbs* this does not mean that the notion of development should be done away with [*Gibbs,* 1979, p. 108]. Rather, he is saying that the development beyond the conventional level exhibits 'a looser sense of development'. *Gibbs's* ideas are pertinent here not only because of his distinction between the cognitive-developmental and the 'existential' levels of morality but also because they allow consideration of the importance of the social environment in the transition from the conventional to the principled level. (In the interest of continuity we have retained *Gibbs's* term 'existential', though in quotations since his use confuses the important distinction of *existentielle* and *existential* in the Heideggerian tradition.)

If young children are exposed to a normal social environment they will, through a complex interaction between the maturational processes and the social environment, go through the preconventional level to stage four of the conventional level. The course of their development will correspond with the general criteria of stage development characterizing the Piagetian genetic structuralist view [*Gibbs,* 1977; *Isaksson,* 1979]. Variation in the social environment will not be crucial in this phase of development, except perhaps to increase or decrease the speed with which the individual goes through the stages [*Kohlberg,* 1973].

On the other hand, only a limited number of people reach the level of principled morality, and the proportion that reach this stage varies from country to country [*Gibbs,* 1979]. There is thus a good reason to believe that the transition from the conventional to the principled level is influenced by social factors.

Kohlberg's formulation of moral development has tended to stress the cognitive-structural characteristics of moral development as opposed to social determinants [*Hoffman,* 1970]. Some critics of *Kohlberg's* moral theory have even gone as far as interpreting any direct influence of social factors on moral development as a refutation of *Kohlberg's* cognitive-structuralist theory of moral judgment [*Kurtines and Greif,* 1974]. As *Broughton* [1978] has pointed out, extreme interpretations of *Kohlberg's* work denying all social influences on moral development are in error. *Kohlberg* has denied not that moral judgment is influenced by social factors, 'but that it is totally the product of social *learning* or copying via contingent or extrinsically imposed conditionings [*Broughton,* 1978, p. 88].

Anticipations in *Piaget* and Their Comparability with *Bernstein*

Piaget himself, in his early work on morality, clearly recognizes the importance of social factors in the development of morality [*Piaget,* 1932]. The crucial variable in the child's social environment, according to *Piaget,* is the degree to which the child's interaction with others is characterized by reciprocal or equalitarian relationships as opposed to authoritarian or unilateral relationships. Although *Piaget* refers repeatedly to the importance of peer interaction in the child's shift from unilateral to reciprocal social interaction, he clearly recognizes the importance of family interaction for the development of higher stages of morality. According to *Piaget,* parents who tend to be authoritarian in their child-rearing practices help consolidate the child's natural tendency toward heteronomy. On the other hand, if parents interact with their children in a reciprocal fashion, they would increase the likelihood of moral autonomy in their children. *Piaget's* view of social interaction and morality is captured in his identification of two major types of social relations.

The first one, which he calls the relationship of constraint, is characterized by conformity to invariant rules that define 'appropriate' behavior. This kind of relationship is unilateral and is commonly based on authority. For example, a child accepts a certain number of commands to which he or she must submit, where right is what conforms with these demands and wrong is what fails to do so.

The second type of social relationship *Piaget* calls relationship of cooperation. The relationship of cooperation is reciprocal and based on mutual respect of rules governing behavior. The rules of social behavior are thus viewed as man-made and negotiable.

Bernstein's [1971] conceptualization of personally versus positionally oriented family interaction bears a striking resemblance to *Piaget's* relationship of cooperation and constraint [*Thorlindsson,* 1978]. According to *Bernstein,* position-oriented families are characterized by interaction patterns and decision-making that are organized around the formal statuses of the individuals involved. The separation of roles in such families tends to be very firm. Formal statuses and ascribed role norms tend to determine the distribution of power and authority. Behavior tends to be regulated in terms of role expectations. Parents, for example, tend to regulate the child's behavior closely in terms of age- and sex-role expectations. Socialization tends to occur unilaterally (from parent to children), rather than reciprocally.

In person-oriented families, interaction and decision-making are organized around the individual qualities of interactants. Decisions are more open to discussion, and there is less reference to formal statuses. Children, for example, achieve position within the family communication system in terms of their unique social, affective, and cognitive characteristics. Indeed, one of the important characteristics of a person-oriented family is that the children learn to make their 'own roles' instead of being formally assigned to them. Also, children tend to socialize their parents as well as to be influenced by them, and the parents are sensitive to their children's unique standpoints[2].

We may summarize the foregoing discussion of social interaction as follows. Two ideal types of social interaction may be identified. The first ideal type, which may be called position-oriented interaction, has four major characteristics: (a) There is conformity to formal role expectations and relatively invariant rules justified with reference to tradition or formal authority. (b) The rules guiding the interaction are relatively nonnegotiable. (c) Power and authority are distributed on the basis of formal statuses and are justified with reference to tradition. (d) The relationship between people holding different positions in the status hierarchy tend to be unilateral, involving one-way accountability, as opposed to a reciprocal relationship involving mutual accountability.

The second ideal type of interaction pattern, which may be called person-oriented interaction, has the following characteristics. (a) The

[2] *Hoffman's* [1970] and *Keller's* [1976] conceptualizations of parent-child interaction tap dimensions analogous to those of *Piaget* and *Bernstein* discussed above, though *Keller,* unlike *Hoffman* and *Bernstein,* argues for a structural/developmental account of these influences.

interaction focuses on the bases and the consequences of the behavior, and the rules guiding the behavior are justified with reference to reasons for the behavior and consequences of it, rather than tradition. (b) The rules are relatively open to discussion and negotiation. (c) The relationships between interactants tend to be reciprocal, involving mutual accountability as opposed to the unilateral relationships in position-oriented interactions.

For the purpose of studying the influence of the family on moral development, family interaction has been conceptualized in terms of position-orientation and person-orientation. The family interaction patterns have been conceived of as two variables that are not necessarily mutually exclusive. An individual could then be viewed as engaging in both interaction patterns within the family setting. In fact, one would expect an individual to engage in both patterns, but to varying degrees, within different social settings, such as the family, school, work, and so on. Even within one such setting, the same individual might engage in both types of interaction. However, it is likely that the two patterns would be negatively correlated when considered within the same social seting – i.e., the family in the present study. Thus one would expect one of the interaction patterns to be more dominant than the other. In line with the discussion above, the following hypotheses may be stated: (a) There should be a positive relationship between mother-child person-oriented interaction and the child's use of principled moral judgment. (b) There should be a negative relationship between mother-child person-oriented interaction and the child's use of conventional moral judgment. (c) There should be a negative linear relationship between position-oriented mother-child interaction and the child's use of principled moral judgment. (d) There should be a positive relationship between position-oriented interaction and the child's use of conventional moral judgment.

Investigating Family Organization in Iceland

Sampling

The data for this research were collected in Iceland. With regard to race and ethnicity, the population is very homogeneous. Everyone speaks the language of Icelandic, and local dialects are practically nonexistent. The Icelanders are very homogeneous with respect to religion; about 92.7% of the population belong to the Icelandic National Church, the Evangelical Lutheran Church [*Tolfraedihandbok*, 1976].

In this century Iceland has rapidly become urbanized. However, only one town has a population of more than 15,000 - Reykjavik, the capital. Reykjavik is situated on the southwest coast of the country, and the pattern of urbanization has centered there: in 1901, 19.1% of the population lived in the urban area of Reykjavik, whereas in 1978 the corresponding figure was 53%.

The design used in sampling was a multistage stratified design including the two major strata of the urban area of Reykjavik and the relatively small fishing communities scattered around the coast of Iceland. The measurement instruments were given to the children in a classroom situation, in groups ranging in size from 13 to 26. Of the 100 subjects that were sampled, 92 subjects returned the material fully completed.

The Measurement Instruments

Moral Judgment

The moral judgment stage was measured by the shorter version of the Defining Issues Test, an instrument developed by *Rest* and his collaborators [*Rest*, 1974, 1975; *Rest* et al., 1974]. The Defining Issues Test has some practical advantages over the less standardized measures of morality, for example, the most widely used method of *Kohlberg* and his associates. It is highly standardized and much less time-consuming. As *Rest* describes it [*Rest* et al., 1974, p. 492]: 'The methodological advantages of the Defining Issues Test format are the following: It is highly structured in that the information from each subject is comparable, it minimizes variance in stage scores due to individual differences in verbal expressivity; and it is objectively scored (can be computerized), thus saving time and minimizing scorer bias.'

In the Defining Issues Test, the subject reads a moral dilemma; he or she is then presented with twelve issues or considerations bearing on the situation. For instance, in one of the dilemmas a woman is dying from a special kind of cancer. The dilemma is whether or not her husband, Heinz, should steal an exorbitantly priced drug from a druggist to save his wife's life. The subject is asked to consider the importance of such issues as 'whether the druggist's rights to his inventions have to be respected', 'is Heinz willing to risk getting shot as a burglar or going to jail for the chance that stealing the drug might help', 'whether Heinz is stealing for himself or doing this solely to help someone else', and so on. Each issue is designed to exemplify some distinctive characteristic of a stage. Each moral dilemma includes statements for stages of moral development (see discussion of the stages above). The subject is asked to rate each issue according to its importance on a five-point Likert scale, that is, 'great importance', 'much importance', 'some importance', 'little importance', 'no importance'. The subjects are then asked to rank their first four choices of the most important issues. This ranking is used as the basis of analysis. There are three of these dilemmas in this shorter version of the test. [The Icelandic version used in this research and the English language equivalent are available in *Thorlindsson*, 1978].

The Defining Issues Test has been developed and tested in the sociocultural setting of the United States and has proven a valid measurement of moral judgment stages in that particular setting [*Rest,* 1974; *Rest* et al., 1974]. However, the instrument may be 'culturally biased' and not a valid assessment of moral judgment stages in the sociocultural setting of Iceland. It is the position taken here that rather than viewing the problem of conceptual equivalence as mainly a problem of translation, it may be viewed as a special case of the more general problem of measurement validity [*Straus,* 1969]. In line with that view, estimating the validity of the Icelandic version of the Defining Issues Test was given some priority. The validation of the Defining Issues Test included the following procedures: An attempt to receive a best translation and to improve the validity of the instrument was undertaken by the use of 'expert judges' [*Straus,* 1969]. Secondly, two other types of validation, known groups and criterion validity, were used as major sources of validation of the instrument. [For a detailed description of these procedures, see *Thorlindsson,* 1978].

The shorter version of the Defining Issues Test was translated into Icelandic by the researcher. Four Icelanders who all spoke good English were then asked to translate the format independently of each other. These four persons were all teachers at the elementary or high school level. The different translations were then compared to each other and problems or disagreements in the different translations were discussed among the translators in order to reach final agreement on what would be the best translation of the problematic Icelandic version of the schedule. It was felt that the teachers might serve as 'expert judges' to evaluate the appropriateness of the indicators of the Defining Issues Test, and that their suggestions, comments, and criticisms would help to provide for content validity of the instrument. In spite of these attempts to secure equivalence between the Icelandic and English versions of the Defining Issues Test, some minor differences exist between the versions. [See *Thorlindsson,* 1978.]

Rest has argued that if the Defining Issues Test is a valid measurement of moral stage development, it should be able to discriminate more 'expert' groups [*Rest,* 1974, 1975; *Rest* et al., 1974]. More specifically, he has argued that junior high, senior high, college students, seminarians, and graduate students in moral philosophy and political science should show significant differences, that the more advanced groups should tend to choose higher stage statements. Studies using the Defining Issues Test have confirmed this hypothesis. [For a summary of a number of these studies, see *Rest,* 1974.]

Based on this line of reasoning, the Icelandic version of the Defining Issues Test was given to two groups, 27 14- and 15-year-old junior high school students and 19 college seniors and first-year graduate students in political science and sociology, in order to test its validity. As cognitive-developmental theory predicts, the stage scores at stages 2 and 3 are higher for the junior-high group than those of the comparison group whereas the P scores are higher for the college-aged sample than for the junior high group. (Note: P scores equal the percentage of maximum scores for combined stages 5 and 6 in *Rest's* morality assessment.) A pooled variance estimate for the difference between the mean stage scores for the two groups also indicates that besides being in the direction hypothesized, the differences are significant. The highest probability of making a type I error is 0.02. Also, table I, which shows the group means as percentages of the maximum possible score for each stage, is directly comparable to results obtained by *Rest* [1974], where stage scores are also presented as percentages of maximum possible scores. Comparisons of the results obtained here and the results obtained by *Rest* and his associates show the same main trends. It may further be noted that the mean scores for the Icelandic and American samples are fairly close. After reviewing a number of studies, *Rest* has concluded that the P scores of junior-high samples 'tend to average in

Table I. Group differences presented as a percentage of maximum scores on the Icelandic version of the Defining Issues Test indices

Student group	Stage			
	2	3	4	5 and 6 (P)
Junior high (N=27)	8.2	37.4	41.1	24.0
College seniors and graduates in political science and sociology (N=19)	3.3	8.2	18.8	60.5

the 20's and low 30's, senior-highs in the upper 30's, college underclass samples in the 40's, college upperclass samples in the 50's, graduate students in the 60's, and academic specialists in the moral-social-political areas in the 70's [*Rest*, 1974, p. 3].

Rest [1974, p. 5] has further argued that: 'The D.I.T. is expected to correlate with certain value positions which are required by a high stage perspective but which may seem paradoxical from a lower stage perspective. In other words, moral judgment is expected to correlate with those attitude tests that key on stage characteristics, but not with all attitude tests [see *Kohlberg*, 1969, p. 390]. In our 1974 studies, two attitude tests were used. One test (the "Law and Order" test) is comprised of 15 controversial public policy issues ...'

A split-half reliability of 0.79, using the Spearman-Brown correction formula, was obtained for an Icelandic translation of the Law and Order Test [*Rest*, 1974]. A correlation of −0.45 was obtained between the Defining Issues Test and the Law and Order Test for a sample of 18 college seniors. This may be compared to a correlation of −0.58 reported by *Rest* [1974] for a sample of 160 between the shorter version of the Defining Issues Test and the Law and Order Test.

In view of the evidence it seems appropriate to conclude that the Icelandic version of the Defining Issues Test has proven to be a valid instrument for assessing moral judgment stages, and to manifest properties that are highly compatible with the original English version (table I).

Table II. Split-half and test-retest reliability coefficients for the main sample and pretests[1]

	Main sample	First pretest	Second pretest	Pretest group test-retest
Mother-child person-oriented interaction	0.87	0.90	0.92	0.91
Mother-child position-oriented interaction	0.86	0.84	0.89	0.87

[1] The Spearman-Brown formula was used to correct the split-half reliability coefficients.

Mother-Child Interaction

Measures of mother-child interaction were obtained by a questionnaire. A detailed description of the operational procedures for development of the instrument and the Icelandic version and English language equivalent have been given elsewhere [*Thorlindsson*, 1978]. The questionnaire was composed of two major parts. Part A included 19 items, 10 measuring person-orientation and 9 measuring position-orientation. The subjects were asked to rate the items on a 5-point Likert-type scale: 'never' (scored 1), 'hardly ever' (2), 'sometimes' (3), 'very often' (4), and 'always' (5).

Part B was also intended to measure the two interaction patterns – i.e., person- and position-orientation – and is compared with Part A for purposes of validation. Unlike Part A, which was based on the subject's rating of the items, Part B was based on the subject's ranking of four items which were intended to measure mother-child position- and person-oriented interaction. The schedule listed four reasons that mothers might give when asked by the subject why he or she was not allowed to do something: (1) 'Because I say so.' (2) She explains in detail why you can't do this. (3) She allows you to do things you want to do, if you give her good reasons for it. (4) Because parents know what is best for their children. The reliabilities of the scale (Part A) are shown in table II. The convergent and discriminant validity of the mother-child measurement instrument was estimated through a multitrait-multimethod matrix as recommended by *Campbell and Fiske* [1959], utilizing the two methods used for measurement of mother-child interaction, each of which measured two traits. The four criteria given by *Campbell and Fiske* for determining both convergent and discriminant validity are adequately met for the rating scale (Part A) [*Thorlindsson*, 1978, 1981].

Mothers, Children and Morality: the Importance of Social Interaction

The correlation coefficients between the variables of the study are shown in table III. The correlation coefficients between the mother-child interaction patterns and the moral judgment variables are all in the direction predicted. The correlations range from − 0.31 to 0.45. All the correlation coefficients are significant at the 0.001 level. The correlation coefficients remain relatively stable between the urban and the rural samples and between the male and female samples. No significant interaction is found between the two social settings and the correlation coefficients involving independent and dependent variables nor is any significant interaction found between sex and these correlations. Examination of a scattergram describing the relationship between the variables does not indicate any systematic departure from linearity, nor does the scattergram suggest an inflation or attenuation of the correlation coefficients for the relationships between the variables due to extreme scores.

Hypothesis 1 states that there should be a positive relationship between mother-child person-oriented interaction and the child's use of principled moral judgments. Table III indicates that this hypothesis is moderately supported. A correlation coefficient of 0.45 is obtained for the relationship between mother-child person-oriented interaction and use of principled morality judgments.

Hypothesis 2 states that there should be a negative relationship between mother-child person-oriented interaction and the child's use of conventional moral judgments. As indicated by table III, a correlation coefficient of − 0.35 is obtained between these variables.

Hypotheses 3 and 4 state that mother-child position-oriented interaction should be related to moral development in such a way that the variables should be positively correlated with conventional morality

Table III. Zero-order correlation among the variables

	Variable			
	1	2	3	4
1. Principled morality	–	-0.47**	0.45**	-0.31**
2. Conventional morality		–	-0.35**	0.38**
3. Mother-child person-oriented interaction			–	-0.34**
4. Mother-child position-oriented interaction				–

** Significant at the 0.001 level.

and negatively related to principled morality. Table III shows that a correlation coefficient of 0.38 is obtained between mother-child position-oriented interaction and conventional morality. Table III further shows that a correlation coefficient of – 0.31 was obtained between position-oriented interaction and principled morality.

Cognitive Development and Social Order: Implications of a Structuralist Alternative

The results show that the empirical evidence, in general, supports the model. The model's four propositions are significantly supported by the data. However, the strength of the evidence may be debated. When the absolute magnitude of the correlation coefficients is considered, the evidence offers moderate support for the model. However, when the magnitude of correlation is considered in a theoretical context, it may be argued that it offers relatively good support for the hypothesis. Even though we have emphasized the influence of the family on moral judgment, we have to bear in mind that the child engages in much interaction outside the home, for example, peer interaction, which affects the child's moral judgment. Thus, the influence of the social variables cannot be expected to be strong unless measurements of the individual's engagement in the same interaction forms across all groups in which he or she participates are used to predict the moral judgment variables. When the empirical evidence is considered in this light, it seems to offer rather good support for our model.

How do these results, which clearly demonstrate the influence of the family on moral thinking, bear on cognitive-developmental theories of morality? Although the direct influence of social factors on moral judgment has sometimes been interpreted as a criticism of *Kohlberg's* cognitive developmental theory of moral judgment [*Kurtines and Greif*, 1974], it is a position taken here that these results are coincident with fundamental aspects of the structuralist developmental view of morality. This position is based on the fact that the family interaction patterns and the morality variables, as well as the relationships between these two sets of variables, were conceptualized from a Piagetian point of view (generic to *Kohlberg's*, *Gibbs's*, and related cognitive development approaches). That is, the two interaction patterns are viewed as involving, reciprocally, different ways of organizing interpersonal relations and different ways of defining a given social-moral dilemma. It is consistent with the cognitive-developmental view of moral judgment to depict the stages of moral judgment as 'successive transformation in the way people view cooperative social arrangements. A moral judgment stage is a conceptual framework for interpreting social interrelationships and mutual responsibilities. Each moral judgment stage therefore has distinctive ways of defining a given social-moral dilemma and of evaluating a crucial issue of a problem' [*Rest* et al., 1974, p. 492]. Correlatively, whereas all social relations require their participants to decenter, to have words and actions be consistent with one another, and to take account of other interactants' viewpoints, different organization of interpersonal relations may foster different levels of operational or reflective thought, different levels of morality development.

Position-oriented social relationships are essentially relationships of constraint where the forms of association between interactants are constrained by existing rules. Behavior is concerted by conformity to ascribed role norms and in terms of formal statuses. The interactants in this kind of relationship are not constantly forced to be occupied with the other's points of view. So long as the interactants conform to the rules defining appropriate behavior, concerted interaction will not be problematic. Behavior will be highly predictable, given the situation, the status, and the social position of the interactant, and the corresponding expectations. The individual organizes the different standpoints of the social group in terms of formal statuses and conventional rules of organization. The role-taking skills involved are obtained in a relatively concrete, unproblematic way, in contrast with the more complex coordination of individual intentions or standpoints involving multiple perspectives as in the more equalitarian relationships of cooperation, where the norms or the rules of social behavior are viewed as human-made and resting on mutual agreement. There is a clear awareness of the fact that there are different ways of organizing a stable social order. Behavior is negotiated by reference to its basis and consequences, for a hypothetical, more or less rational, group of people.

In person-oriented interaction, the individual is thus constantly forced to take the points of view of the other interactants and to organize or coordinate them in various ways. In general, person-oriented social relations seem to involve higher levels of operational and reflective intelligence. This conclusion is in agreement with both *Mead's* [1934] and *Piaget's* views that participation in groups of more complexity and participation in networks of groups that involves coordination of diverse points of view will foster higher levels of reflective intelligence. It is further in line with *Piaget's* argument that relationships of an equalitarian nature tend to foster higher levels of operational thought and morality than unilateral relationships built on authority and arbitrary tradition. *Piaget* has noted in particular that it may be the case that only people in complex societies employ formal operational thought, whereas people in traditional societies may not move beyond the level of concrete operational thought [*Inhelder and Piaget,* 1958; *Piaget,* 1971].

It is the view taken here that too little attention has been given to a Piagetian structuralist view of social organization and the interplay between social organization and cognition. *Piaget* has again and again emphasized that thought comes from action. Interpersonal relations are the originating source of knowledge, especially moral and social knowledge. Thought is rooted in interpersonal interaction, in the relations in which interactions are organized. These relations are later organized into rule systems that explain (define) these relations. If the cognitive structuralist tradition is to benefit from approaching cognitive and moral development from a more sociological point of view, social organization needs to be conceptualized from a constructivist point of view. This means, among other things, that social organization has to be conceptualized in terms of different forms of social relations involving different typologies of social interaction patterns. Further, the empirical relationship of these typologies to cognition and morality needs to be investigated further.

In conclusion, the general theoretical status of the conceptualization and findings here might best be articulated in terms of a tripartite arrangement of alternative origins of social structure provided by *Piaget* [1970]. One alternative, 'genesis without structure', is *preformed* as in archetypes *(Jung)*, biologically-based dispositions in *Freud* [as described in *Sulloway*, 1979], or the genetic determinism of sociobiologists [e.g., *Wilson*, 1975]. Clearly, here, the prospect of social environmental influence as demonstrated in this chapter tends to be obviated. Secondly, there is 'structure without genesis' where *organizational structures are taken as given*, as, for example, *Durkheim's* social facts or notions of the Gestalt in cognitive psychology. Here the contributions of natural, developmental features of human cognition (whether Piagetian or as elaborated by *Kohlberg*) are begged. Thirdly, *Piaget* describes genetic structuralism which sees social organization arising, consolidating, and constraining itself as the production of an interaction between properties of actors and properties of the social environment. It is this third alternative which encompasses and illuminates the features of our conceptualization and research. The natural foundations of morality, and the extreme importance of a just social order, as suggested by *Rawls* [1971] and elaborated by *Condon* [1976] and *Condon and Wieting* [1980], exist in the developmental potential of the human organism. However, since the development of the competence is interconnected with the organism's interaction with features of the social as well as the physical environment, the prospects of social factors accounting for behavioral and cognitive variations as we have found are foretold. (That is, that social conditions are necessary for elements of development implies different settings will lead to different patterns – here, in levels of principled morality.) In short, the thrust of our statement is that cognitive development and social organization mutually imply one another, pointing to the satisfactory character of the genetic structuralist alternative where environmental effects are not obviated (as in the preformed alternative) and where origins are not begged (as in the emergentist alternative which possesses structure without genesis).

Summary

The authors investigated the influence of mother-child interaction within a family setting in Iceland on levels of moral development. Questionnaire items measured interaction, and the short version of *Rest's* Defining Issues Test assessed moral development of 92 boys and girls aged 14 and 15 years. Using *Bernstein's* conceptualization it was hypothesized: position-oriented interaction would be negatively associated with principled moral judgment and positively associated with conventional moral judgment; person-oriented interaction would be positively associated with principled moral judgment and negatively associated with conventional moral judgment. Correlation coefficients between the interaction and moral judgment variables were in the directions predicted, ranged between -0.31 and 0.45, and were significant at the 0.001 level. Theoretical implications regarding cognitive development and political and social order are drawn.

References

Bernstein, B.: Class, codes and control, vol. I (Routledge & Kegan Paul, London 1971).

Broughton, J.: The cognitive-developmental approach to morality. A reply to Kurtines and Grief. J. moral Educ. *7:*81–96 (1978).

Campbell, D.; Fiske, D.: Convergent and discriminant validation by the multitrait-multimethod matrix. Psychol. Bull. *2:*81–104 (1959).

Condon,T.: Comment on Coleman's Inequality, sociology and moral philosophy, Am. J. Sociology *82:*205–217 (1976).

Condon, T.; Wieting, S.: Morality, justice, and social choice. Natural foundations for the construction of social order. Unpublished manuscript (Guelph University, Guelph, Ont., 1980).

Erikson, E.H.: Identity: youth and crisis (Norton, New York 1978).

Flavell, J.P.: Cognitive change in adulthood; in Goulet, Baltes, Life span developmental psychology: research and theory (Academic Press, New York 1970).

Fromm, E.: Escape from freedom (Holt, Rinehart & Winston, New York 1955).

Gibbs, J.C.: Kohlberg's stages of moral judgment. A constructive critique. Harvard educ. Ref. *47:*43–61 (1977).

Gibbs, J.C.: Kohlberg's moral stage theory. A Piagetian revision. Hum. Dev. *22:*89–112 (1979).

Hoffman, M.: Moral development; in Mussen, Carmichael's manual child psychol. *2:* 261–360 (1970).

Hoffman, M.: Moral internalization, parental power, and the nature of parent-child interaction. Devl. Psychol. *2:*228–239 (1975).

Inhelder, B.; Piaget, J.: The growth of logical thinking from childhood to adolescence (trans. Parsons, A., Milgram, S.) (Basic Books, New York 1958).

Isaksson, A.: Kohlberg's theory of moral development and its relevance to education. Scand. J. educ. Res. *23:*47–63 (1979).

Keller, M.: Development of role-taking: social antecedents and consequences of school success. Hum. Dev. *19:*120–132 (1976).

Kohlberg, L.: The development of children's orientations toward a moral order: 1. sequence in the development of moral thought. Vita hum. *6:* 11-33 (1963).

Kohlberg, L.: Stage and sequence: the cognitive-developmental approach to socialization; in Goslin, Handbook of socialization theory and research (Rand McNally, Chicago 1969).

Kohlberg, L.: The child as a moral philosopher; in Chazan, Soltis, Moral education (Teachers College Press, Columbia University, New York 1973).

Kohlberg, L.: Moral stage and moralization. The cognitive-developmental approach; in Lickona, Moral development and behavior (Holt, Rinehart & Winston, New York 1976).

Kohlberg, L.: Gilligan, C.: The adolescent as a philosopher. The discovery of the self in a postconventional world. Daedalus *100:* 1051-1086 (1971).

Kurtines, W.; Greif, E.B.: The development of moral thought: review and evaluation of Kohlberg's approach. Psychol. Bull. *81:* 453-470 (1974).

Mead, G.H.: Mind, self, and society (University of Chicago Press, Chicago 1934).

Piaget, J.: Le jugement moral chez l'enfant (Presses Universitaires de France, Paris 1932).

Piaget, J.: Structuralism (trans. Maschler, C.), (Harper Torchbooks, New York 1970).

Piaget, J.: Genetic epistemology (trans. Duckworth, E.) (Norton, New York 1971).

Rawls, J.: A theory of justice (Havard University Press, Cambridge 1971).

Rest, J.: Manual for the Defining Issues Test, an objective test of moral judgment. Unpublished manuscript (University of Minnesota, Minneapolis 1974).

Rest, J.: Longitudinal study of the Defining Issues Test of moral judgment. A strategy for analyzing developmental change. Devl. Psychol. *6:* 738-748 (1975).

Rest, J.; Cooper, D.; Coder, R.; Masanz, J.; Anderson, D.: Judging the important issues in moral dilemmas. An objective measure of development. Devl. Psychol. *4:* 491-501 (1974).

Sulloway, F.J.: Freud, biologist of the mind: beyond the psychoanalytic legend (Basic books, New York 1979).

Straus, M.: Phenomenal identity and conceptual equivalence of measurement in cross-national comparative research. J. Marriage Family *31:* 233-241 (1969).

Thorlindsson, T.: Social organization, role-taking, elaborated language and moral judgment in an Icelandic setting. Unpublished PhD diss. (University of Iowa, Iowa City 1978).

Thorlindsson, T.: The quest for mind: family interaction, role-taking ability and use of elaborated language. J. comp. Family Stud. *12* (1981).

Tolfraedihandbok: Statistical abstract of Iceland (Hagskyslur Islands II, Reykjavik 1976).

Wilson, E.O.: Sociobiology (Harvard University Press, Cambridge 1975).

Contr. hum. Dev., vol. 5, pp. 131–144 (Karger, Basel 1981)

The Development of Concepts of Self: An Interpersonal Perspective[1]

Jacqueline Smollar Volpe
The Catholic University of America, Washington, D.C., USA

A major assumption underlying most investigations of self-concept and self-concept development is that individuals have an idea about 'who they are' or 'how good they are' which remains constant across variations in interpersonal contexts [*Wylie,* 1974]. While such an assumption may be tenable with respect to physical characteristics or particular ascribed roles, its validity is questionable when applied to behavioral aspects of the self or to a sense of self-worth [*Gecas,* 1972; *Monge,* 1973; *Kokenes,* 1974]. As a result, studies concerning developmental aspects of the self-concept have often focused on age-shifts in the nature of the adjectives generated to describe the self (i.e., concrete vs. abstract; global vs. articulated) rather than on the characteristics of the concept of self per se [*Mullener and Laird,* 1971; *Montemayer and Eisen,* 1977; *Mohr,* 1978; *Keller* et al., 1978].

An alternative to the notion of self-concept constancy is offered by *Youniss* [1980] in his presentation of the Sullivan-Piaget thesis – a combination of the theoretical perspectives of *Harry Stack Sullivan* and *Jean Piaget*. This thesis provides a framework for conceptualizing cognitive-social development based on the proposition that primary objects of social knowing are not 'other persons' or 'selves' but interpersonal relations. These relations come to be known in much the same way as logical relations – through interactions between subject and 'object'. Interpersonal relations are constructed by individuals through mutual reflection on the interactions between subject and subject. Just as interactions with objects can be conceptualized in generalized forms and ordered with respect to various types of logical relations, the generalizable aspects of interactions with persons may be organized with regard to different types of interpersonal relations.

[1] This research was supported in part by a grant from the W.T. Grant Foundation.

A corollary to this proposition is that knowledge of 'self' and of 'other' develops along with construction of relational knowledge. That is, knowledge of self and other depends upon the form of the relation that exists between self and other. Others are known in the context of the self's relation to them, and the self is known in the context of its relationships with others. An implication of this notion is that to the extent that individuals participate in various types of interpersonal relations, their self-conceptions will differ accordingly.

While there are several ways in which interpersonal relations can be classified [*Hinde*, 1978; *Watzlawik* et al., 1967], the concern for *Youniss* [1980] and others [*Piaget*, 1932; *Sullivan*, 1953] has been with a system which differentiates relations according to the form of interacting that typifies the ongoing process of the relation. To this end, the Sullivan-Piaget thesis proposes the general categories of relations of authority and relations of equality, and discusses the two relations which perhaps best exemplify each of these categories - parent-child relations and friendship. According to the thesis, parent-child relations (as well as other authority relations) involve interactions which are unilateral in form while friendship is characterized by reciprocal forms of interacting. These disparate forms of interacting result in different conceptions of relations and eventually of 'self' and 'other' within the relations.

An interaction may be termed 'unilateral' when one member of the relation imposes his or her mode of interacting upon the other and, conversely, when the other member conforms his or her actions to meet the directives or expectations of the authority. Parents, for example, frequently intervene in children's activities and direct their behavior. They tell children how to behave with others (share with friends, be polite to adults, obey parents, etc.), what to do in various social situations, and what activities the child can expect to be praised or punished for. Within parent-child relations, directives flow in one direction. Children do not, as a rule, instruct parents with regard to social or interpersonal behavior, nor do parents conform their own behavior to meet children's directives, although they may adapt their role in response to children's needs or styles [*Bell*, 1968]. Maintenance of an authority relation, then, involves compliance rather than cooperation.

In peer relations, interactions are reciprocal. Children do not unilaterally impose their modes of interacting upon one another (at least not successfully), but instead exchange them for eventual comparison, validation, or alteration. To the extent that adults do not intervene, each participant in the relation is free to act in whatever way he or she pleases. Children quickly learn that to maintain a relation with a peer it is necessary to set limitations on behavior or develop 'rules' of interacting. Since this process involves a mutual effort it requires cooperation rather than compliance.

Previous research efforts have provided support for the notion that parent-child relations are perceived as involving unilateral interactions while peer relations are conceptualized in terms of equality and reciprocal interactions [*Youniss and Volpe,* 1978; *Youniss,* 1980]. The purpose of the present study is to determine whether concepts of self within these relations will reflect this distinction. It is proposed that a self-concept constructed in the context of cooperation and equality will be disparate from a view of self developed in the context of compliance and authority. In addition, since earlier research has found that concepts of parent-child and friend relations change with increasing age, it is expected that self-conceptions within these relations will demonstrate age changes.

Investigating Self-Concepts

In order to study self-concepts from an interpersonal perspective, 80 subjects were individually interviewed using two standard self-report tests modified to incorporate a relational context. There were 20 subjects in each of four age groups – preadolescents (10–11 years), mid-adolescents (14–16 years), late-adolescents (18–19 years), and young adults (22–24 years) – with males and females equally represented at each age level. The first test was the 3-question Way-I-Am test. In its original form, the test involves having subjects provide 3 responses to the stem: I am _____. For this study, the form was altered by specifying another person and requesting explanations for self-descriptions. The stem presented to the subjects in this study was: 'When I am with my mother (father, close friend), I am _____ because _____.' Subjects were required to give 3 responses to each of the 3 relational contexts. This test was given orally and responses were written down by the interviewer.

Following the Way-I-Am test, research participants were asked to fill out a 'true-false' test involving two scales of the Interpersonal Style

Inventory (ISI) [*Lorr and Youniss*, 1973]. The scales chosen were the Sensitivity to Others Scale and the Independence Scale. The Sensitivity to Others Scale is designed to measure the level of an individual's sensitivity to the feelings, moods, and attitudes of others. It is comprised of 20 statements about the 'self'. Examples are: 'Other people tell me I am quick to sense when they are troubled', and 'I can nearly always tell when I have offended someone'. Each statement of this scale was modified to include the specification of 'parent' and 'friend'. Thus, the two statements above were changed into the four following statements: 'My parents tell me I am quick to sense when they are troubled'; 'My friends tell me I am quick to sense when they are troubled'; 'I can nearly always tell when I have offended my parents'; and 'I can nearly always tell when I have offended my friend'.

The 20 statements on the Independence Scale are concerned with an individual's willingness to 'openly' express one's own opinions and to resist pressure to conform. Examples of statements included in this scale are: 'I say what I believe no matter what other people think'; and 'Other people can easily change my opinion even after I have made up my mind'. These statements were presented to subjects as: 'I say what I believe no matter what my parents think'; 'I say what I believe no matter what my friends think'; 'My parents can easily change my opinion even after I have made up my mind'; and 'My friends can easily change my opinion even after I have made up my mind'.

Each subject received all 80 of the modified statements and 10 additional items chosen at random from other scales of the ISI. These additional items were not modified and were not scored. All statements were arranged so that there were at least 5 statements in between modified versions of the same statement.

During the pilot study it was discovered that the vocabulary of many of the scale items was unfamiliar to 10- to 11-year-olds. As a result, for subjects at this age level a separate 'True-False' test was prepared with simplified vocabulary and sentence structure. For example, the statement 'I am genuinely glad when I see my parents are happy' was changed to read 'I am really happy when I see that my parents are happy'. And the statement 'I often misjudge my friends' intentions' was changed to read 'I often make mistakes when I try to guess why my friends do some of the things they do'. Once altered, these items were given to another group of 10- to 11-years-olds. Each statement was read to the pilot subject, and the subject was asked to indicate if he or she understood it. Before the True-False test was administered, subjects were asked if they were familiar with this type of test (all said 'yes') and were told that they must answer all statements either 'true' or 'false'.

Self-Concepts in Three Interpersonal Contexts

Responses to the 3-question Way-I-Am test were separated into descriptions of self and reasons for descriptions. These were then categorized on the basis of content similarity without knowledge of age or sex of subjects or type of relational context. Once categories were established, their reliability was checked by having an independent rater assign appropriate category numbers to each of the 720 responses. An interrater agreement score was then calculated. The categories of descriptions of self are shown in table I with frequency distributions across relational contexts. The category miscellaneous includes idiosyncratic responses such as 'good at things', 'envious', and 'idolizing'. Interrater agreement on assignment of response to categories was 0.96.

As shown in table I, categories 1, 2 and 3 include 62% of self descriptions given in mother-child contexts; categories 1, 2, 4 and 7 account for the majority (72%) of descriptions in father-child contexts; and categories 1, 3 and 6 incorporate 80% of descriptions generated for close friendships. Parent-child relations are differentiated from one another by the relative frequency of category 7 responses in the father-child relational contexts as compared to the mother-child context. In addition, category 5 descriptions occurred more often in mother-child than in father-child relational contexts. The close-friend context is distinguished from parent-child relations by the absence of category 8 descriptions, the infrequent occurrence of category 2 and 7 descriptions, and the relatively high frequency of category 6 descriptions which characterized close friendships.

Reasons for self-descriptions were classified into the 5 categories presented in table II. Interrater agreement on assignment of reasons to the 5 categories was 0.88. As shown in the table, category 1 includes over 50% of the reasons given in parent-child relational contexts, but only 12% of those provided in close-friend relations. The reverse of this pattern occurs for category 5 reasons, which appeared particularly infrequently in the father-child context. In addition to these cross-relational differences, the close-friend context produced an age difference

Table I. Description of self in three interpersonal contexts

Description of self	Interpersonal relations					
	mother-child		father-child		close friend	
	n	%	n	%	n	%
1. Positive feelings (happy, loved, comfortable, relaxed)	66	27	50	21	86	36
2. Negative feelings (angry, defensive, unhappy, cold, uncomfortable, rebellious)	48	20	59	25	8	3
3. Extroverted (playful, outgoing, talkative, rowdy)	34	14	25	10	64	27
4. Nice (polite, obedient, attentive, considerate)	28	12	34	14	16	7
5. Warm (loving, affectionate, caring)	24	10	10	4	6	3
6. Open (honest, trusting, 'free')	14	6	4	2	42	17
7. Mature (serious, intellectual, quiet)	5	2	31	13	8	3
8. Circumspect (guarded, not open, careful about what I say)	15	6	17	7	0	0
9. Miscellaneous	6	3	10	4	10	4

between the preadolescents and older subjects. In close friendships, category 5 accounts for at least 42% of the reasons offered by each of the three older age levels, but occurred only 2 times at the preadolescent level. These younger subjects, in contrast, generated primarily category 3 reasons. Within parent-child relations a major age shift did not occur until young adulthood. Category 2 reasons were generated more often by young adults (45%) than by younger subjects.

Scores on the two scales of the ISI – Sensitivity to Others and Independence – were analyzed using a mixed design 4(Age) × 2(Sex) × 2(Relation) analysis of variance (ANOVA) with repeated measures across relations. Sensitivity scores were found to increase significantly

Table II. Reasons for descriptions of self in three interpersonal contexts

Bases for reasons	Interpersonal relations					
	mother-child		father-child		close friend	
	n	%	n	%	n	%
1. Reactions – other person's actions or feelings toward the self (actual, expected or possible) Because I don't want to get into trouble Because he likes me to be that way Because that's how she is with me	123	51	139	58	28	12
2. Feelings – feelings for or attitudes about the other person Because I like her Because I respect him Because I feel I can trust her	65	27	55	23	42	17
3. Interactions – the mode of interactions established in the relationship Because that's the way we are together Because we are like that with each other Because we have fun together	18	8	33	14	71	29
4. Personality – personal qualities of the self Because that's the way I am Because that's just my personality Because I think it's fun	14	6	7	3	14	12
5. Acceptance – mutual understanding, intimacy, and acceptance etablished in the relations Because I am completely accepted Because we understand each other so well Because I know he won't judge me	20	8	6	2	85	35

Table III. Mean Independence scores for Age and Type of Relation[1]

Relation	Age, years			
	10–11	14–16	18–19	23–24
Parent-child	12.2	14.9	13.8	16.8
Friend	11.0	15.0	17.0	17.4

[1] Score range, 0–20.

as a function of increasing age [$F(3, 72) = 6.41$, $p < 0.001$], with differences occurring between preadolescents and each of the other age levels (Duncan's Multiple Range Test; Alpha 0.05). Sensitivity scores were also significantly higher in the friend context than in the parent-child context [$F(1, 72) = 66.80$, $p < 0.001$]. Although this relational distinction was apparent for both sexes, it was significantly greater for females than for males [$F(1, 72) = 7.77$, $p < 0.01$] (difference for females = 2.9 points; difference for males = 1.43 points).

Independence scores were also found to increase significantly with increasing age [$F(3, 72) = 24.02$, $p < 0.001$] with differences occurring between all age levels (Duncan's Multiple Range Test; Alpha 0.05). Although there was no main effect for relational context with respect to Independence scores, there was a significant effect for the interaction of age and relational context [$F(3, 72) = 4.52$, $p < 0.01$]. As shown in table III, the scores for preadolescents, mid-adolescents, and young adults were similar across relational contexts, while the scores for late-adolescents were higher in the friend context than in the parent-child context.

The data reported above indicate that conceptions of self change considerably as the interpersonal context shifts from parent-child to close-friend relations, and, in some cases, as the age level shifts. Within close friendships, individuals reported that they are happy, comfortable, outgoing, open, and trusting.

Adolescents and young adults attributed these feelings and behaviors primarily to the mutual acceptance (intimacy, understanding) which characterized the close-friend relation. This is consistent with their perceptions of themselves as highly sensitive to the feelings and moods of their friends. Preadolescents, however, explained similar feelings and behaviors in terms of the actual mode of interacting established in their close-friend relations. Subjects at this age level also produced lower sensitivity scores in friendship than did their older counterparts.

While the parent-child relational contexts frequently elicited such self-descriptions as happy, comfortable, and outgoing, individuals rarely described themselves as open, honest, and trusting in these relations. In addition, self-concepts within parent-child relations often included descriptions such as uncomfortable, defensive, guarded, and unhappy. In further contrast to close friendships, the feelings and behaviors generated to describe the self in parent-child contexts were, for the most part, 'reactive'. That is, they were perceived as a product of expected or actual feelings and behaviors of the parent toward the self. This 'explanation' was applied to positive as well as negative self-descriptions. The concept of mutual acceptance as an explanation for feelings or behaviors was rarely mentioned in either parent-child context, although it was more frequent in the mother-child than in the father-child context. Although young adults still perceived themselves as primarily 'reactive', at this age level feelings and behaviors of the self were also frequently attributed to the self's feelings and attitudes toward the parent, i.e., love, respect, admiration.

The analysis of Independence Scale scores presents a less clear picture than the other data with respect to cross-relational differences. Preadolescents, mid-adolescents, and young adults appear to be equally comfortable expressing their opinions and ideas regardless of relational context (although scores did increase with increasing age). Late-adolescents (18–19 years), however, apparently feel more at ease expressing opinions and ideas in their friendships than in their parent-child relations. One possible explanation for this finding may be that it is during late adolescence (early college years) when children begin to develop opinions and ideas which are distinct from those of their parents, while at the same time they may not be secure enough with these new opinions to defend them against possible challenges from parents. As a result, late-adolescents may be more likely to decline to express their ideas and opinions if they think their parents will not agree or approve.

The 'Unilaterality' of Self-Concepts

In order to add to the descriptive analysis of the implications of parent-child and friend relations for self-conceptions, responses to the Way-I-Am test were individually coded with respect to whether they were or were not 'unilateral'. A response was judged to be 'unilateral' and given a score of '1' if the self-description incorporated the actions of the 'other' person toward the self (i.e., obedient, rebellious) or was actually attributed to the feelings or actions of the 'other' toward the self (i.e., category 1 reasons, table II). All other responses were judged 'non-unilateral' and assigned the score '0'. Scores were assigned to each of the 3 test responses given by each subject for each relation and then summed within relational contexts. Each subject was thus given a 'unilaterality' score (ranging from 0 to 3) for each relationship. Interrater agreement or assignment of unilaterality scores to responses was 0.89.

A statistical analysis to compare unilaterality scores between parent-child and close-friend relations was not necessary and, in fact, not feasible. Only 28 of the 240 responses given in the close-friend context could be scored as 'unilateral', while over 50% of responses in the parent-child contexts were so scored. Unilaterality scores were analyzed for parent-child relations, however, using a mixed design 4(Age) × 2(Sex) × 2 (Type of Parent-Child Relation) ANOVA with repeated measures across relations. Unilaterality was found to decrease significantly with increasing age [$F(3, 72) = 2.70$, $p < 0.05$], with young adults differing from pre- and mid-adolescents but not late-adolescents (Duncan's Multiple Range Test; Alpha 0.05). While there was no main effect for type of relation, same-sex parent-child relations were found to elicit lower unilaterality scores (mean score = 1.52) than did cross-sex parent-child relations (mean score = 1.85) [$F(1, 72) = 8.32$, $p < 0.001$].

The rare instances of 'unilateral' self-concept responses in the close-friend context serve to underscore the distinctions found in the descriptive analysis between self-concepts in this relation and those generated in parent-child relational contexts. While unilaterality appears to be a major component of the self-concept in parent-child relations, it is practically nonexistent in the self-concepts of close friends. Within parent-child relations, however, young adults perceive themselves as less 'reactive' or unilateral than the younger subjects do. This suggests that some shift in the relationship may occur at this point.

Another important result is the finding that self-concepts within mother-daughter and father-son relations are less unilateral than those developed within mother-son and father-daughter relations. Similarity of sex, then, appears to reduce the 'reactive' aspects of the self-concept, possibly because it allows for the self to identify with the authority in a way that is not feasible in cross-sex parent-child relations. However, the reverse of this may also be true. That is, similarity of sex may permit a perception of a child of the same sex as more of an 'equal' than a child of the opposite sex. This finding clearly requires further research and has important implications for the study of parent-child relations and family processes.

Discussion

The variations in self-conceptions across relational contexts reported in this chapter lend strong support to the thesis that the self-concept cannot be perceived as a static or consistent cognitive construction about 'Who I am'. Instead, 'Who I am' appears to be a function of 'Who I am interacting with' and 'What type of relation exists between us'. Thus, individuals can be quite different 'selves' in different interpersonal contexts. This statement is not meant to imply that perceptions of self change with each new social or interpersonal situation, but that interpersonal situations themselves are ordered with regard to generalizable forms, i.e., relationships, and it is these generalizable forms which allow for both consistency (within similar relational forms) and variation in self-conceptions.

The data also support the proposition that self-concepts within authority relations (parent-child) and reciprocal relations (friendship) will not only differ from one another but will be consistent with the forms of the relations themselves. Within parent-child relations, for example, the self is primarily perceived as unilaterally determined. That is, the feelings and behaviors of the self are seen as determined by the feelings, behaviors, or expectations of the parent toward the self. This 'unilaterality' of self-concept corresponds to *Piaget's* [1932] and *Youniss's* [1980] descriptions of parent-child relations and to an earlier research finding [*Volpe,* 1980] that parent-child interactions are described by adolescents as unilateral in form. In contrast, the self in close-friend relations is seen as 'co-determined' [*Piaget,* 1932]. Feelings and behaviors of the self are attributed to the relationship that the self and the other have co-constructed. Again, this concept of self is consistent with research findings with regard to concepts of friendship relations as involving interactions which are reciprocal rather than unilateral [*Youniss and Volpe,* 1978] and with the descriptions of peer relations offered by *Piaget* [1932] and *Sullivan* [1953].

The evidence regarding changes in self-concepts as a function of increasing age from preadolescence to young adulthood suggests that within parent-child relations and close friendships, self-conceptions may develop along parallel, not intersecting paths. That is, it may be quite rare that the self-concept in parent-child contexts becomes integrated with that in the close-friend context. Developmentally, in close-friend relations preadolescents attribute the self's feelings and behaviors to the modes of interacting established in the relation. While this attribution is maintained by adolescents and young adults, these older subjects also explain their feelings and behaviors in terms of a more general principle governing the relation – the principle of mutual acceptance. This means that in adolescence participants in close-friend relations understand that within that relation they will not be 'judged'. Such knowledge permits an openness, intimacy, and understanding that could not exist otherwise. Mutual acceptance may also permit the development of a sense of self and other as valued entities and lead to a more general principle of the respect for human life [*Piaget,* 1932].

The principle of mutual acceptance appears rarely in the self-concepts generated in the context of parent-child relations, even among young adults. Instead, the developmental shift apparent in these relations was that young adults tended to provide less 'reactive' self-conceptions than the younger subjects and were more likely to attribute the self's feelings and behaviors in the parent-child context to the way they felt about or the attitudes they held toward their parents, whether it be love, respect, hate or admiration.

It is entirely possible that in most cases the principle of mutual acceptance may never become an aspect of either the parent-child relation or the concept of self within that relation. A relation that begins as one of unilateral respect or authority may not ever reach a state of mutual respect or acceptance simply because neither participant can fully relinquish the 'critical' or 'judgmental' aspect of the relation and accept the other as a 'person'. The demands of the parents as authorities are for respect and compliance. In return, the child 'demands', at the least, security and 'wisdom about the world'. Both the parents and children 'judge' one another with respect to each person's ability or willingness to meet these demands. The possible prevalence of this judging process in parent-child relations would certainly impede any development of mutual acceptance. Thus, even in adulthood, while individuals may become less 'reactive' with respect to their conceptions of self in parent-child relations, they do not attribute either to themselves or to the relation a sense of mutual acceptance.

In conclusion, the results of this study support the research hypotheses and provide several possible channels for future research and theoretical development. The contrast of the principle of mutual acceptance with that of unilateral respect suggests that relations of authority and equality have quite different implications not only for the development of self-concepts but also for the development of the individual's understanding of the social world he or she lives in. In addition, since there are obviously other relational forms existing in society than those studied here, these forms need to be explored to expand our understanding of how people conceptualize themselves and others and how these conceptualizations serve the individual in the context of a larger society.

Summary

From *Piaget's* suggestion that parent-child and peer relations involve different interactive forms, it was hypothesized that self-concepts within these relations would vary and correspondingly reflect the unilaterality of parent-child relations and the mutuality of peer relations. 80 adolescents and young adults were administered modified versions of the Way-I-Am test and the Sensitivity to Others and Independence Scales of the Interpersonal Style Inventory. Self-descriptions were found to be primarily unilateral in parent-child relations, but unilaterality decreased with age ($p < 0.05$). Females generated unilateral self-descriptions more often in the father context than in the mother context, while this pattern was reversed for males ($p < 0.001$). Self-descriptions in close-friend relations were rarely unilateral, but focused on acceptance. Scores on the Sensitivity to Others Scale varied across relations ($p < 0.001$). Subjects reported greater sensitivity in friendship than in parent-child relations, with the difference greater for females than for males ($p < 0.001$). These results support the view that self-concepts are differentiated across relational contexts, and that they reflect the interactive forms of interpersonal relations.

References

Bell, R.Q.: A reinterpretation of the direction of effects in studies of socialization. Psychol. Rev. *75:*81–95 (1968).

Emler, N.P.; Hogan, R.: Developing attitudes to law and justice: an integrative review; in Brehm, Kassin, Developmental social psychology: theory and research (Oxford University Press, New York 1981).

Gecas, V.: Parental behavior and contextual variations in adolescent self-esteem. Sociometry *35:*332–345 (1972).

Hinde, R.A.: Interpersonal relations: inquest of a science. Psychol. Med. *8:* 373–386 (1978).

Keller, A.; Ford, L.H.; Meacham, J.A.: Dimensions of self-concept in preschool children. Devl Psychol. *14:*483–489 (1978).

Kokenes, B.: Grade level differences in factors of self-esteem. Devl Psychol. *10:*954–958 (1974).

Lorr, M.; Youniss, R.P.: An inventory of interpersonal style. J. Personality assessm. *37:* 165–173 (1973).

Mohr, D.: Development of attributes of personal identity. Devl Psychol. *14:* 427–429 (1978).

Monge, R.H.: Developmental trends in factors of adolescent self-concept. Devl Psychol. *8:*382–393 (1973).

Montemayer, R.; Eisen, M.: The development of self-conceptions from childhood to adolescence. Devl Psychol. *13:*314–319 (1977).

Mullener, N.; Laird, J.D.: Some developmental changes in the organization of self-evaluation. Devl Psychol. *5:*233–236 (1971).

Piaget, J.: The moral judgment of the child (Routledge & Kegan Paul, London 1932).

Sullivan, H.S.: The interpersonal theory of psychiatry (Norton, New York 1953).

Volpe, J.S.: The development of concepts of parent-child and friend relations and of self within these relations; unpublished doctoral diss; The Catholic University of America, Washington (1980).

Watzlawik, P.; Beavin, J.H.; Jackson, D.D.: Pragmatics of human communication (Norton, New York 1967).

Wylie, R.C.: The self-concept (University of Nebraska Press, Lincoln 1974).

Youniss, J.: Parents and peers in social development (University of Chicago Press, Chicago 1980).

Youniss, J.; Volpe, J.: A relational analysis of friendship; in Damon, Social cognition, pp. 1–22 (Jossey-Bass, San Francisco 1978).

Contr. hum. Dev., vol. 5, pp. 145–159 (Karger, Basel 1981)

Understanding of Social Rule Systems in Adolescence

Kathleen McConville, Hans G. Furth[1]

The Catholic University of America, Washington, D. C., USA

The present study explored adolescent understanding of social rules. An important issue in the study of social rules is the extent to which rules pertaining to different domains of social life are conceptualized as distinct systems. According to *Piaget* [1965] and *Kohlberg* [1969, 1976], social rules are initially conceptualized as a unitary system and in the course of development differentiation occurs. Specifically, children become able to differentiate between conventional and moral rules. *Turiel* [1978a,b] argues that rules governing different domains of social life are differentiated from each other early in development. He contends that conventions seek to regulate social functions, but there is nothing inherently right about conventions; they are dependent upon the context. Morality, however, refers to principles of justice and moral considerations are related to factors intrinsic to the action. Morality involves issues such as harming others and violating other's rights. The findings of *Turiel* [1978] and *Nucci and Turiel* [1978] indicate that young children are aware of this distinction between conventional and moral violations. Conventions are understood to be arbitrary and therefore a violation of a convention is only wrong to the extent that it represents a violation of a rule. If there was no rule prohibiting the act, it would not be wrong. Moral transgressions are regarded as wrong, regardless of whether there are specific rules prohibiting them. Children understand that it is intrinsically wrong to hurt others.

The present study was an attempt to further explore this domain of knowledge, specifically by examining the extent to which older and

[1] This research was done at and partially supported by the Boys Town Center for the Study of Youth Development, Catholic University of America. Thanks are expressed to *Debbie Harris*, research assistant, and to the schools that cooperated in the research.

younger adolescents conceptualize rules from different domains as distinct systems. In addition to moral and conventional rules, situations of legal and interpersonal rules as well as rules pertaining to home and school were explored. These latter are here called 'ascriptive' since they are associated with the status of being a minor in this society.

The Study and Its Main Results

80 adolescents participated in this study. There were 5 male and 5 female students each from grades 7 through 12. These adolescents attended Catholic schools in the New York metropolitan area and in suburban Maryland. The college group consisted of 10 men and 10 women who were freshmen at the Catholic University in Washington, D. C. All subjects came from a similar social class and educational background.

The adolescents were presented with a sequence of 10 sets of three cards. On each card was a written description of a situation that was an infraction of social rules. The situations were drawn from five rule systems, namely, legal, moral, conventional, ascriptive, and interpersonal rules. In each set two situations illustrated violations of one rule system, while the third situation illustrated a violation of a contrasting rule system. The situations were combined as follows: two legal violations versus one conventional (set 1) and one interpersonal (set 5) violation; two ascriptive violations versus one legal (set 6) and one conventional (set 9) violation; two moral violations versus one ascriptive (set 2) and one legal (set 8) violation; two conventional violations versus one interpersonal (set 3) and one moral (set 10) violation; two interpersonal versus one ascriptive (set 4) and one moral (set 7) violation. For reasons of time and fatigue only two of the four possible main contrasts were explored for each rule system with the remaining two contrasts implicitly given in two other triads. Thus, law was directly contrasted (two situations versus one) with conventions (set 1) and interpersonal rules (set 5) and indirectly (one situation versus two) with ascriptive (set 6) and moral rules (set 8). In short, in each set adolescents were presented with a triad of rule violations. The complete set of situations is presented in table I. The adolescents had to indicate which two of the situations were alike and together differed from the third. Following this they were asked to explain their choice.

Table I. Ten sets of triads (A,B,C,) describing events 'that usually do not or should not happen'

1	A	A girl frequently goes into department stores and takes clothes and records without paying for them.
	B	A group of children slash the tires of several cars that are parked on the street.
	C	Two friends eat dinner in a restaurant. When they are finished, they pay for their dinner, but do not leave a tip for the waiter.
2	A	Jim is a college student. He wants to get an A in his history course. On the day of the exam, he sits next to the smartest guy in the class and copies from him.
	B	An elderly couple were driving along a country road. The man had a heart attack. The woman cannot drive, so she goes to a nearby house and asks if she can use their phone to call for help, but they refuse.
	C	Mr. Brown is accused of robbing a bank. His neighbor, Mr. Smith, knows that Mr. Brown was at home at the time the robbery was committed and therefore could not have done it. Mr. Smith, however, doesn't bother to tell anyone that Mr. Brown is innocent, because he doesn't like him.
3	A	The Smith family doesn't exchange Christmas presents.
	B	A couple's wedding is arranged by their parents. They do not meet until the day of the wedding.
	C	John's friend is in the hospital but John doesn't bother to go visit him.
4	A	Mary is eating lunch with a group of girls. Another girl, who is a friend of Mary's, asks if she could sit with them. Mary says she can't.
	B	Terry frequently neglects taking his assigned turn in household chores.
	C	A boy promises his friend that they would go to the movies but, when it is time to go, the boy decides not to go.
5	A	Jack lets Fred use his bicycle on the condition that he can use Fred's skateboard the next day. Fred, however, refuses to let Jack use his skateboard when he asks for it.
	B	A group of guys steal a car, ride around in it for a few hours and then return it.
	C	A man sells liquor to guys who aren't old enough to drink.
6	A	Tom likes to drive fast and frequently goes above the speed limit.
	B	Bill often stays out later than his parents permit.
	C	John cuts classes because he doesn't like school.
7	A	Ann is the smartest girl in the class and she frequently reminds the other girls that she is smarter than they are.

B Mr. Smith drops a $20 bill but doesn't realize it. Mr. Jones sees him drop the money but doesn't tell him. Later when Mr. Smith is not looking Mr. Jones picks up the money and keeps it.

C Jim asks his classmate, Bob, if he could borrow a pen. Bob refuses to lend it to him even though he has an extra pen.

8 A A group of friends smoke marijuana at a party.

B Carol knows that Mary would be upset if people found out that her father had been in jail but Carol tells people anyway.

C A woman withdraws money from the bank and by mistake the clerk gives her $100 extra. The woman doesn't tell the clerk about the mistake and keeps the extra money.

9 A Ted is 15. His parents don't want him to go out unless he has finished his homework but he goes out anyway.

B Jane is frequently late for school.

C Sally wears a red gown on her wedding day.

10 A The Garrett family doesn't have turkey for dinner on Thanksgiving.

B Mary frequently makes up stories that hurt other people.

C Mr. Jones is married. He stays home and takes care of the children while his wife works.

The explanations accompanying the choices were grouped into three categories which are here called *Irrelevant, Partial and Systemic.* In the Irrelevant category were explanations of a personalistic type, frequently an evaluation of events in terms of global 'badness'. In these explanations there was no direct or indirect reference to appropriate rule systems as a basis for the pairing. Partial explanations made indirect reference to these rule systems; they suggested but did not explicitly mention the relevant sources of similarities and differences. In contrast these criteria or sources were explicitly mentioned in the comments grouped into the Systemic category. Take as an illustration the triad of set 7 where A and C are interpersonal violations while B is a moral violation. An explanation of 'A and C happen in school, B not in school' was classified as Irrelevant; 'A and C both selfish, want to feel more powerful, B is just dishonesty' as Partial; 'A and C inconsiderate toward friends, B almost like stealing, involves moral decision' as Systemic. Generally comments of the Irrelevant category were offered where the pairing was with the original design. However, even with the expected pairing, as shown in the first example above, the explanations

Table II. Frequency of pairing two rule violations of the same rule system for each age group (n=20) in ten sets of three situations

Set No.	Rule System	Contrast rule	Age, years			
			13	15	17	19
1	legal	conventional	17	16	13	18
5		interpersonal	11	11	14	18
6	ascriptive	legal	6	8	2	8
9		conventional	15	17	13	12
2	moral	ascriptive	14	16	20	17
8		legal	10	11	16	16
10	conventional	moral	13	18	20	18
3		interpersonal	3	2	4	2
4	interpersonal	ascriptive	11	13	11	9
7		moral	8	7	6	8

could fall into the Irrelevant category. Inversely, there were few cases where an unexpected pairing was explained by comments of the Partial or Systemic category. The classifying of explanation was done by one investigator and checked for reliability by a second person with an initial 90% agreement.

The frequency of pairing two situations belonging to the same rule system in each of the triads is presented in table II. Contrary to expectation no age trend was found. On the other hand, in seven triads the majority (55–86%) of pairings were in the same rule system. In two sets (6 and 7) the proportion of rule pairing was around chance level (33%) and in set 3 it was well below (11%). In terms of rule systems the legal and moral rule situations were most frequently paired, the interpersonal situations least frequently, and in the ascriptive and conventional areas one set showed high, the other low pairing.

With regard to the categories for the explanations in each set table III presents the pertinent frequencies for the age groups. Chi-square tests (d. f. = 6) applied to each set revealed significant age effects for sets 1, 5, 6 and 10 ($p < 0.01$) and sets 8 and 9 ($p < 0.05$). Note that all four triads involving legal rules (sets 1, 5, 6 and 8) showed age changes; three triads with conventional rules (sets 1, 9, 10), two triads with moral rules (sets 8, 10), and only one triad each for ascriptive (set 5) and interpersonal (set 6) rules showed significant age changes.

Table III. Adolescents' explanations of pairing rule violations distributed into three categories: irrelevant (I), partial (P), systemic (S)

Set	Rule system	Contrast rule	Age (years) and category											
			13			15			17			19		
			I	P	S	I	P	S	I	P	S	I	P	S
1	legal	conventional	3	16	1	4	12	4	7	6	7	2	8	10
5		interpersonal	9	9	2	9	5	6	6	8	6	2	3	15
6	ascriptive	legal	12	5	3	13	5	2	15	2	3	2	2	16
9		conventional	10	10	–	4	12	4	5	10	5	8	3	9
2	moral	ascriptive	10	4	6	6	10	4	2	9	9	4	7	9
8		legal	10	9	1	12	6	2	4	14	2	4	11	5
10	conventional	moral	8	9	3	4	11	5	–	4	16	1	3	16
3		interpersonal	20	–	–	16	4	–	15	2	3	9	8	3
4	interpersonal	ascriptive	10	7	3	9	7	4	9	3	8	11	3	6
7		moral	13	3	4	13	5	2	14	2	4	11	3	6

To facilitate an overview across the four ages and the five social rule systems table IV was constructed. Scores of 1, 2 or 3 were assigned to the three categories of Irrelevant, Partial and Systemic explanations respectively – a not unreasonable translation of qualitative into quantitative categories. Further, the two sets comprising two situations of the particular rule system were combined so that a maximum score of six and a minimum of two could be obtained. These combined scores were divided by two so that they can be readily translated back into the original qualitative categories. These data were tested by five separate 2 × 4 analyses of variance for differences associated with sex or age. First, male-female differences were found to be nonsignificant. Second, largely confirming the earlier chi-square analyses, four of the five rule systems yielded significant ($p<0.01$) age effects, the Interpersonal being the one rule system where no significant age effect was found.

Adolescents' Explanations of Social Rules

The question whether or not adolescents recognize different social rule systems is affirmed by the generally high frequency of expected pairing (see table II). These pairings were obviously a function of the particular situations presented and especially of the particular rule system with which the expected pair was contrasted. Unexpected low frequencies of pairing require explanation. In set 3 one of the conventional infractions involved a prearranged marriage. This in itself was seen as altogether outlandish and resulted in the pairing (86%) of the two other situations, one of which was conventional, the other interpersonal; moreover, the interpersonal rules were the one system least clearly articulated. Sets 6 and 7 had a low frequency of pairing (chance). In set 6 this was apparently due to the qualitative similarity in frequency and minor consequence of breaking a traffic law and a school or house rule. In set 7, as mentioned before, the interpersonal situation was not clearly separated from its contrast; rather the more common (59%) pairing was in terms of causing material harm to others (interpersonal: refusal to lend; moral: keeping lost property) versus 'no harm done' (interpersonal: show-off behavior).

In contrast to the lack of age differences in systematic pairing, the typical explanations differed with age. Older adolescents tended to give responses in which the violations were conceptualized on the basis of appropriate rule systems and referred to different underlying sources of authority. These type of comments were grouped into the Systemic category. They increased from a low range of 8–18% at age 13 to a high of 30–63% at age 19. The majority of the youngest adolescents, however, explained their choice by degree of badness, separating acts that were 'seriously wrong' from those that were 'not that serious, not that bad'. These Irrelevant explanations prevailed at age 13 in all except the legal areas and at age 15 were still the modal response. The criteria for deciding which acts were seriously wrong were largely arbitrary and reflected the adolescents' personal feeling about particular acts. References to systemic sources of rules were absent. Between these two extremes, Partial explanations showed familiarity with the more obvious distinctions between rule systems, but rather than referring to the underlying system, particular differentiating qualities were stressed.

In comparing the different rule areas, the legal area stands out as best recognized and articulated with the interpersonal area at the other end as most poorly recognized and articulated. As pointed out in connection with table II, in the two triads (set 1 and 5) with pairs of legal violations these pairs were chosen in the majority of cases for all age

Table IV. Mean scores (1–3) for five rule systems across four age groups

Rule system	Sets	Age, years			
		13	15	17	19
Legal	1, 5	1.77	1.92	2.00	2.52
Ascriptive	6, 9	1.52	1.72	1.70	2.38
Moral	2, 8	1.67	1.70	2.12	2.15
Conventional	10, 3	1.37	1.62	2.10	2.22
Interpersonal	4, 7	1.60	1.60	1.72	1.75

groups, particularly also in set 5 which included the unclear interpersonal rule area as contrast. The same was also true for set 8 where the moral system was paired against the legal system. Further, significant and consistent changes in type of explanation were observed in all the four sets that included legal situations. The progress is illustrated (table III) in the increasing percentage of Systemic explanations (8, 25, 33, 63%) with increasing age groups for sets 1 and 5 combined, a corresponding decrease in Partial explanations starting from a very high 63% at age 13, down to 43, 35 and 28% at age 19, and an equally exceptional low of 30% for Irrelevant explanations at age 13 which dropped to 10% at age 19. An example of Systemic explanations for contrasting legal from conventional rules was a simple '(These two) are both illegal. (This one) is discourteous but it's not illegal' (set 1) or '(This one) is a violation of a friend's trust' (set 5). Corresponding Partial explanations were '(These two) are alike because they are both doing things they shouldn't do. (This one) isn't that serious, he should lend the friend the skateboard, but it's not really wrong' (set 5) or '(This one) is different... not leaving a tip... isn't wrong' (set 1). Table IV illustrates this steady progress in the gradual increase of the mean score for the legal system that corresponds at age 13 to the Irrelevant category and at age 19 to the Systemic category.

Ascriptive rules are similar to legal rules in important respects, such as explicit formulation and articulated sanctions, except of course that the authority of the school or the parent is of different quality and familiarity than that of the state. Table III illustrates that in fact the quality of explanations of ascriptive rules trailed behind the legal rules most closely, notably in the increase of Systemic explanations from age

17 to age 19 (after staying stationary between ages 15 and 17). It seems that just when they have almost outgrown the jurisdiction of child-ascriptive rules, adolescents are able to understand the rationale for these home and school rules. Ascriptive rule violations were contrasted with a legal (set 6) and conventional (set 9) violation. In set 9 the majority of adolescents paired the ascriptive violations and recognized the difference between ascriptive and conventional rules. In the three younger groups Partial explanations were dominant. Typically younger adolescents thought that the ascriptive rule violations 'were wrong because they are hurting their parents. Parents are probably paying for their education and they are wasting their money when they don't do their homework and are late for school'. Systemic explanations were dominant (9/20) in the 19-year-old group.

In contrast, few of the adolescents paired the ascriptive violations when contrasted in set 6 with a legal one. The probable reason, as mentioned before, was the personal familiarity with breaking the particular law of speeding. Consequently, in the three younger age groups the explanations were generally of a less advanced type than in the previous set and the difference between the rule systems was not recognized. Typical Irrelevant explanations were that speeding (the legal infraction) was similar to one of the ascriptive rule violations (staying out beyond the curfew set by one's parents) 'because in both cases people can get hurt; speeding can cause accidents and staying out late may cause parents to worry'. Cutting classes (the second ascriptive violation) 'isn't that bad if he doesn't like school'. Nearly all adolescents at age 19 gave comments of the Systemic type, even when they did not pair the two ascriptive situations, because they referred to the appropriate rule systems and different sources of authority involved in enforcing the ascriptive rules. For example, cutting classes and speeding were considered as 'more similar because they both may involve the law. If the child is under 16 cutting classes could be a legal matter; staying out late is simply a family matter'.

In comparison with the two systems of legal and ascriptive rules moral and conventional rules are less explicit. As is clear from table III and particularly table IV, the age trends in these areas were similar. Note that in stark contrast to the legal and ascriptive rules there was no advance in quality of explanation between ages 17 and 19. As Table 1 shows, there was a strong trend at all ages to spontaneously pair the moral violations as against ascriptive (set 2) and legal rules (set 8), and also conventional violations as against moral rules (set 10). Nevertheless, for sets 2 and 8 combined - the two moral rules situations - there was a relatively high frequency of Irrelevant comments at ages 13 (50%) and 15 (45%). These youngsters typically thought that - in contrast to clearly promulgated legal or ascriptive rules - moral infractions 'are okay, you don't have to do these things' or else that one moral infraction was wrong but not the other. Since the rules violated in the moral situations are relatively abstract, it seemed to be difficult for children to recognize that injustice and infringement of others' right had occurred. That young adolescents give more weight to the violation of concrete rules was clearly illustrated in the moral-ascriptive set 2. Here an ascriptive rule violation (cheating) was contrasted with the moral violations (refusing to let an elderly woman use a telephone to call for help for her ailing husband or failing to provide information that would save an innocent man from jail). Younger adolescents thought 'cheating was really wrong, you shouldn't do this, these (the moral violations) aren't bad, you don't have to do these things if you don't want'.

Interestingly, the type of explanation given varied as a function of whether the moral violations were contrasted with an ascriptive or legal violation. As is shown in table III, Systemic explanations were more frequent in the moral-ascriptive triad (set 2) than the moral-legal triad (set 8). Apparently, the adolescents' low frequency in systemic explanations in set 8 may be related to their attitudes concerning the legal violation (i. e., smoking marijuana) rather than a lack of understanding of the moral issues. In the 17- and 19-year-old groups, a majority expressed the idea that 'there is nothing wrong with smoking marijuana, it doesn't hurt anyone. It's up to the individual to decide'. In contrast the moral infractions were 'wrong because they hurt others'. While it was not determined whether the adolescents knew that smoking marijuana was against the law it is unlikely that a majority of the 19 year olds were unaware of this fact. Since this practice is so prevalent, it is probably treated as a convention and not conceptualized as belonging to the same category as other illegal acts which are not as immediate to their experience. The failure to refer to legal sanctions and the statements that this violation was not wrong because 'it didn't hurt others' may represent an attempt to rationalize either their own or their peers' rule-violating behavior. At the least the statements appeared to question the legitimacy of the law.

The difference in typical moral reasoning between the younger and older adolescents is striking. The younger ones, cited above, take what *Kohlberg* [1976] would call a preconventional stance. They imply that one moral violation – cheating – may get them in trouble, while the other – not helping a person in need – does not have these consequences. This would be like stage I, fear-of-punishment reasoning. In contrast, the older adolescents seem to approach a post-conventional level and in their reasoning about the use of marijuana show the beginning of principled thinking (stage V).

Concerning the two sets involving breach of conventions the data indicate that both pairings and type of explanations varied greatly. When conventions were contrasted with a moral situation (set 10), the majority of adolescents recognized that the conventional violations were similar. Consequently 45 and 50% of the adolescents in the 13- and 15-year-old groups gave Partial explanations. Typically, they suggested that the conventional violations 'weren't really wrong because they don't hurt anyone'. On the other hand, the moral infraction 'was wrong, you have no right to hurt others'. Systemic explanations were prevalent in the 17- and 19-year-old adolescents, who generally referred to 'traditions' and 'conventions'. However, in the conventional-interpersonal set 3, few adolescents paired two conventional violations. Further, in all but the oldest group, the majority gave Irrelevant explanations. This poor result may be due to the adolescents' attitude towards one of the conventional violations, namely arranged marriage. As mentioned earlier, it was considered a serious moral offense for parents to select a marriage partner for their children. The example of arranged marriages was said to 'violate the couple's rights', and was not considered comparable to the other conventional violation (not exchanging Christmas presents). Even when older adolescents were aware that arranged marriages were acceptable in other societies they still contended 'it is not done here so it is wrong'.

The findings on conventional violations clarify previous claims [*Turiel*, 1978a, b] that even young children differentiate between conventional and moral rules. Nevertheless, in the present study 35% of 13-year-old adolescents paired one of the conventional violations with a moral one. For example, in set 10, they considered it wrong for a man to stay home and take care of his children (a conventional violation) because it's 'unfair to his wife. He should work. It is like this one (the moral violation) because it is unfair of the girl to make up stories'. Furthermore, the responses to the conventional-interpersonal contrast (set 3) suggest that the majority of the adolescents at all ages thought that the conventional violation (arranged marriage) was not just conventionally uncommon but morally wrong. Of major importance is *Turiel's* suggestion that young children understand the arbitrary nature of conventional rules. However, the adolescents in this study seemed to express the well-known fact that violating a – theoretically arbitrary – convention, once established in a society's world-view, may have moral implications. The oldest group typically recognized that the method of mate selection was essentially arbitrary and can be different at other times and places, but violation of the convention of one's society is a grave infringement of young people's rights and this constitutes a moral issue.

Finally, as said before, interpersonal rules were found to be most difficult to recognize or explain in a systematic fashion. Like moral and conventional rules, they differ from the legal and ascriptive rules by being less explicit in formulation and sanctions. But in addition they are experienced less as constraints, whether imposed from outside or from the personal conscience, and as expressing personal habits of relating to others. Within this study of other rule systems the adolescents had difficulties placing interpersonal rules. This is most vividly apparent from tables III and IV which show no significant age progress. In fact, Irrelevant explanations for the combined sets 4 and 7 hover closely around the grand average of 57%.

Interpersonal violations were contrasted alternately with ascriptive (set 4) and moral (set 7) violations. Typical Irrelevant explanations indicated that an interpersonal infraction was similar to either the ascriptive or moral violation because 'others were hurt'. For example, in set 7, not lending a pen to a classmate (an interpersonal violation) was said to be comparable to the moral violation (keeping extra money that a man dropped) 'because they both are causing harm to another. The boy may get in trouble in school if he doesn't have a pen, and the man may need the money for food or medicine'.

Conclusion

In conclusion this study has provided some pointers towards exploring the process of social rule understanding and differentiation. By early adolescence a global recognition of different rule systems seems well established; however, understanding as revealed in the adolescents' comments is quite poorly articulated and changes substantially between ages 13 and 19. Early in adolescence there appears to be a general sense that breach of rules is wrong because it hurts others and as such is 'bad'. A notion of global moral badness was a chief criterion by which rule violations were grouped. Recognition of different sanctions attached to rules from different domains and of different institutions involved in the enforcement of separate rule systems is obviously a slow process that covers the adolescent years and is related to a growing understanding of societal and personal relations. It makes sense that the legal system turned out to be the best articulated and contrasted system, since it is most clearly promulgated and connected with specific societal structures. Not surprisingly, interpersonal rules were most poorly conceptualized since they involve an area of practical personal living which does not require theoretical reflection and formulation.

This lack of reflective differentiation should not be interpreted as immaturity in personal relating. There is a big difference between an implicit know-how of personal interactions and the explicit articulation of this know-how. If this study failed to discover an appreciable progress in the differentiation of the interpersonal rule system between ages 13 and 19 and found the majority of explanations in the global Irrelevant category, this should be seen in the context of the study. The explicitly promulgated rules of a legal and ascriptive type are experienced as social rule models. Only after their functions are well comprehended can a differentiated understanding of conventional customs be attained. Over against these are rules of moral obligations which indirectly touch on all rule systems and provide them with their ultimate justification.

All these four rule systems have an 'abstract' character, they pertain to 'knowledge' as imposed from without or, in the moral sphere, from within. The interpersonal sphere, in contrast, is the arena of 'practical' actions. It is quite characteristic of development [*Piaget*, 1965] that the practice of rules-in-action precedes the consciousness of principles, particularly a reflective consciousness. Hence, there is no contradiction to hold that these same youngsters who showed no progress in interpersonal rule differentiation would in fact develop considerably in interpersonal know-how.

The study confirms the complexities in working out an adequate differentiation of rule systems. Personal attitudes or feelings about a particular event may interfere with judgment of that event. This point was demonstrated by the 19-year-old adolescents who did not refer to legal sanctions against smoking marijuana, and their failures to consider the example of the arranged marriage as an instance of a conventional violation. It appears that in matters that concern them directly even young adults failed to be logical; rather, they resorted to subjective evaluations of the acts.

The findings also raise a question concerning the utility of *Turiel's* [1978a, b] distinction between conventions and moral rules. It may be theoretically important to determine that adolescents know that moral rules are intrinsic, while conventions and ascriptive rules are context-bound. However, adolescents are operating within a certain context, where the rules are in existence. Apparently any rule-violating behavior is seen to have an impact on others, and in terms of judging acts or in guiding behavior, the social context takes on critical importance. Regardless of whether a rule is arbitrary, violating it may still have moral consequences.

Summary

80 adolescents, aged 13–19 years, paired stories of rule violations in contrast to a third one. The explanations were classified in terms of the adolescents' explicit understanding of differentiation between the five rule systems studied: legal, ascriptive (school/home), moral, conventional, interpersonal. A gradual advance in the first four systems was observed. Some context conditions are described that contribute to the quality of rule conceptualization and differentiation.

References

Kohlberg, L.: Stage and sequence. The cognitive-developmental approach to socialization; in Goslin, Handbook of socialization theory and research (Rand-McNally, Chicago 1969).

Kohlberg, L.: Moral stages and moralization. The cognitive-developmental approach; in Lickona, Moral development and behavior: Theory, research and social issues (Holt, Rhinehart & Winston, New York 1976).

Nucci, L. P.; Turiel, E.: Social interactions and the development of social concepts in pre-school children. Child Dev. *49*: 400–407 (1978).

Piaget, J.: The moral judgment of the child (Free Press, New York 1965).

Turiel, E.: The development of concepts of social structure; in Glick, Clarke Stewart, The development of social understanding (Wiley, New York 1978a).

Turiel, E.: Social regulations and domains of social concepts. New Direct. Child Dev. *1*: 45–74 (1978b).

Contr. hum. Dev., vol. 5, pp. 160–181 (Karger, Basel 1981)

The Development of Natural Rationality: Can Formal Operations Account for it?

Karen Strohm Kitchener, Richard F. Kitchener

University of Denver, Denver, Colo. USA; Colorado State University, Fort Collins, Colo., USA

Adults are confronted daily with problems of a complex and difficult kind. One need only look at a daily newspaper or the agenda of a scientific or philosophical meeting to become aware of numerous examples of the following kind: In what ways do chemical additives affect the safety of particular foods? How can we have a cheap but indefinite source of energy that is also safe and nondetrimental to the environment? Is the thinking process in adults the same as in children? etc. These are obviously examples of questions that require careful answers and the formulation of such an answer is obviously a case of reasoning (making an inference, forming a judgment, etc.). What is the nature of such reasoning? How can it be best described and explained?

In attempting to characterize this process of reasoning it is tempting to appeal to logic as a model and to think that this reasoning is (or must be) logical in nature (e.g., an example of deductive reasoning or inductive reasoning). But is formal logic an adequate model of this process of reasoning? Several philosophers have argued that logic alone cannot account for such processes [*Toulmin,* 1958; *Harman,* 1980]. But psychological studies of reasoning continue to be dominated by models of formal logic, for example, mathematical probability models [*Brinbaum,* 1975; *Pitz,* 1975; *Castellan,* 1977], and especially in the case of cognitive development, the model of formal operations [*Inhelder and Piaget,* 1958].

Only in the last 10 years have psychologists begun to question the ability of hypothetical-deductive reasoning [as *Inhelder and Piaget* (1958) have characterized it] to account for the reasoning processes that occur in adult life [*Strauss and Kroy,* 1977; *Gilligan and Murphy,* 1979; *Schaie,* 1977–78; *Niemark,* 1979]. *Broughton* [1975, 1977], for example, has argued that an awareness of the 'self as knower' arises in adolescence and cannot be explained by a deductive model of reasoning. Furthermore, he argues that people's assumptions about the self, reality, and knowledge change markedly from early adolescence to adulthood. *Kitchener and King* [1981] also argue that a network of concepts related to the rational justification of decisions develops markedly between late adolescence and adulthood and that these categories provide descriptions of major differences in how adolescents and adults solve problems related to life. Others [*Arlin,* 1975; *Riegel,* 1979] have argued that formal operations must be superceded by a fifth stage of cognitive development in order to account for the complexity of adult thinking. In particular, *Riegel* has suggested that adult thinking is better characterized by its integrative characteristics than by its logical ones.

Although these criticisms have received little attention from the Genevan group, a reply has recently been formulated by *Monnier and Wells* [1979]. First, they suggest that the criticisms of people such as *Broughton* are not generalizable, since they do not describe the thinking strategies of 'normal' groups of people. Formal operations presumably are supposed to be more basic and essential and common to everyone, whereas the nonformal reasoning processes are specific to special (and unusual) people or situations. In short, the alternative models are not descriptive of how the 'average' person reasons. Secondly, they claim that those aspects allegedly not accounted for by formal operations have not been precisely or clearly delineated nor has it been adequately shown why formal operations cannot account for these processes.

By contrast, we will argue first that formal operations, characterized as hypothetico-deductive reasoning, is not sufficient to account for those thinking processes which *Inhelder and Piaget* [1958] suggest are typical of adolescents, i.e., the construction and evaluation of theories and ideologies, nor for similar but even more complex reasoning found in young adults. Secondly, we will suggest that an individual's epistemological assumptions about the nature of evidence, knowledge, and justification play a critical role in reasoning. Different assumptions lead to different conclusions about identical content even if the reasoning is equally valid logically. We will offer examples of the kinds of assumptions that lead some adults and some adolescents to reason in different ways and suggest that these assumptions develop sequentially in adolescents and adults.

The Nature of Formal Operations

In this section we attempt to show that Piaget's theory of formal operations is not able to describe and/or explain all types of reasoning carried on by adolescents and that even in those rather simple contexts in which adolescents reason about physical problems, Piaget's account of this process is defective.

Piaget's discussion of formal operations is not known for its conceptual clarity [*Flavell,* 1963; *Bruner,* 1960; *Parsons,* 1960]. [See *Piaget* (1967a) for a reply to these criticisms]. In general, however, Piaget characterizes formal operations as dealing with hypothetico-deductive reasoning [*Inhelder and Piaget,* 1958, pp. 56, 190, 251; *Piaget,* 1975, pp. 213, 228]. It has the properties of dealing with propositions (as opposed to concrete operations), of dealing with what is hypothetical (rather than actual), and of being a combinatorial system.

Confusions Surrounding Formal Logic

Piaget's theory of formal operations is a model of the cognitive structure or reasoning process of adolescents. Thus, there is a important distinction to be made between the model (formal operations) and what it is a model of (the actual thinking processes of individuals and the underlying structure) [*Piaget,* 1953, pp. xvii, 25; 1967a, p. 269]. The individual's actual reasoning, together with the mental processes producing it and the underlying structure, represent the factual or objective domain *to be explained* by a model of reasoning (be it Piaget's model or another one). The psychological reality is what our theories or models are tested against for an adequate fit and our model is an adequate one (according to Piaget) to the extent that it describes this psychological reality in a correct way. Since we are interested in the development of reasoning, we might characterize this as the development of *formal thought* understood in a theoretically neutral way as opposed to *formal operations,* which is a theoretical construct. Whether formal operations adequately explains formal thought would be an open question, since it would depend upon how well the model characterized the actual reasoning of the individual. But in any case, we would not want to identify formal operations with formal thought, since this would presuppose that our abstract model was not only correct but the last word on the subject. Piaget himself is not always clear about maintaining this distinction (since he often uses 'formal operation' and 'formal thought' interchangeably) and the average reader may also be lulled into thinking that formal operations *is* equivalent to formal thought, but this would be a conceptual mistake. The fundamental question that must always be kept in mind is: is formal operations an adequate model of 'natural reasoning'?

If the average reader of Piaget tends to equate formal thought with formal operations, he or she might also tend to equate formal thought with formal, *deductive* logic [see *Monnier and Wells,* 1979, p. 16]. Standard propositional logic – a major part of formal operations – is deductive and *Piaget* also writes [1967a, p. 269] that the Klein (IRNC) four group is a part of propositional logic and hence deductive, too (we may presume). In fact, in one passage *Piaget* [1975, p. 236] even claims: 'Once reasoning has been acquired, that is, reasoning as it is presented in balanced states of thought, it is always deductive and deduction rests on systems of logical-arithmetical or spatial-temporal operations which consist partially of groups and groupings' [cf. *Inhelder and Piaget,* 1958, p. xxi]. There is also a good deal of historical precedent behind the association of 'formal thought' with 'deductive logic', since formal thought and formal logic usually are thought of as being deductive in nature by most philosophers, logicians, mathematicians, etc. This need not be the case, however, if we understand 'formal thought' and 'formal logic' in a sufficiently broad way, as dealing with the *form* of thinking (as opposed to its *content*). For in this case we could talk about the possibility of nondeductive logics (e.g., inductive logic) belonging to formal logic, and we could also cite attempts that have been made to formalize inductive logic [e.g., *Carnap,* 1962], as well as mention so-called epistemic logics, deontic logics, etc., as falling under the purview of formal logic.

Although in a broad sense formal logic can be thought of as dealing merely with the logical form or structure of thinking and as ignoring the content, the term formal logic was understood in a somewhat narrower way by logicians in the late 19th and early 20th centuries. Formal logic was construed to be the attempt to *formalize* thought by constructing a *formal* system, that is, producing a set of axioms (containing primitive undefined terms) and inference rules, such that the axioms are consistent, complete, independent, etc. [see *Mendelson,* 1964]. Historically this led to the program of Hilbert's *formalism* according to which logic and mathematics were to be 'formalized' using only certain restricted meta-mathematical principles: constructive consistency proofs via finitary methods only, a purely syntactical interpretation of all terms, etc. [For a discussion of Hilbert's formalism and related issues see *Kneebone,* 1963; *Luchins and Luchins,* 1965]. Much of the confusion surrounding formal operations is due, in our opinion, to the confusion between the various senses of 'formal logic', 'formal thought', 'formal system', 'formalization', 'formalism' and finally 'formal operations'.

Gödel's Proof

In 1931 Hilbert's program of formalism was dealt a death blow by the famous incompleteness proofs of Kurt Gödel [see *Davis* (1965) for a collection of these and related papers]. Recently, there have been several discussions of the relevance of Gödel's proof to the critical evaluation of formal operations, and some psychologists [*Gilligan and Murphy,* 1979; *Labouvie-Vief,* 1980] have claimed that Gödel's proof shows that formal operations are inadequate. Since these same authors proceed to draw conclusions very similar to ours concerning the limitations of formal operations, it might seem that we are claiming nothing new since 'Gödel has already shown that'. Since we believe this is wrong and, moreover, that many psychologists misunderstand Gödel's proof, a brief comment concerning the relevance of Gödel's proof for formal operations is necessary.

Gödel actually has two proofs that are relevant to this issue. Gödel's first proof (roughly put) is that in a formal system rich enough to encompass number theory, there exists a true but undecidable proposition. A corollary of this (Gödel's second proof) is that the consistency of such a formal system cannot be proved within that system itself. What these proofs show (along with Church's theorem and Tarski's theorem) is that there are inherent limitations in the attempt to formalize mathematics into a signale formal system à la Hilbert and thus that formalism is impossible. Formal systems are inherently limited since humans can 'intuitively' see the truth of certain propositions (the Gödel sentence) that cannot be proved within a formal system; hence 'truth outstrips provability'. If the consistency of a formal system is to be proved, one must use a higher-order, extended system which contains the lower-order one but is 'richer' in that it is a meta-system that can mention the lower-order one. However, this higher-order system in turn can also be proved to be incomplete.

Several individuals have discussed the relevance of Gödel's proof [see *Myhill* (1952) for an excellent, nontechnical discussion], but its precise relevance for psychology remains very controversial. This may be illustrated in recent discussions by *Gilligan and Murphy* [1979] and *Labouvie-Vief* [1980]. First, these authors suggest that somehow Piaget recognizes that Gödel's proof throws formal operations into doubt. Piaget is clearly aware of the limits of formalization and has often [*Piaget*, 1967b, 1967c, 1970] discussed these. But he does not seem to think they are a criticism of formal operations, but rather a decisive objection to Hilbert's formalism, which he also rejects on other grounds. What Gödel's proof shows, according to Piaget, is the need to pursue a nonformalistic constructivism (a genetic constructivism). But Piaget does not claim that Gödel's proof shows the limitations of formal operations.

Secondly, *Labouvie-Vief* [1980] and *Gilligan and Murphy* [1979] claim that Gödel's proof shows the need to embed or 'contextualize' formal logic in a system of higher generality, a dialectical one. *Labouvie-Vief* [1980, p. 144] for example, concludes: '*Logical validation, therefore, demands that logic be contextualized within a system of higher generality*. For example, only by placing Newtonian physics in the context of *Einstein*'s relativistic space-time model could the absolute Newtonian notions be validated; and this validation of necessity also demonstrated the logical *limits* of its applicability. Similarly, only by placing the logic of the concrete operational child in the context of formal operations are the limits of concrete logic exposed'. *Labouvie-Vief* claims that this follows from Gödel's proof. But although it might well be true, it does not *follow* from Gödel's proof as a logical consequence, for (as she correctly points out) Gödel's proof shows that a logical system 'can only demonstrate its consistency if it refers to the language of a higher order system within which it is but a constituent part' (p. 144). Gödel's point here is that the *consistency* of a formal system S can only be shown in an extended meta-system S′ containing S as a part. But nothing about the consistency of such a formal system (which is a property of formal logic) has anything to do with the limits of the applicability of Newton's theory or its empirical validation, issues which are not logical in nature but empirical. The same applies to the limits of concrete operations as shown by reference to formal operations: Gödel's proofs have nothing to do with this at all, since presumably the limits we are talking about are something more than merely formal consistency or decidability. Likewise, nothing in Gödel's proofs shows anything about the impossibility of setting logical limits to the progressive changes in adulthood, nor does it follow that by Gödel's argument any claim for a universal standard of developmental competence must be logically vulnerable and replaced by a socio-historical contextualism [*Labouvie-Vief*, 1980, p. 145].

Finally, since nothing in Gödel's proof has anything to say about the necessity of embedding every formal logic in more comprehensive systems consisting of methodological, philosophical, or epistemological assumptions, nothing about Gödel's proof has any direct relevance to what we are claiming about the nature of natural reasoning and formal operations. Formal operations, we claim, are inadequate as a model of adult thinking essentially because the simple hypothetico-deductive model cannot adequately mirror the complex reasoning of adults. Even if there were (contra Gödel) a completeness proof for formal logic, this would in no way affect our claim, which is that adult reasoning and rationality are not co-extensive with formal operations (nor with the algorithms of formal logic). The process of inquiry, critical deliberation, and reflective judgment involve reasoning in ways that transcend formal operations conceived either as a hypothetico-deductive method or merely as a set of deductive algorithms. In addition to formal rules of inference (formal logic), 'natural reasoning' involves, we will suggest, epistemologial and methodological assumptions which are not properly a part of formal logic. Gödel's proof has relevance only to the formal dimension and has nothing to say about meta-logical assumptions about the nature of reality, knowledge, and evidence.

Deduction, Induction and the Hypothetico-Deductive Method

A crucial distinction for our purposes is that between deductive logic (or deductive inference) and inductive logic (or inductive inference). Deductive logic is concerned with inferences from premises to a conclusion that are absolutely certain or necessary, whereas inductive logic is concerned with inferences that are not certain, but only probable or likely. Hence, in deductive logic there is a relation of entailment between premises and conclusion (in which case the argument is said to be valid), whereas in inductive logic the premises do not entail the conclusion but only render it likely (probable) or confirm it, etc. Thus, in deductive logic it is impossible for the premises to be true and the conclusion false, whereas in inductive logic it is possible. The simplest example of an inductive inference would be an inference from 'some Ps are Qs' to 'all Ps are Q' (although there are several other types of inductive inference). A simple example of a deductive inference would be an inference from 'all Ps are Qs' and 'all Qs are Rs' to 'all Ps are Rs'.

The question to be raised, therefore, is whether formal operations in Piaget's theory is supposed to include inductive inferences or not. Although there has been perhaps some misunderstanding on this point, formal operations must include inductive inferences. Piaget himself clearly recognizes this and often speaks of his (and Inhelder's) research on adolescents as involving inductive inferences or experimental induction [*Piaget*, 1975, pp. xiii, 82, 100; *Inhelder and Piaget*, 1958, pp. 43, 107, 224–225]. But even when he doesn't use these latter terms, formal operations must involve induction, since formal operations is hypothetico-deductive in nature and the hypothetico-deductive method involves inductive inferences.

One very simplified way to conceptualize the hypothetico-deductive method is to divide it into three stages [*Hempel*, 1966; *Popper*, 1959]: (1) the creation or formation of a hypothesis; (2) the derivation (deduction) of observation statements from such a hypothesis (these observation statements thereby serving as predictions that can be used to test the hypothesis), and (3) the deductive falsification of the hypothesis or the nondeductive confirmation of it, depending on whether the predicted observation occurred or not. The second step in the hypothetico-deductive method is clearly deductive and so is one part of the third step, the inference from a nonobserved prediction to a false hypothesis (*modus tollens*), the classical case of 'falsification' [*Popper*, 1959]. But induction (and inductive inferences) enter (or can enter) at two points: in step three when one infers that a positive outcome confirms a hypothesis and in step one when one arrives at a hypothesis from some experimental data. Although Piaget is not always clear about this model, he often characterizes it in just this way [e.g., *Inhelder & Piaget*, 1958, pp. 39, 251]. But even when he doesn't characterize the hypothetico-deductive model as being inductive, it is easy to show that it must be. Consider step three: if one obtains a positive outcome (the predicted outcome is observed), one cannot *deductively* conclude that the hypothesis is true (for this would be the formal *fallacy of affirming the consequent*). So, if one is to conclude *anything* about the hypothesis it must be an inductive inference. Thus, any confirming instance or positive evidence for a hypothesis must be construed as an inductive relation (the observation confirms the hypothesis, renders it likely or probable, increases its chances of being true, supports it, etc.). The logic of confirmation, therefore, is an inductive logic.

Inductive inference also seems to be involved in step one. In fact, one can easily construe the various experimental tasks assigned by *Inhelder and Piaget* [1958] to their subjects as tasks of *discovering* what the likely causes or relevant variables are which produce, cause, or explain some phenomenon. For example, *Inhelder and Piaget* [1958, p. 182] say: 'The task is to predict the movements or equilibrium position of the wagon as a function of three variables - the weight it carries, the counter-weight suspended by a cable fastened to the wagon, and the inclination of the track.' In doing so, the subject must identify relevant (causal) variables, and then construct all the possible combinations of the values of these variables (usually their absence or presence) and then identify which ones are relevant. This is the experimental determination of 'other things being equal'. As Piaget says:

> 'At the level of formal thought... on the other hand, proof consists in demonstrating the truth or falsehood of a particular or general assertion which takes into account (or tries to take into account) the total number of possible combinations, thus permitting the subject to group combinations in a demonstrative fashion. However, grouping these combinations is exactly the same as selecting the cases where a single factor varies (the other being held constant) so as to isolate universal relationships from simple contingent conjunctions and above all so as to be able to discover necessary relationships between variables' [*Inhelder and Piaget*, 1958, p. 43].

Aside from the questionable (or misleading) use of words such as 'necessary' and 'demonstrable', this description, together with the lattice structure of the 16 binary operations involving the possible presence (absence) of p and q, has much in common with John Stuart Mill's 'Methods of Experimental Inquiry' or 'Cannons of Induction' for identifying the cause of a phenomenon [For an elementary introduction, see *Skryms*, 1975, chapter 4]. But Mill's methods, which seem to be appropriate to the first step of the hypothetico-deductive method, are inductive methods since, for example, knowing that factor A is present and factors B, C, and D absent whenever the effect is present does not allow one to rule out the possibility that one has overlooked a possible cause of a phenomenon (e.g., F). Which factors to select as possible causes is based on experience and there is no deductive guarantee that one has a list of all the relevant variables or possible causes. Thus, induction enters into the selection of the relevant variables.

If this is correct, and if formal thought is characterized as hypothetico-deductive reasoning, then it essentially involves nondeductive inferences. Hence, models of reasoning restricted to deductive logic will not be able to adequately characterize the reasoning process of adolescents (since they reason inductively). Insofar as the Piagetian model of formal operations (incorporating propositional logic, the INRC group and the operational schemata) is exclusively deductive, then the model will be inadequate. In short, a purely deductive model of formal thought will fail simply because, as Piaget insists, adolescents sometimes reason in a nondeductive way.

But even if we allow Piaget's theory of formal operations to incorporate inductive reasoning so as to explain the reasoning of adolescents who solve physical experiments involving pendulums, balances, etc., such a combined deductive-inductive model, although more powerful than a simple deductive model, will also be inadequate as a model of adolescent reasoning and will require further extension and modification. The *basic* reason that it is inadequate is rooted in the natural and spontaneous reasoning of adolescents, activities that *Inhelder and Piaget* [1958] describe in the last chapter of The Growth of Logical Thinking. As these authors say, the typical kind of thinking that occurs in adolescence is the construction of theories, systems, and ideologies which are predominantly philosophical, not scientific, and have virtually nothing to do with pendulums and balances.

> Consider a group of students between 14 and 15 years and the *baccalaureate*. Most of them have political or social theories and want to reform the world; they have their own ways of explaining all of the present-day turmoil in collective life. Others have literary or aesthetic theories and place their reading or their experiences of beauty on a scale of values which is projected into a system. Some go through religious crises and reflect on the problem of faith, thus moving toward a universal system – a system valid for all [*Inhelder and Piaget*, 1958, p. 340].

Especially crucial for adolescents, Inhelder and Piaget later say, is a *life program* and their *plans for changing the society they see*.

Piaget nowhere shows that formal operations is adequate to explain or characterize these philosophical activities. True, formal operations (even construed as deductive-inductive) may be *necessary* for this kind of adolescent philosophical or ideological thinking, since it does depend upon an ability to reason about these issues in a particular combinatorial way. But although it might be a necessary condition, formal operations will not be a *sufficient* condition for adolescent reasoning. The crucial issue here is the subject matter of adolescent reasoning. On the one hand, it might seem that formal operations is adequate to characterize reasoning about causal relations between experimental variables and their empirical effects (e.g., weight, distance, angle, force). Here we might say that our criterion for correctness is rather unproblematic because the relation itself is empirical: our criterion is something like successful empirical prediction. We look to see what variables are absent and present when our effect is present and thus have a reliable (although not infallible) criterion for deciding upon the correct variable. Here, hypothetico-deductive reasoning might seem to be a sufficient condition. But in other contexts (e.g., ideological disputes), the direct empirical observation of the presence or absence of a predicted occurrence is not necessarily an appropriate criterion. What other criteria of evaluation are relevant and how are they related to the hypothetico-deductive model? We will suggest that even in the context of scientific reasoning (e.g., which scientific model offers a better explanation of the origin of the universe?), the hypothetico-deductive model is not an adequate characterization of the reasoning process and hence (although necessary) is not sufficient. We then will show that in reasoning about more complex issues (philosophical, religious, ideological), formal operations is also an inadequate model.

When confronted by the question concerning which astronomical theory was better, the Ptolemaic or the Copernican, astronomers in the 16th and 17th centuries made observations, collected data, reasoned about this question, and came to various conclusions. The hypothetico-deductive model seems to be inadequate here largely because the relevant criterion of evaluation used in this context was not the simple presence or absence of experimental evidence [*Kuhn,* 1957]. It is not clear what the relevant criteria were for assessing the competing theories, but we might suggest the following: quantity of evidence, precision of predictions, novelty of predictions, variety (heterogeneity) of evidence, explanatory power, simplicity, theoretical support, coherence with philosophical and religious views, agreement with certain epistemological assumptions, aesthetic satisfaction, etc. Whether these were actually present or not, they would certainly seem to be relevant in evaluating the scientific question. It remains unclear how the hypothetico-deductive model can incorporate all these various criteria, since they are not subsumed either by inductive or deductive logic, nor is it clear how such a model can incorporate higher-order criteria to be used in weighing the relative merits of these lower-order criteria (e.g., suppose a theory T_1 is simpler than T_2 but T_2 has more evidence in its favor). When our first-order criteria conflict, we need second-order criteria for weighing them. In short, the hypothetico-deductive model might be appropriate as a model for *testing* a theory but when it comes to the *comparison* and *evaluation* of theories and the acceptance of one theory over another, other criteria of evaluation are relevant and necessary [*Swinburne*, 1973]. If formal operations are equivalent to the hypothetico-deductive model, as Piaget suggests, then it is not even adequate to characterize all types of scientific reasoning.

If this is true in the context of competing scientific theories, it applies with even greater force to ideological, religious, and philosophical contexts. When an adolescent is debating the issue of science versus religion, the above scientific criteria will not be of much help since it is precisely in this context that the adequacy of these criteria themselves arises. What will be debated, for example, will be precisely whether quantity of evidence or technological power should be a criterion for evaluating a worldview, or whether perhaps criteria such as 'meaningfulness' or 'emancipatory potential' are better ones. Here we will not be able to apply these 'scientific' criteria *tout court* but only (if at all) after considerable deliberation and reflection, and this reasoning process will surely involve criteria other than the scientific ones mentioned above. Hence, the hypothetico-deductive method (formal operations) is not sufficient as an account of all or even the typical reasoning of scientists or adolescents (even though it may be necessary). What additional elements, therefore, need to be included in a more adequate model of adult rationality?

Important Assumptions in the Reasoning Process

Let us begin by positing two possible responses to the evidence for and against the Ptolemaic (geocentric) and Copernican (heliocentric) models of the solar system. Person A may reason that the church (or the

Bible) is the ultimate authority and what it (the Pope or the Bible) decrees is the truth in an absolute or dogmatic sense. Secondly, Person A may assume that, in questions involving issues of science versus religion, religious sources are the ultimate authority. If, therefore, the church decrees that Ptolemy's theory is correct, then he or she reasons that since the two are incompatible, Copernicus must be wrong. Any scientific evidence that is presented in Copernicus' favor is disregarded as irrelevant (since this is not a relevant criterion). Given this person's assumptions, his or her conclusion logically follows, even though at a later day we may bring in more scientific evidence (showing on scientific grounds that the Copernican theory is better) and even though we judge his or her reasoning process to be inadequate since the Copernican model was not evaluated on the basis of its scientific merit alone.

Person B may hold an entirely different set of assumptions. First, he or she may assume that empirical evidence is more relevant in answering such questions than are a priori claims based upon authority or religious dogma. Secondly, it may be assumed that both Ptolemy and Copernicus offer reasonable models about the relationship of the earth and sun, and both have some evidence in their favor. Since both models offer possible explanations for astronomical observations, person B must decide how to weigh the evidence in their favor. The assumption that there are two possibilities or candidates entails a more complex sorting and evaluation process in order to draw a reasonable conclusion about the best model.

Person B must decide (for example) if the quantity of evidence for the Ptolemaic model outweighs the alleged simplicity of the Copernican one. In addition, the accuracy of predictions, the novelty of predictions, the agreement with current physics, etc., must be evaluated against the other variables or criteria. Here the conclusion depends upon the weighing of the various factors. If, for example, the Copernican system was simpler but its predictions were less accurate person B might decide in favor of Ptolemy. Similarly, if the quantity of evidence was overwhelmingly in favor of Ptolemy, the other two criteria might be discounted. What this process involves is a complex set of highly refined (explicit or implicit) decision rules about when to accept or believe in a theory [see *Hempel*, 1966]. These decision rules lead to rationally defensible conclusions, but not to absolutely certain ones. In other words, while person B may reject the claim that 'truth is manifest', he or she does not abandon the claim of an objective reality [*Popper*, 1963,

1972]. Person B's knowledge claims thus avoid the absolutism or dogmatism of person A's claim, since absolutely certain and incorrigible knowledge is not assumed but rather what is assumed is something like the pragmatic fallibilism of Peirce or Popper.

The arguments person A and B use reveal very different assumptions about the nature of knowledge and truth, as well as different criteria for evaluating two or more systems. In other words, their epistemological and metaphysical assumptions influence the interpretation of the problem itself and color the basic principles they use in solving these problems. These differences occur despite the fact that each may be able to argue in a deductively correct and logically impeccable way about propositions. The significant differences between their reasoning processes, therefore, are ones that have to do with prior assumptions and criteria of evaluation, and not with the correctness of formal logic. Even though both persons may use hypothetico-deductive reasoning equally well, their conclusions may not be equally warranted, reasonable, or plausible when judged against further evidence, scientific productivity, the reasonable judgements of other reasonable people, etc. Perhaps the most important difference between persons A and B is that person B allows for the possibility of an alternative solution. As *Toulmin* [1958, p. 18] has pointed out, 'to speak of a particular suggestion as a possibility is to concede it has the right to be considered'. Within an absolutistic frame of reference, this right is denied since alternatives are denied. Contrary to *Piaget's* [1972] claim that it is the development of formal operations which necessitates this ability to consider alternative hypothesies, we are suggesting it is a change in epistemological or metaphysical assumptions.

We are not suggesting that theoretical assumptions are the only aspects of thinking which may be relevant when evaluating adolescent or adult reasoning, nor are we claiming that formal operations are not important. What we are suggesting is that we must ask what tacit theoretical assumptions people begin with and how these assumptions color their perceptions of the problem, their evaluation of the evidence, and their solutions. *Karmeloff-Smith and Inhelder* [1974–75] have suggested that concrete operational children's implicit theories or 'theories-in-action' may initially lead them to ignore the implications of negative actions when trying to solve a simple physical problem and to conclude that contradictory evidence is irrelevant. Here we are arguing that a similar process occurs with formal operational adolescents and adults.

Their epistemilogical and metaphysical assumptions influence their interpretation of data, what they admit as evidence and how they justify their conclusions.

Are There Differences in Philosophical Assumptions That Occur Over the Life Span?

Although data are only beginning to accumulate on this issue, *Kitchener and King* [1981] have presented evidence for an age-related sequence of epistemological and metaphysical assumptions which have corresponding principles of evaluation and justification. Their work is based in part on *Perry* [1968]. They found significant differences in the assumptions of high school students, college students, and graduate students, despite the fact that 98% of the total sample scored as transitional or fully formal on either the pendulum task or the chemicals task or both. *Broughton* [1975] has similarly argued for an age-related sequence of epistemological assumptions and has presented data that suggest that the highest stages cannot be fully accounted for by the presense of formal operations. What makes both of these schemas interesting in this context is that they suggest that major differences in adolescent and adult reasoning can be attributed to differences in theoretical assumptions rather than the presence or absence of formal logic.

As a way of illustrating how differences in assumptions lead to different principles of evaluation, as well as styles of reasoning in real life, examples based on positions 2, 4 and 7 in the *Kitchener and King* [1981] model will be given. These three positions illustrate dogmatic, skeptical, and rational attitudes, respectively, about the nature of knowledge. The subject statements were produced in response to dilemmas about the effects of chemical additives on foods, the construction of the pyramids, the creation of the human race, and the nature of news reporting.[1] An example follows:

> Many religions of the world have creation stories. These stories suggest that a divine being created the earth and its people. Scientists claim, however, that people evolved from lower animal forms (some of which were similar to apes) into the human forms known today.

[1] See *King* [1977] or *Kitchener* [1978] for a complete description of the measurement procedure. All examples have been taken from interviews reported in these sources.

Subjects read the statements and were asked a series of standardized questions such as: What do you think about that issue? How did you come to hold that point of view? or Can you say you know for sure? The questions were designed to elicit assumptions used to form opinions about the dilemmas.

Position 2: Dogmatism
Assumption: There is an objective reality and what it is can be known. Knowledge is both possible and certain.
Assumption: Authorities (e.g., the Bible, science) are the source of absolute knowledge.
Principle of judgement: Believe what the authorities say.

Person 1: High school junior
Person (P): If scientific studies say they cause cancer then, yes, they cause cancer.
Interviewer (I): What about things like red food dye No. 2?
(P): I haven't heard about it. If scientists prove that it does [cause cancer][2] and if they put it on TV, on national news and that it's against a big company, then it's [the big company] got to be doing something wrong because the big companies would sue if it was wrong.
Person 2: High school junior
(P): Somebody had to start this world – so I'd have to believe in my religion that there's a god.
(I): Have you ever doubted that?
(P): Now, I'm not a religious freak or nothing. I just go to church. I just think it's common knowledge, somebody had to start it.

For these 2 late adolescents there is no question that science and the church are absolute sources of knowledge. If science and/or the church says something is correct, then it is correct. In the case of person 1 the negative evidence *presented in the dilemma* (i.e., that some scientists may not agree about the effect of chemical additives in foods) is ignored. The person's theory that knowledge is certain and that scientists have an answer to scientific questions is stronger than contradictory information. For person 2, the absolute belief that God created the universe is so strong that the individual assumes that everyone holds a similar belief.

[2] Words in brackets have been added for clarification.

Position 4: Skepticism

Assumption: Absolute knowledge is not possible. Neither time nor money nor evidence can be relied upon to ultimately lead to the truth.

Assumption: There are many possible answers to every question. Without certainty and without a way of adjudicating between different answers, there is no way to decide which one is true or better than the others.

Principle of judgement: The individual is the ultimate judge of (his or her own) truth.

Person 1: College student

(P): I'd be more inclined to believe it [evolution] if they had proof. It's just like the pyramids [dilemma]. I don't think we will ever know. People will come up with different interpretations because people will differ – who are you going to ask – because no one was there.

Person 2: College student

(I): Would you be in a position to judge between which one is a better opinion and which one is a worse opinion?

(P): Well, the thing about this is that anybody can be a judge, but even your decision is an opinion.

Here the individuals express a practical skepticism, i.e., since we will never have absolute proof, we can not really decide between different interpretations of the same event because, as person 2 suggests, our interpretations are merely our opinions. Frequently subjects go on to say 'and who is to say one opinion is right and one opinion is wrong?' Since conflicting data and opinions exist, since our minds are inherently limited, since many times there is no way to absolutely decide between conflicting interpretations, and since they assume that no amount of evidence less that the total amount would be adequate to argue for an objective view of knowledge, they conclude there is no rational way to decide between different points of view. Individuals are trapped by their assumptions into a skepticism and an implicit view that there is no objective reality. Here they may even point to the inherent limitations of logic to provide absolute answers to many questions and use this limitation as an argument in support of skepticism.

Position 7: Rationalism

Assumption Knowledge is possible, but it is not absolutely certain. Knowledge is a consequence of the process of reasonable inquiry.

Assumption: Although there is something called objective truth the process of inquiry is fallible and thus individuals may be wrong. Knowledge statements must, therefore, be evaluated as more or less likely approximations to the truth and be open to the scrutiny and criticisms of other rational people.

Principle
of judgement: Decide on the alternative that can be justified as most or more reasonable. Criteria for judgment may vary from domain to domain (religion, ethics, science) but the assumption that ideas, theories, beliefs, etc., may be judged as more or less reasonable and better or worse approximations to reality remains the same.

Person 1: Advanced graduate student
(P): It's my belief that you have to be very skeptical about what you read for popular consumption – even for professional consumption.
(I): [How do you ever know what to believe?]
(P): I read widely – of many points of view, partly (it's) reliance on people you think you can rely on, who seem to be reputable journalists, who make measured judgments – then reading widely and estimating where the balance is – where reputable people line up or where the weight of the evidence lies.

Person 2: Advanced graduate student
(P): It's [the view that the Egyptians built the pyramids] very far along the continuum of what is probable.
(I): Can you say one [point of view] is right and one is wrong?
(P): Right and wrong are not comfortable categories to assign to this kind of item – more or less likely or reasonable – more or less in keeping with what the facts seem to be.

Here, the subjects imply that knowledge is neither absolute nor unobtainable. What they suggest is that other opinions must be judged to the extent that they are reasonable and thay they cannot be accepted as categorically correct. On the other hand, both the opinions of experts and other evidence need to be weighed in deciding which alternative is most reasonable.

What the Kitchener and King research suggests is that the thinking of adolescents and post-adolescents about certain kinds of theoretical-philosophical issues can be characterized as progressing through a series of stages (only three of which have been discussed here). These stages represent the development of a kind of thinking that culminates in what we have called the stage of *rationalism*. This kind of thinking can be called *natural rationality* – the development of reason as it occurs naturally (psychologically) in the person rather than the ideal rationality sketched by philosophers and logicians. This corresponds roughly to Piaget's distinction between the logician's logic (axiomatized) and logic as it develops naturally in the person (natural logic or psycho-logic). Such rationality, according to *Hiley* [1979, p. 139], 'entails the idea that self-criticism and self-correction will yield ultimate convergence on the true or best representation of reality'. It is consistent with beliefs being rational, according to *Hiley*, that significantly different sets of beliefs could be the outcome of rational inquiry without the implicit assumption that further inquiry will decide between them. In addition he suggests that such rationality represents a mid-point between or dialectical synthesis of the tensions involved in dogmaticism and relativism.

What our research tentatively shows and what we have been arguing here is that the development of natural rationality cannot be accounted for by formal operations (conceived narrowly as purely deductive or broadly as deductive-inductive), nor can it be accounted for by stronger models of formal logic such as modal logic [*Strauss and Kroy*, 1977]. What is needed is something which perhaps includes modal logic but goes beyond it in the direction of an epistemic logic [*Chisholm*, 1977; *Hintikka*, 1962]. Our own theoretical attempts [*Kitchener*, 1977; *King*, 1977] have been in the direction of a pragmatism of fallibilism (a 'logic of inquiry'), the roots of which are in *Peirce* [1931–35] and *Dewey* [1915] and extend to the current work of *Popper* [1963, 1972], *Quine* [1953], *Rorty* [1979] and others.

Conclusion

The ability to use formal operations and to reason about propositions frees individuals to think in more abstract and valid ways about the issues that surround them in daily life. It does not, however, provide them with valid and reasonable assumptions from which to reason. What is misleading about the simple physical experiments about which *Inhelder and Piaget* had their subjects reason is that they lead to relatively clear-cut solutions (if individuals are arguing in logically valid ways). They do not throw metaphysical, epistemological, or theoretical assumptions into conflict and it is here that individuals reason in the most complex and uniquely human ways.

Issues in real life are not nearly so simple to resolve as Archimedes' principle of the pendulum. Evidence may not be readily accessible; it may be inherently limited by historical factors or by the process of empirical inquiry; there may be debate about what may be admitted as evidence, etc. Formal logic (formal operations) may play an important and necessary role in the reasoning processes of adults confronted with real life issues and theoretical decisions. Historically, it took humankind centuries before they even developed this relatively simple ability and we should not depreciate or minimize it. But it must be seen in its correct perspective.

Inhelder and Piaget point out, in the final chapter of *The Growth of Logical Thinking* that the reasoning of formal operational adolescents is still marked by egocentrism and that it must undergo a process of decentration. It is this decentration, they argue, that accounts for the differences in reasoning between adolescents and adults. However, what they have failed to pursue, either theoretically or empirically, is the possibility that this process has developmental regularities which cannot all be traced to less egocentric applications of the logic of deduction (or even induction). The differences in assumptions and their roots are interesting and important in and of themselves, since many issues which confront adults, as we have shown, are not ones that rely on logic alone for solutions. *Popper* [1963] has even argued that it is the difference in these kind of assumptions that differentiates free and totalitarian societies. Whether or not he is correct, they clearly are differences which need further investigation and explanation.

Summary

In this theoretical chapter, it is argued that the Piaget and Inhelder model of formal operations must include both deductive and inductive logic. Even when it is understood to include both types of logic, however, it cannot fully account for developmental differences in adult rationality. It is suggested that while different adults may reason in ways that are equally valid logically, they may draw very different conclusions because of differences in metaphysical and epistemological assumptions. Examples of differences in assumptions are offered from a model of the development of concepts of justification. Actual transcripts of adult reasoning are given as evidence for the use of these assumptions in ordinary life.

References

Arlin, P.K.: Cognitive development in adulthood: a fifth stage? Devl Psychol. *11:* 602–606 (1975).

Brinbaum, M.H.: Expectancy and judgment; in Restle, Shiffrin, Catellan, Lindman, Pisoni, Cognitive theory, vol. 1 (Erlbaum, Hillsdale, 1975).

Broughton, J.: The development of natural epistemology in adolescence and early adulthood. Harvard University (1975, unpublished dissertation).

Broughton, J.: Beyond formal operations: theoretical thought in adolescence. Teachers Coll. Rec. *79:* 88–97 (1977).

Bruner, J.S.: Inhelder and Piaget's the growth of logical thinking. Br. J. Psychol. *50:* 363–370 (1960).

Carnap, R.: The logical foundations of probability (University of Chicago Press, Chicago 1962).

Castellan, J.J., Jr.: Decision making with multiple probabilistic cues; in Castellan, Jr., Pisoni, Potts, Cognitive theory, vol. 2 (Erlbaum, Hillsdale, 1977).

Chisholm, R.: Theory of knowledge (Prentice Hall, Englewood Cliffs 1977).

Davis, M.: The undecidable (Raven Press, Hewlett 1965).

Dewey, J.: The logic of judgments of practice. J. Phil. *12:* 504–515 (1915).

Flavell, J.: The developmental psychology of Jean Piaget (Van Nostrand, Princeton 1963).

Gilligan, C.; Murphy, J.M.: Development from adolescence to adulthood: the philosopher and the dilemma of the fact. New Direct. Child Devl. *5:* 85–99 (1979).

Harman, G.: Reasoning and explanatory coherence. Am Phil. Q. *17:* 151–157 (1980).

Hempel, C.G.: Philosophy of natural science (Prentice Hall, Englewood Cliffs 1966).

Hiley, D.R.: Relativism, dogmatism and rationality. Int. Phil. Q. *19:* 133–149 (1979).

Hintikka, J.: Knowledge and belief (Cornell University, Ithaca 1962).

Inhelder, B.; Piaget, J.: The growth of logical thinking from childhood to adolescence (Routledge & Kegan Paul, London 1958).

Karmeloff-Smith, A.; Inhelder, B.: If you want to get ahead get a theory. Cognition *3:* 195–212 (1974–75).

King, P.M.: The development of reflective judgment and formal operational thinking in adolescents and young adults. Diss. Abstr. Int. *38:* 7233A (1977).

Kitchener, K.S.: Intellectual development in late adolescence and young adults: reflective judgment and verbal reasoning. Diss. Abstr. Int. *39:* 936 B (1978).

Kitchener, K.S.; King, P.M.: Reflective judgment: concepts of justification and their relationship to age and education. J. Appl. devl Psychol. (1981).

Kneebone, G.T.: Mathematical logic and the foundations of mathematics (Van Nostrand, Princeton 1963).

Kuhn, T.: The Copernican revolution (Harvard University, Cambridge 1957).

Labouvie-Vief, G.: Beyond formal operations: uses and limits of pure logic in life-span development. Hum. Dev. *23:* 141–161 (1980).

Luchins, A.S.; Luchins, E.H.: Logical foundations of mathematics for behavioral scientists (Holt, Rinehart & Winston, New York 1965).

Mendelson, E.: Introduction to mathem. logic (Princeton University, Princeton 1964).

Monnier, C.; Wells, A.: Does the formal operational stage exist? A review and critique of recent works on the subject of formal operations (1979, unpublished).

Myhill, J.: Some philosophical implications of mathematical logic. Rev. Metaphysic *6:* 165–197 (1952).

Niemark, E.D.: Current status of formal operations research. Hum. Dev. *22:* 66–67 (1979).

Parsons, C.: Inhelder and Piagets the growth of logical thinking. Br. J. Psychol. *50:* 75–84 (1960).

Peirce, C.S.: Collected paper of Charles Sanders Peirce, vol. I–VI; in Hartshorne, Weiss (Harvard University, Cambridge 1931–35).

Perry, W.G.: Forms of intellectual and ethical development in the college years (Holt, Rinehart & Winston, New York 1968).
Piaget, J.: Logic and psychology (Manchester University, Manchester 1953).
Piaget, J.: Logique formelle et psychologie génétique; in Fraisse, Faverge, Bresson. Les modèles et la formalisation du comportement (CNRS, Paris 1967a).
Piaget, J.: Introduction et variétés de l'épistémologie; in Piaget, Logique et connaissance scientifique (Gallimard, Paris 1967b).
Piaget, J.: Epistémologie de la logique; in Piaget, Logique et connaissance scientifique (Gallimard, Paris 1967c).
Piaget, J.: Structuralism (Harper & Row, New York 1970).
Piaget, J.: Intellectual evolution from adolescence to adulthood. Hum. Dev. *15:* 1–12 (1972).
Piaget, J.: The origin of the idea of chance in children (Norton, New York 1975).
Pitz, G.F.: Bayes' theorem: can judgement and inference do without it? in Restle, Shiffrin, Catellan, Lindman, Pisoni, Cognitive theory, vol. 1 (Lawrence Erlbaum. Hillsdale 1975).
Popper, K.: The logic of scientific discovery (Basic Books, New York 1959).
Popper, K.: Conjectures and refutations (Harper & Row, New York 1963)
Popper, K.: Objective knowledge (Oxford University, Oxford 1972).
Quine, W.V.O.: From a logical point of view (Harper & Row, New York 1953).
Riegel, K.F.: Foundations of dialectical psychology (Academic, New York 1979).
Rorty, R.: Philosophy and the mirror of nature (Princeton University, Princeton 1979).
Schaie, K.W.: Toward a stage theory of adult cognitive development. Int. J. Aging and Hum. Dev. *8:* 129–138 (1977–78).
Strauss, S.; Kroy, M.: The child as logician or methodologist? A critique of formal operations. Hum. Dev. *20:* 102–117 (1977).
Skryms, B.: Choice and change: an introduction to inductive logic (Dickenson, Encino 1975).
Swinburne, R.: An introduction to confirmation theory (Methuen, London 1973).
Toulmin, S.: The uses of argument (Cambridge University, Cambridge 1958).

Author Index

Subject Index